So Long as You're Healthy

(ABEE GEZUNDT)

HARRY GOLDEN

So Long as You're Healthy
(ABEE GEZUNDT)

G. P. PUTNAM'S SONS
NEW YORK

To my grandsons,
Michael, Danny, Barney, Rex, and John

Author's note

I am again grateful to Harry Golden, Jr., of the Chicago *Sun-Times* for putting this book together, editing the essays, and writing the headings for them.

And I am grateful to my eldest son, Richard Goldhurst, the novelist, of Westport, Connecticut, who did special research for the essays "Lynching in America" and "Adam Clayton Powell."

Contents

CONTENTS

PART 1

While God Laughs

So long as you're healthy

Abee gezundt—so long as you're healthy. The affectionate greeting among Jewish people on the Lower East Side of New York was "*Gezundt un parnosseh*" (livelihood). But if the livelihood was not so good, and even if the shopkeeper went bankrupt, his relatives and friends would say, "*Abee gezundt*" (so long as you're healthy).

Abee gezundt could reach unreasonable heights—as for instance when a relative was told she had cancer, the answer was invariably, "Cancer schmancer—*abee gezundt*."

And good health was closely associated with food. In the sweatshop era, tuberculosis was endemic on the Lower East Side of New York. The immigrant women correctly associated this disease with loss of weight. And so the tables literally creaked under the weight of the food—"*ess, ess, mein kindt*" was the mother's watchword—eat, eat, my child.

The Jews anticipated Medicare by seventy-five years. The Jews brought the idea of organized self-help to America out of the Pale of Settlement of Europe. By 1900 there were several hundred Eastern European societies of self-help in New York, as well as dozens of smaller *vereins*. These societies and vereins provided a sophisticated program for the health of the entire family. Young doctors often vied with one another for election as the verein doctor. The member of the verein paid fifty cents every

19

two months, which provided him with medical care for his entire family, when needed, as well as a flat cost of fifty cents for prescriptions. There was a special tax for confinement cases—a special tax of eight dollars.

The solicitors for the society never sold memberships with the stated contingency, "...in the event of your death, your family will get...." They sold only "benefits." The most famous English word in the ghetto was "benefits," which replaced such words as death, sickness, and unemployment. It was a way to deceive the Evil Eye. "If, God forbid, something should happen to you after one hundred and twenty years, the benefits would give your wife...."

The Evil Eye had much to do with *abee gezundt*. If a visiting neighbor so far forgot himself as to say, "Your little boy looks very healthy," the grandmother was quick to divert attention from the little boy by saying, "That lampshade looks good."

And yet all these things paid off. The food and the religion helped the Jew through critical periods of his life. The washing of the hands before eating or before praying was really a health measure. One of the accusations that a man was a practicing Jew before the Spanish Inquisition was that he was seen washing his hands before he sat down to eat.

And so I say to all my friends, no matter what befalls you, *abee gezundt*.

Evaluating the century

It would be nice to wonder what happened to the twentieth century, except that we know what happened. The century started off like a precocious child filled with the promise of achievement. Now the century is 70 percent gone, and it looks like a middle-aged dropout, the shrewd old jealous geezer who had always had potential but never realized any of it.

We had a lot of action but no gloriana.

I would guess the three men who most characterize the original promise of the century are Mohandas Gandhi of India; Albert Einstein of Zurich, Berlin, and Princeton; and Sigmund Freud of Vienna.

Gandhi and his disciples were the first group of men to come up with a new political idea since some English nobles wrested the Magna Carta and the institution of Parliament from King John. The tactic of nonviolent resistance was a way of expression for millions of the poor and the exploited by which they could demonstrate their very massiveness to the oppressors and still save their own lives for better days ahead. One way or another, with many innovations and modifications, Gandhi's nonviolent resistance has been the single most effective stratagem for the rising wave of nationalism throughout the world.

I speak of Einstein generically, the physicist-scientist who discovered at the beginning of the century that we always had seen things grossly. $E = mc^2$ is another way of looking at the universe, a way which banishes matter and insists there are only events, collections of energy clustered together in different combinations. For all their seeming variety, these events are at core electric impulses. By unlocking these impulses, separating them, we have literally found the way to destroy the whole shebang if we choose.

Sigmund Freud and his disciples found another way of interpreting behavior and the human animal. At base, psychoanalysis is simply the insistence that everything is motivated, from the advent of disease to certain kinds of social structure. The motivation for these situations can be discovered by a psychological investigation. It is this investigation that also yields certain remedies.

Yet the salient difference between the twentieth and previous centuries has been the growth of the world population.

John Maynard Keynes has evolved a system for financing these peoples, dictators and democrats have offered different methods of governing them, but no one has devised the crucial system for having the world accommodate all of them in some degree of comfort. That is the one gift the old dropout could bestow upon us before he quits in the next thirty years.

My mother's funeral

ONE OF the Latin letters through which English school-boys must struggle was sent by Cicero to a friend on the occasion of the death of the friend's daughter. Cicero, who always struck me as a pompous type, told his pal not to worry, the daughter was better off because she would not live to see Rome's decay. Whether Cicero had his eye on posterity or not is hard to see. I know of no staunch Republican who wrote any pal on the occasion of a loved one's departure that at least the deceased was missing the ministrations of the Roosevelt New Deal. If anyone did so write, someone generously burned the letter.

I have thought, chauvinistically, of course, that the attitude of the Hebrews is the most sensible expression of grief. The loved ones wail and weep. The paid mourners outdo even them. But no one weeps for the widows. No one weeps for the orphans left to defend themselves in this world. Everyone weeps for the one laid away forever in the earth.

Significantly, my pious mother always uttered the ghetto prayer for the dead—not a promise or hope of future life, but "May all the earth be sealed with this body." It is the wish, certainly futile, but a wish nevertheless, that no one else ever die again. It is a wish expressed toward the eternal, implacable enemy —death.

The dead should be the center, the focus of grief. Orphans survive, and widows and widowers know ecstasy again.

I did not know my mother had cancer of the spine until she was already in the hospital and I happened to overhear the doctor's diagnosis accidentally.

My mother died in the early 1920's, a time when cancer was a taboo word. You never told anyone a relative had cancer. It was tantamount to revealing that someone had a venereal disease or leprosy.

Thinking back, I am amazed at how recent our enlightenment is. In the early 1900's tuberculosis was also a taboo subject. It was not until people felt safe in confessing its affliction that successful treatments came in profusion, and it is no longer always a lethal disease.

My mother never smoked, and I think the only wine she ever drank was on Passover, when she said, "I only wet my lips with it." I recall no accident to her, no sudden blows or bad falls. She rarely left the kitchen except to attend the synagogue and to do the shopping.

In those days all the women worked hard at sewing and cooking and preparing the kids for school. Her leisure consisted of an hour on a rocking chair, looking out the window with her arms folded, sometimes leaning on the sill.

My mother's cancer caused her death, of course. From the time of her first pain until she succumbed was less than two months. By that time, my brother Jacob was doing well, and the family could afford to take her to famous Mount Sinai Hospital and engage one of the great surgeons of the day, Dr. A. A. Berg.

It was Dr. Berg whom I overheard. He told my brother, "We dare not operate. The cancer has already affected the brain."

We told everyone my mother was suffering an infection of some kind resulting from a bout with pneumonia. People talked about pneumonia. They whispered about cancer.

Cancer is no longer taboo. It is still a great killer. It would certainly kill twice as many if people feared mentioning it. I shall enter no discussion here about the proposed cures so far offered except to say that a scientist in the Weizmann Institute in Jerusalem told me he was sure there would have to be many cures for cancer eventually. This disease may very well have multiple origins, and each cause will need a separate discovery.

I was particularly devoted to my mother. But I remember within a month after her funeral I was at the Polo Grounds watching Artie Nehf throw left-handed strikes across the plate.

I remember Nehf gave the batter very little motion. He pitched with his wrist. Christy Mathewson was at the tuberculosis sanitarium in Saranac Lake, Rube Marquard was then playing for Brooklyn, and John J. McGraw was still the top manager, developing such future managers as Bill Terry and Frankie Frisch.

Out in center field for the Giants was a dandy ballplayer from the South whom the fans used to razz because his temper was so short. One day they really got under his skin, and he shouted back at them something silly about "New York Jews," and he was on the train that night, traded off somewhere. Interestingly enough, the bleachers were populated mostly by Irishmen.

I remember all these names, but outside of our immediate family I couldn't tell you who went to the graveyard the day we buried my mother.

Charles Francis Murphy, the big boss of Tammany Hall, and my mother had their funerals on the same day. It was, in fact, the first day of Passover in 1924. The district Tammany leader, Solomon Goldenkrantz, put in a full day. He attended both funerals, my mother's and Murphy's. That night Goldenkrantz marched in the Santa Lucia fiesta to the Madonna in "Little Italy." It was a full day indeed.

The miser's objective

JACK SASSO, according to the brief news dispatches, was eighty years old and lived in a thirty-dollar-a-month walkup apartment on New York's West Side. He wore shabby clothes. Every afternoon he bought an evening newspaper and a can of tuna fish for his supper. He never threw away the newspapers and never cleaned up the empty cans. The police had to wade through these to find Mr. Sasso, who had succumbed to natural causes. In his pockets the cops found ninety-three cents. In his bureau drawers they found fifteen bankbooks with deposits totaling more than $200,000.

In a society as commercially oriented as ours, a miser has an affliction hard to understand. Money becomes an end in itself and ceases to have any utilitarian value. The miser saves much as a boy collects marbles or a connoisseur collects paintings, but marbles and paintings have an esthetic value.

I know of no psychoanalytic or psychological account which explains the motivations of misers, but Arnold Bennett's novel *Riceyman Steps* is the best clinical study I have ever read. Riceyman Steps is a square in London in which Henry Earlforward runs a secondhand book shop. Henry lives on tea and stale bread, and though he has six decent suits, never wears any of them. What disturbs his existence is his marriage to Mrs. Arb, a neighbor with a private income, whom Henry finally makes miserly, too. They save their money in separate places, and Mrs. Arb admires Henry's packet filled with new pound notes and his bag of gold sovereigns.

Earlforward is so miserly he refuses to call a doctor for himself or his wife when they both fall seriously ill. Mrs. Arb is finally spirited to a hospital for surgery but dies from malnutrition. Henry dies the next day when he discovers the housemaid has stolen six shillings from his horde to pay for his wife's taxi fare. Earlforward's estate, together with that of his wife's, goes to a brother he has not seen in thirty years. This inheritance needless to say makes the brother quite happy.

Bennett had a long career as a novelist, which stretched from Victorian times into the 1920's. *Riceyman Steps* was published in 1923 and reveals the new psychoanalytic techniques then in vogue. Bennett hit upon the real in this book: The miser is trying to deprive himself of sustenance in the same way the alcoholic is trying to deprive himself of sense. The alcoholic consciously seeks the unconscious, and the miser subtly seeks death, a secret which he masks from himself by accumulation, but it is an accumulation he never intends to use, not even to save himself.

The old-timers

ONE OF the surprises about growing old is the abrupt, all-too-sudden realization that the old-timers you remember are not immortal after all.

A high school editor in Charlotte, North Carolina, came around for an interview in the course of which I delivered my customary eulogy of Enrico Caruso. He nodded perfunctorily, and presumptuously I asked, "Haven't you ever heard of Caruso?"

"He was a singer?" the young man ventured.

"The greatest opera singer of his time," I said.

"I guess that was before Ezio Pinza," said the high school editor.

Ezio Pinza was this fellow's idea of an old-timer. I had to admit from where he sat Ezio Pinza was an old-timer. To this young man World War I and the Civil War are almost simultaneous conflicts.

High school students today think of Shaw and Ibsen as classics, fellows who wrote plays about which English teachers tirelessly expatiate. Yet I saw the American premieres of both Shaw and Ibsen, and I saw them on the Lower East Side. In these days Shaw and Ibsen entertained ideas so new and radical Broadway couldn't stand it. Now Shaw's works are an unending source for musical comedies, and though A Doll's House has passed into the language, I doubt there's an American woman anywhere who lives in one.

In a civics class over fifty years ago, I read William Jennings Bryan's "Cross of Gold" speech. Whenever he ran for President, which was fairly often, Bryan brought down the rafters by repeating his ringing peroration, "You shall not crucify mankind upon a cross of gold." Although I understand what he meant now, we students couldn't fathom it then. Would an American President really dare to pass a law that made one ounce of gold equal to sixteen ounces of silver.

William Jennings Bryan lives on in this high school editor's imagination not because Bryan was the first Presidential candidate to champion an eight-hour day or the first major political figure to condemn American imperialism or because he was a teetotaling Secretary of State but because he proved so inept upon Darrow's cross-examination in the Scopes Monkey Trial.

As a matter of fact, William Jennings Bryan was sort of a Democratic Barry Goldwater. You know what the high school editor said about ex-Senator Goldwater? He said he was old hat. "Old hat" is an expression all the old-timers ought to remember.

The birthday of Cassius

EVERY TWENTY seconds one American turns sixty-five. Every hour one hundred and eighty Americans turn sixty-five. Five thousand people every day celebrate their sixty-fifth birthdays; one and a half million a year qualify at last for Social Security.

These statistics come from the President's Council on Aging.

The Eternal Enemy is death. No one thinks, When will I die? We all think, How long will I live? You can see the old folks cautiously spending money on the cafeteria lines. For along with the question "How long will I live?" is the attendant worry, under what conditions?

The old folks lived with even greater worry in the days when they had to depend on children to take care of them.

No one expects to die suddenly. No one wants to be a burden on the children. But age sixty-five keeps descending upon us.

As a boy, I considered sixty-five old. A sixty-five-year-old man was an elderly gent. When I myself turned sixty-five, I saw it is not so old as I imagined when I was playing on the streets of the Lower East Side. Eventually, seventy-five will be considered but ripe middle age.

There is a great deal of sentiment attached to birthdays. Shakespeare, I suspect, makes the best use of this sentiment in *Julius Caesar*. Caesar is the hero of the play, and when he is assassinated, the audience cheers on Antony and pities Brutus and thinks the real villain of the piece is the lean and hungry Cassius. On the day Cassius dies, he says to his second-in-command, "Mesalla, this is my birthday; as this very day was Cassius born. Give me thy hand, Mesalla. . . ." There is magic in the expression of Cassius's sadness. One realizes he was a politician, a little more desperate than most, mixed up with other desperate politicians in an assassination. There is something singular about a man who is born and dies on the same day. (Shakespeare himself was born and died on April 23.)

In the Orthodox Jewish home on the Lower East Side, no birthday meant much. Orthodox Jews steer shy of numbers, dates, and years, hoping thereby to ward off the Evil Eye. To fool the Evil Eye every mother invented circumlocutions to avoid specificity in names and thereby lend anonymity to a loved one.

When a crass census taker asked, "How old is your son?" mothers ruminated and finally said, "He was nine when we came to America." The rule was never give a direct answer.

When the Jews began having occasional banquets at the McAlpin Hotel, they never let the maître d'hôtel count heads. When the headwaiter asked the chairman how many wanted seats, the chairman would point one by one to his party and answer, "Not one, not two, not three, not four. . . ," and finally say, "*Not* fifty-two dinners."

But all this superstition is behind us. And anyway, I am very careful in everything I do to ward off the influence of the Evil Eye.

Freud, Jung, and Reik have written about the "normal" fear of death! But my father was just as brilliant as these men. At age eighty-five he anticipated my concern, and he said, "Look who else has gone: Maimonides, Jefferson, Henry George. . . ."

In one year we lost three of the greatest voices of our age:

Churchill, Ed Murrow, and Adlai Stevenson. And amazingly, Murrow and Stevenson were my good friends, my *personal friends!* Am I better than these men? Their deaths have "diminished me," as the poet has said, but their deaths have also taken the fright out of dying.

Composers' forte

ROSSINI, WHO wrote *Stabat Mater*, an awesome requiem to the Virgin Mary, lived for weeks at a time in a brothel. He was a big wine, women, and song man.

Giacomo Puccini—the composer of *La Bohème* and *Madama Butterfly* as well as *Il Tabarro*, which has the most inspired love duet in all grand opera—was also on better than speaking terms with most of the divas. His wife once accused him of making love to every soprano in Italy.

"What can I do?" sighed Puccini. "It is my destiny."

The father of Johannes Brahms determined his son would be a musical prodigy just like Mozart. The trouble was that in Brahms' time, dukes, barons, marquises, even kings were not only going broke but going out of style. Brahms senior couldn't secure a place for his little prodigy. Except in a whorehouse. Quite literally Johannes Brahms grew up playing piano in a house which was not a home. His talents were of such proportion the girls often expressed their appreciation.

The experience colored his whole life. One had to cross the street to avoid Johannes Brahms, the composer of four symphonies each the equal of Beethoven's, and of the Violin Concerto, because invariably he was accompanied by a tart with a merciless giggle.

Reading the paper

OVER THE years I have discovered that a man can place which of Shakespeare's seven ages of man he populates by what he reads first in the newspaper.

The schoolboy reads the comic strips straight off. The comic strips remain an unfortunate addiction for many. Newspapermen hate comic strips like they hated the Liz Taylor-Richard Burton affair. Newspapermen hate anything which usurps valuable space which could be devoted instead to downtown corruption, uptown murder, or the shipping news, depending on which desk a reporter works.

The young man, Shakespeare's lover, turns to the sports pages. God bless you if you still turn to the sports pages first. It means you are perpetually young and understand the important changeless things. If the world is going to be saved, it will be saved by the lifetime subscribers to the *Sporting News*. It wasn't until President Nixon asked the moon walkers if they knew the score of the All Star game that I began to have hope for him.

The soldier, "full of strange oaths and bearded like the pard," reads the front pages. As a matter of fact, once a man settles down, he tends to read two or three newspapers, even though they all are reporting the same thing.

And the justice, with plump round belly, zips to the editorial pages. Middle-aged men, by the way, read more magazines than newspapers because magazines have more editorials, which don't make any more sense than newspapers'.

I am now the expert on the last age for reading, the sixth age. There is some debate about whether a man in his late sixties goes straight to the obituaries or straight to the stock market report. I go to the obits. I recommend my practice for all contemporaries. Today, for instance, I hit it lucky. Three prominent men died yesterday, a musician, an actor, and a writer—all of them in their eighties. Longevity is the best news any paper can hand a reader. With that kind of obituary reporting, I can bear reading about the vigorous plunge of common stocks. I can even follow with interest the financial writer's grim prophecy that the Dow-Jones industrial average will fall to 750.

This you call news?

BARNARD COLLEGE, a prestigious school for young ladies up in New York City, discovered one of its sophomores, a twenty-year-old girl, was living in a state of sin with a twenty-year-old junior from neighboring Columbia University. Imagine that! What secrets are left? What thrills? Nothing, I guess, except to get tattooed.

The relationship made front-page news. The New York *Times* reported the whole matter in exquisite detail.

New York City is a sophisticated town by its own admission. It has survived in the past few years a subway strike, a garbage strike, a riot or two, even a sunshine tax on buildings with windows. Two people living together without benefit of clergy really shakes the place up.

Many years ago Mark Twain, as head of a committee, invited the Russian novelist Maxim Gorky to America. The great writer would lecture to tumultuous audiences and tour the entire continent. When Gorky arrived in New York, however, the reporters discovered he was accompanied by a woman who was not his wife. They put this news in the paper, and the hotel evicted Gorky. He had to sit on the curb, his luggage stacked around him, while he and his middle-aged girlfriend wondered what the devil got into everybody.

Not long after Gorky quit our shores, thereby undefiling New York City, Countess Cathcart from England paid the big town a visit. She wasn't even going to lecture, but when an enterprising snoop found out she was consorting with a man younger than she, the attendant scandal sent her packing.

I dread the day when the papers discover why those vital businessmen register for fancy suites at noon at the midtown hotels. Usually these gentlemen have evacuated the suites by three and are back at the shop, no doubt refreshed but a step closer to hell. The revelation ought to bowl the town over.

About the only refreshing disclosure in the whole incident was the declaration by the two school kids that they hoped to live in their own specially established community and educate their children without benefit of compulsory schooling. No, they still don't believe in marriage, but it does my heart good to realize there are still folks who want to move into Plato's Republic.

While God laughs

A FRIEND in Miami calls me on Sunday.

"Harry," he asks, "will you be home Tuesday? I'm passing through Charlotte, and I'd like to stop off."

"Stop off," I say. "We'll have a drink and do some talking."

Tuesday he doesn't appear. I wonder: Maybe he didn't have the time after all.

Then on Friday his brother calls me. My friend died of a heart attack on Monday night.

During that same week, the prime minister of India, Lal Bahadur Shastri, signs a peace protocol with the prime minister of Pakistan. It is the great achievement of Shastri's career. Within nine hours, however, Shastri too has succumbed to a heart disease.

Man makes plans, says the ghetto proverb, and God laughs.

The truth is we all think we are immortal. That is why electronic, refrigerative, missile, cosmetic devices keep ever improving. That is why technology has far outstripped medical and pharmaceutical research. We think when we buy something, we will own it forever.

But we can die at the moment of our great success, and we

can never make that trip to Charlotte. My friend from Miami was rich beyond his wildest early imaginings. Shastri was to come home to wild acclaim. But we are never rich and never quite successful.

A man is successful only when he himself is satisfied.

And _Thoreau_ laid down the principle: "A man is rich in proportion to the number of things he can afford to let alone."

There is a vast number of things I can afford to let alone and haven't the faintest interest in. What I must have every day, besides at least two good meals, are: the Charlotte _Observer_, the Charlotte _News_, the New York _Times_, ten cigars, half a pint of bourbon, and a few hours of solitude. The rest, as Rabbi Hillel said, is "commentary."

Great exit lines

WHEN VOLTAIRE, who was a scandalous skeptic, lay on his deathbed, one of his close friends thought it might be time to reconcile the philosopher with God. His pal hurried to the cardinal's residence. The prospect of uniting an articulate atheist with God was enough inducement to His Eminence. As the cardinal, in red beret and cape, swept into the sickroom, Voltaire moaned, "Ah, the devil already."

The Roman Emperor Nero felt his mother was balking him, so he sent a couple of Praetorian thugs around to do her in. She saw them coming, bared her womb, and said, "Strike here! In the womb that gave birth to a Nero."

Some of the folks have a gift for the final phrase. Beethoven is supposed to have awakened from his coma, raised his fist, and as lightning flashed across the heaven, shouted, _"La comedia finita est!"_ But I always wonder if these are not the inventions of butlers or casual acquaintances.

I wonder why Beethoven would refer to life as a _comedia_. Fellows who read Immanuel Kant and write Ninth Symphonies obviously think life is full of meaning and purpose. Did the cardinal really bother with Voltaire? And isn't it more reasonable to suppose Nero's mother shouted, "When I get my hands on that lousy kid . . ."?

Years ago, I was with my best friend, John Duff, when his father died. Duff senior had been a fireman, a precinct captain, and now he was on the farthest limb of old age. Just before he died, Duff senior opened his eyes and very patiently sang "Oh believe me if all those endearing young charms." I remember it as a terribly sad and moving moment because that old Irish lay is precisely what an old man would think of as light begins to fade.

Eugene O'Neill was born while his father, James, was on tour with *The Count of Monte Cristo*. O'Neill spent most of his valuable youth in the wings of a theater, living out of trunks and suitcases. In his old age, he was afflicted with Parkinson's disease and so debilitated that he had to live in a hotel because he needed day and night service. He knew he was dying when he remarked grouchily to his wife, "Damn it, born in a hotel room, died in a hotel room."

The best last line I ever heard was in a movie and was uttered by W. C. Fields. The townsfolk are about to lynch Fields, whom they mistakenly suspect is the masked bandit. They have him mounted on the scaffold, and the sheriff asks if he has any last requests. "Always wanted to see Philadelphia before I died," said Fields.

The abuse of wives

Of ALL the allusions to which the English-speaking world resorts, the most abused is the expression about "Caesar's wife." The full expression is "Caesar's wife must be above suspicion." The allusion to Caesar's wife does not refer to purity but to the victim of circumstances.

Milo, a *cives Romani* but a conniver of the worst sort as well as a lecher, conceived a passion for one of the ladies-in-waiting who attended Caesar's wife. There not being motels in classical antiquity, Milo took matters into his own hands by sneaking into Lady Caesar's bath and, as it were 'twixt earnest and joke, enjoyed his lady. But he was spotted leaving. Caesar promptly instituted divorce proceedings.

Her lawyer pointed out to the general that his wife was perfectly innocent, that she had not conspired in the affair, that she had ordered her handmaiden boiled in oil, that she despised Milo and wouldn't say hello to him if he were the last man in the world, and wasn't the divorce carrying things too far? Mighty Julius replied, "Caesar's wife must be above suspicion," admitting the truth of her defense but insisting that she was out of luck because he, Caesar, was big time.

Everyone knows that Lot's wife, who is otherwise nameless, is turned into a pillar of salt. Her crime was to look back at the destruction of Sodom after the Lord had given Lot the warning to flee to Zoar.

Why the jealous God of the Old Testament changed her into *salt* I leave to the Freudians and the Higher Critics. He changed her because in looking back she longed for possessions which God was destroying. See, when the Lord warned Lot of the imminent destruction of the city, Lot lingered. He lingered until the vicious Sodomites started to seize his lands. Even then he was able to make a deal with God to flee to another city instead of the mountains. God was giving him a better than fair shake.

Wives of the men in receivership: Take due notice. That's what the expression "Lot's wife" is about.

"Potiphar's wife" is always referred to as the seductress of Biblical times. Potiphar, one of the Pharaoh's captains, took Joseph into his house and made him the majordomo of the estate, the overseer.

But Potiphar's wife began making eyes at Joseph, who spurned her advances. She tried again. And again. And at last Joseph told her to lay off, if Potiphar found out they would both be in the soup. She grabbed Joseph's cloak. He ran out. Whereupon she accused him of attempted rape, and Potiphar threw him in the dungeon.

Potiphar's wife has had a life in all literature since then because the underlying sense of the situation is that Joseph led her on a little bit, Shakespeare not having yet warned him that hell hath no fury like that of woman scorned. If she entrapped Joseph, it was a spur of the moment entrapment. She wanted a jet-set swinger, while he was all for forecasting the future through dream analysis.

The generation gap in the dictionary

School: a place or institution for teaching or learning; establishment for education; specifically an institution for teaching children.

School: a crowd, a school of fish; a large number of fish or water animals of the same kind swimming together, going in the same direction.

Women at parties

No man I have ever known can do right by his wife at a party. There's something about marriage that makes her think a jovial evening should be instead a disciplinary exercise in self-restraint. My pal took his wife to the ballet and from the ballet to the reception at the Bulgarian Embassy. Now that's an evening for the little woman, right? He put up with the ballet, than which he hates nothing more, and did she ever dream of attending embassy receptions when she was a substitute French teacher twenty-eight years ago? But she is still insisting the evening was a total disaster. Why? Because after he had enjoyed several slivovitzs, which, mind you, the Bulgars pressed upon him, he told the Italian ambassador he liked olive oil.

She insists it was a gaffe, a blunder of severe international proportions. How many people think to tell the Italian ambassador how they admire olive oil? Very few.

Nothing makes a wife as unreasonable as getting stuck in the snow when leaving the party. To a woman, they will say, "You're always getting stuck." This is a big help when the tires are sliding on the ice. When you have to retreat to the house, there to call a wrecker, she will say, "I thought maybe once we could get through an evening without other guests realizing he was a boor. I was hopeful when I noticed he did not spill coffee on the tablecloth. My heart leaped up when he did not put on another lady's hat. I was transported by delight when he declined a drink for the road. Alas."

I cannot imagine why anyone would go to a party simply to catalogue the vices of the guests. But it seems that is why they go. They come home from the bridge club with gossip, but they leave the party with their dear little hearts filled with complaint.

It is useless to argue that they have their faults. They do not reform when you point out they are forever closing your newspaper and losing your place. They keep rearranging the living room furniture with the regularity of the tides. They remain incapable of making a left-hand turn. What spirit is so ungenerous as to keep reminding them of their charming foibles?

A friend has confided in me that many, many years ago at a party his wife discovered him in the kitchen kissing his hostess. "Ever since, I have labored under a crippling restriction. No matter where we go," he said, "I am never allowed in the kitchen."

The generation gap

WHEN HARVEY HADDIX of the Pittsburgh Pirates pitched twelve perfect innings against the Milwaukee Braves, it was big news not because he lost on a double by Del Crandall in the thirteenth, but because Harvey was thirty-three years old.

I had a friend whose sole ambition was to become the youngest member of Congress. Well, he not only didn't win the election, he didn't win the nomination. Now he's campaigning again, and his theme is that we need "experience," "calm wisdom," and "moderation," all of which he suddenly developed when he passed thirty-five.

Part of my inspiration comes out of the realization that I am in my late sixties. I still, however, deliver over thirty lectures a year at various colleges describing the course of civil rights and integration.

At a girls' college I asked several of the students if there was any relationship between the academic revolution and the sexual revolution. One of the girls pursed her lips and said, "The C-minus students are interested in the academic revolution. The boys who want to be doctors, physicists, or engineers are interested in the sexual revolution." The Phi Beta Kappas always mean business. Students do not always regard me as antique. When we talk later, they do so regard their fathers.

The Talmud speaks about venerating the old and the young. I do not want to take up cudgels solely for the old. We practice dreadful inequities among the young.

The draft, for instance, with the changes of late 1969, remains demonstrably unfair.

There are cities built specifically for the old, like St. Petersburg, Florida, where there is not a curb. This is what we do with the aged: We shove them into this incubator where they wait for the small joys of isolated life, fretting about all the annoyances of the day.

One of the reasons for this division is that we do not believe merit affects the quality of life. Yet Winston Churchill was in his sixties when he became Britain's wartime prime minister. When Sophocles was ninety and his sons wanted the courts to declare him mentally incompetent, he read his jurors the verses of *Oedipus at Colonus*.

On the Lower East Side, in the crowded tenements, still we had a pretty good idea of what life looked like. We lived with kid brothers, maiden aunts, and grandparents. The result was that we didn't think people belonged in the categories of young, middle-aged or old—we all of us communicated one way or another. Today, in most suburban complexes, the town at midday is populated only by the women, the kiddies, and the dogs.

We have victimized ourselves by subscribing wholeheartedly to our own myths. We all retire at sixty-five not because that is when we should retire but because sixty-five is the most advantageous retirement age for the insurance premiums. We really believe that poets and mathematicians get their gifts early and are washed up at thirty. Goethe wrote *Faust* in his seventies. When a forty-seven-year-old bishop becomes a cardinal, we say he is young. I submit that our universe is viciously relativistic when it comes to age.

The trouble with all of us is that we believe life is like a business graph. We imagine life as a slowly ascending line which reaches a peak at roughly fifty and then abruptly descends into senility or bankruptcy at seventy. I submit life is a continuum, an ever-circling curve, every point of which is as near the end as the beginning. Only if it is thus can the old learn from the young, just as the young learn more handily from the old.

There is little reverence for the old in our society. And because there is none, there is probably less reverence for the young.

Morals of the mother country

THERE IS a ministerial convention going on in my home-town of Charlotte. The reverends are considering the quality of life in the 1960's and what this quality portends for the 1970's. Their prognostications I fear are dim. One of the subjects the ministers came down hard on was our morals—a word loosely used to describe our sex habits. No good, they say, no good a-tall.

I always like to remind conventions that our morals are no worse than those which flourished in England, the mother country, during the reign of Charles II. It was from Charles's reign, 1660–85, that England went on to Gloriana.

In Bonny Charles's heyday it was important for a man to prove he had never been in sympathy with the Puritans. So the boys went all out. Englishmen had a wild time. So did wives, sons, brothers, and daughters. A wild time was *prima facie* evidence of loyalty to the king.

The wildest of all the Englishmen was the king himself, who established an "orange girl" in one of his castles.

The orange girls ostensibly sold fruit to the theater audiences, but in reality they were soliciting. The first two rows of the theater were reserved for them, and the chairs were arranged backs to the stage so the girls could flirt with the patrons.

The king was a devoted theatergoer, and after a time he threw discretion to the winds and waved to the orange girls as enthusiastically as the coarsest commoner. Once the queen was outraged. She left the theater indignant. But after a while she said, "What's the use?" and she used to sit through the plays while the king made merry.

Nell Gwyn was an orange girl who caught the king's fancy. From all accounts she was a pretty good actress, but when she became a courtesan, she went into orbit. The king took her away "from all this" and started paying rent on a castle. Nell was more to him than a great and good friend.

To impress his subjects, Charles never made a fetish of marital fidelity. He had more than one great and good friend, but Nell proved as tolerant of his defection as the queen. Things went along swimmingly until King Charles conceived an affection for a Frenchwoman who had been married to an Englishman. Her name was Mrs. Carwell, and Nell might have had to share the castle with this new inamorata except Mrs. Carwell was a Catholic, a religion not very popular among the English constituency.

Charles's flirtation with Mrs. Carwell made a lot of folks cluck their tongues. In fact, Charles's liaison came near to putting an untimely end to poor innocent Nell Gwyn.

Nell was passing through Oxford one bright day when her carriage was beset by a mob of toughs. They heaped insults upon her, and she feared for the safety of her footmen and horses. She stuck her head out of the carriage window and shouted, "I'm not the Catholic whore, I'm the Protestant whore," and thus saved her pretty white neck.

I like to repeat this story when some do-gooders want to revoke Richard Burton's entrance visa.

Joy of the presence

I RECALL a note from Carl Sandburg some time back: "Come to see me, I'd like to see your face."

I thought of *darshana,* the power of "the presence." Our Talmudists knew all about it, and of course it is part of the religion of India. Gandhi sat there weaving cloth and thousands of people came and they just sat down and looked. When Nehru consulted with his political aides from throughout that vast subcontinent, he called them in, and they sat with him and often did not exchange more than a few words.

There is no mysticism about this at all. Think back and you will recall many of your own moments of darshana, the great relaxation you have found in the presence of someone who was very dear to you. The more relaxed, the less need to talk.

What we need today is a bit of darshana, communication and fellowship, without that terrible need to knock each other out with whiskey and then turn on the TV.

Women alcoholics

THE FEMALE alcoholic is protected, insulated, kept remote and at a remove. The children are told, "Hush, Mommy has a sick headache." When she stumbles, no one mutters, "Drunk again," but instead all cluck sympathetically about the bad carpeting or the treacherous footing. The more she is protected, the more her indulgence increases. Women drunks literally retire into the vaguely conscious world of the alcoholic where there are no clocks, no duties, no shame, only the next drink, which everyone, she included, pretends she will not take but which she always does.

A tradition of bribery

I FOLLOWED the Carmine DeSapio case with the typical attention of an American citizen. Scandals in this country always revolve around bribery and the prospect of bribery.

There are countries in this world where government officials and authorities are paid by the amount of bribes they can collect. This is, fortunately, not true in America, yet bribery is one of our most cherished and one of our oldest traditions.

We bribe our children, although we are forever telling each other it is a bad habit. We bribe high school athletes with fringe benefits on their scholarships, but for all this, most of us do not compromise ourselves.

I remember the magazine articles that used to ask, "How Far Should a Girl Go?" and after you read enough of them you realized a girl could go as far as she wanted as long as she didn't tell magazine editors about it. I suspect this is the reasoning that overtakes the boy who accepts the five hundred dollars from a gambler to shave points in the basketball game and the government official who lets a businessman pay his clothing bills or give his wife a vacation.

What the Americans worry about most

1. Calories
2. Communism
3. Body odor

PART 2

Swimming in the Ghetto

First came the Yankees

THE FIRST to occupy the Lower East Side were the Yankees. The Yankees named all the streets—Eldridge, Delancey, Orchard, Forsythe, Houston, Allen. After the Yankees came the Germans and then the Irish, the Bohemians, the Jews, the Russians, the Greeks, the Italians, the Poles. The colonial Yankees left their cemetery, which was in the heart of the ghetto I knew as a boy. This was the old Marble Cemetery on Second Street and Second Avenue. Here rested the bodies of old New Yorkers —John Ericsson, who built the *Monitor* in the Civil War (I think his body was later moved to his native country, Sweden). Here was the grave of President James Monroe, with the marker indicating that the body had been moved to his native Virginia. This was all a Protestant stronghold once—then Roman Catholic, then Jewish—and now the Negroes make it Protestant again.

In 1908 the illuminated cross on the steeple of St. Augustine's Chapel on Houston Street dominated the ghetto. It could be seen for blocks against the deep night sky, forever a fixture in our minds.

A half mile up Second Avenue was St. Mark's Lutheran Church. Everybody on the East Side knew the story that the body of A. T. Stewart, original owner of Wanamaker's Department Store, had been stolen from its resting place in the church's graveyard.

Later the entire East Side went into mourning because of the great tragedy that afflicted St. Mark's Lutheran Church. The parish lost most of its children in a terrible disaster when the *Slocum*, a holiday ship, caught fire. Many of the children who jumped overboard were caught by the big knifelike paddles of the excursion boat. The Jewish organizations marched in the St. Mark's funeral procession.

Second Avenue was the Great White Way of the Lower East Side, a promenade for the young people. On Sunday afternoons it was a gay sight. Up this street we sold our newspapers as newsboys among the thousands of factory workers who poured out of the tenements in the morning, all moving toward the clothing factories and department stores beyond Union Square.

On the corner of Second Avenue and Fourteenth Street was the Labor Temple. I remember the signs *Lecture Tonight* that daily announced the evening's activities. I heard Margaret Sanger there, Will Durant, and Clarence Darrow. The Labor Temple was founded by Charles Stelze, a Presbyterian clergyman, one of the many Christians who worked among Jewish immigrants to help them into the open society of America. Frances Perkins came to the East Side early, as did Eleanor Roosevelt and Mrs. August Belmont, and I remember volunteer social workers from the fashionable St. Thomas' Episcopal Church on Fifth Avenue.

Nothing was disposable

I DON'T remember that the Lower East Side of New York ever had much of a problem with garbage. Certainly 100,000 tons wouldn't have littered the streets in a few days if trouble came. There were garbage cans in the hall—that I remember—and they were emptied into horse-drawn wagons by muscular draymen who, it seems to me, came once a month into our neighborhood.

The real difference between the administrations of Mayor

William J. Gaynor and John V. Lindsay was that in Gaynor's day nothing was disposable. Garbage was at a minimum. My mother carried a leather shopping bag to the market. She bought fresh vegetables with no cellophane wrapper; she bought fresh cuts of meat with no cardboard tray to throw away; she bought fresh bread, so there was no waxed paper to discard. I don't remember seeing tin cans or plastic bottles or any of the paraphernalia which clutters the kitchen today.

Today, I understand, the proud papa can buy baby's formula in nursettes which Mommy throws away when baby's through. The diapers are used only once.

My mother boiled everything for my baby brother and emptied the drip pan under the ice box to boot. Life was harder for her but easier for the mayor. The mayor had to contend with grafters and crooks but never with contumacious union leaders and governors with their own ideas.

We slept on tough horsehair mattresses and envied Emperor Franz Josef of the Austro-Hungarian Empire. Royalty owned feather mattresses, downy pads which surrounded the incumbent with immediate soft sleep. About the time I could afford one of these mattresses, my doctor told me I'd be better off sleeping on a board. Now I own a bed off whose mattress anyone can bounce ping-pong balls. The beds last longer, I suppose, but I don't know how kids can have a pillow fight with foam rubber pillows. Getting a whack over the head with foam rubber is like getting socked with a wet towel.

Every noon, my father poured himself a thimbleful of brandy and held it to the window to see the glass refract the light, just as a diamond expert would hold a jewel to see its reflections. My father studied that brandy for two minutes, and then with a motion as delicate as a ballet dancer's he downed it and said, "Ah!" as though man were first discovering a new taste thrill. In my father's home I never saw any man take more than one thimbleful.

Well, that's changed. I take my first bourbon at ten in the morning and my last at five in the afternoon. I never drink after

sundown, and I consider myself moderate. I've watched vital
businessmen leave New York restaurants at two in the afternoon
so groggy the doorman has to pour them into cabs. It's a good
thing there are no more drip pans to be emptied, or the little
woman might have to empty it over said vital businessman to
sober him so he could see the kids before they grow up.

A table for New Year's

NEW YEAR'S DAY celebrates the circumcision of Christ. It
is an important religious holiday, a day venerated by Christians.

But New Year's Eve is the only religious holiday that other
religions have no inhibitions about celebrating. Some of our
holidays are meaningless to others. The Sikhs, for instance, who
come here from India to study, are interested in Christmas and
Thanksgiving Day only as cultural phenomena.

Everybody gets the idea of New Year's Eve. After all, the year,
like the week, has to start some place. January is a convenient
time. We live in a business world. People count up profit and
loss on December 31. What could be a happier thought than
starting the New Year with a party, profit or no?

If you're young, you can worry about whether *she'll* spend
New Year's Eve with you, and if she will, you can start worrying
how much she'll eat. If you're old, you and the wife can stay up
and toast the coming year with hot milk. On New Year's Eve
we all have one thing in common: We're all up until midnight.

On the Lower East Side we all looked forward to New Year's
Eve. It made no difference whether you were a hat presser or
a tailor or a law student or a peddler who tramped New Jersey
with a pack of needles and thread on your back. New Year's Eve
made everyone a sophisticate.

The question you heard all over the East Side was, "Have you
got a table?" People rented tables for a New Year's Eve party.

They rented them in halls, in restaurants, in coffee shops, even in kosher delicatessens.

These tables were free and vacant any night in the year. Many of them would have been free and vacant on New Year's Eve, too. But young men put a special emphasis on the table for their party. So you went into Moscowitz's or Katz's and told them you wanted a table for New Year's Eve. This was assurance you'd have a good time.

It is true that for many of these places you took potluck. The table that was empty when you came in was the very one you had reserved.

"Have you got a table?" was what they asked. If you didn't have one, you got one. You asked a friend to split the cost with you, and if neither of you had a sweetheart, well, it was worth the price so you could answer, "Yes, I've got a table. Have you got a table?"

If you had a sweetheart *and* a job, you'd met her family and she'd met yours and neither family complained much about the other, you not only were expected to have "a table," but you were expected to go to a show. You went uptown to see Frank Bacon or Ethel Barrymore or Walter Hampden. Or you went to the Yiddish theater on Second Avenue and applauded David Kessler or Boris Thomashefsky or Jacob Adler, the peer of them all. And if you were a music lover you went to the Metropolitan to hear *Les Huguenots*. The theater impresarios saved the real tragedies for New Year's Eve. No one ever has a complaint about a play he sees on New Year's Eve.

After the play you went to where you'd reserved your table, and later you walked your sweetheart home. You felt dwarfed by the quiet of the big city and small and minuscule, but you knew you were part of it and part of the year that had just come.

The "less desirables"

IN OUR country we have this tremendous mobility, a mobility not only from place to place but from one income level to another income level, from one social level to another social level, from a tenement to a suburb, from the ghetto of the Lower East Side of New York to the most American society on this continent.

But there's more to this symbol than meets the eye. The philosophers have offered us a basic truth: The less satisfaction we derive from being ourselves, the greater is our desire to be like others, and we therefore are more inclined to imitate those who have found such great favor in our eyes.

It is the particular good fortune of the United States of America that she welcomed 17,000,000 immigrants from what some of our legislators have regarded as "less desirable" origins. America was very lucky. Had all our millions of immigrants continued to come from what we call "superior cultures," there would have not been one United States of America but a balkanized string of lingual and cultural groups right up to World War I. The more desirable immigrants from northern Europe insisted, for example, that their Old World languages be taught in our public schools. They asked how this new country could compare with Goethe and Schiller and Mozart and Charles Dickens. They felt terribly sorry for us—no Henry VIII, no Queen Elizabeth, no Shakespeare.

But God was on our side, and while Senator McCarran was not looking, there came these 17,000,000—the lowest, the poorest, the despised, and the rejected. They came with the ardent desire to shed their Old World identities. The strangeness of the new country attracted rather than repelled them. They had the enthusiasm that comes to the man who is born again. To the non-Anglo-Saxons the strangeness of the language was the added attraction; to have to learn to speak again enhanced this illusion of being born again. They were people in a hurry, and people who are in a hurry will imitate more readily than people who are at leisure.

They came off the gangplank, looked into the face of the first American they saw, and said the same thing in eleven different languages: "Ah, when will I be like him?"

This stream of vitality came into being because these less desirable immigrants knew they must make good. They knew they dared not relax. The operations they performed, the pupils they taught, the styles they created and manufactured, the songs they wrote and sang, the books they wrote, the lives they gave, these were not because these immigrants were better than the natives. Their success in entering the American middle class so quickly came because they did not think they were as good as the natives. The "less desirable" immigrant knew that the only way he could escape being forever alien was to achieve a special individual worth. He knew that a stethoscope in his ear would enable him to jump from fifteenth-century eastern Europe into the American twentieth century. His patients would no longer call him alien. They would merely say, "My doctor has such a cute accent."

The Jewish Bronx

IN 1917 when my family moved from the Lower East Side to the Bronx, there were still goats on Vyse Avenue. There were still wagons pulled by drays wending from Yonkers and New Rochelle to the markets. The subway went only to Simpson Street. From there I had to take the Huckleberry Line, a Toonerville trolley conveyance to our apartment—not tenement, mind you, apartment—on 174th Street. I remember on winter mornings the conductor stopped the trolley often to collect kindling for the potbellied stove. If a passenger sat near the stove he roasted to death, and if he sat far from it he froze.

I doubt seriously if we immigrants thought we were seeing the end of something, an era or a way of life. "Modern" as a concept of the environment did not gain popularity or meaning until the 1930's, when the architects discovered chrome and aluminum. But in the early years of the last century I suppose we were witnessing the end of rural America. Not all the immigrants moved to the South Bronx. Many went to Brooklyn, others to Fordham Road, and the luckiest of all to Riverside Drive in Manhattan.

That area of the South Bronx, the old Jewish enclave, was the subject of a feature story in Look magazine. Charles Mangel, in prose and picture, reveals the old synagogues are now littered with debris, that the families have moved to New Jersey or Connecticut; only the old people are left. Someone else, another group of people, is watching the end of something. One only hopes that the Negroes and Puerto Ricans who have invested the South Bronx will have as much luck as the Jews who are leaving. It is a hard place to live in now. Addicts walk its streets, and muggers. I would not say there is no hope. For there didn't seem that much hope when the Jews first moved there, alien people trying to escape the dirt and filth of the ghetto downtown, bringing new ways and sometimes annoying habits uptown.

Neighborhoods and cities change constantly. When I came to Charlotte, North Carolina, there was one Jewish temple, on Seventh Street. I doubt there were three shules in the entire state. In 1939 there were two hundred and fifty Jewish families in Charlotte. Now there are over one thousand, and the Reform temple is a tribute to modern design and planning. There are no arguments about whether the rabbi needs an air-conditioned study or the Hadassah a steam table. The temple is completely air-conditioned and has steam tables that will never be used.

When I came to Charlotte there were still farms and dairies within the city limits. There still are, but they are fewer and fewer every year, for land here as elsewhere is at a premium. In the years just before World War II, everyone I met had been born and bred on the red clay dirt of North Carolina. Now I have friends who grew up in Bangor and Terre Haute and who work here, and many of them do not plan to live the rest of their lives in Charlotte. Where they will spend their lives is never definite. I wonder if, when my friends leave Charlotte, they will change as other people leaving other places change.

Christmas every Friday

My Lord, our army is dispersed already:
Like youthful steers unyoked, they take their courses
East, west, north, south; or, like a school broke up,
Each hurries toward his home and sporting-place.

THE QUOTATION, of course, is Shakespeare's, from *King Henry IV*, Part II. Shakespeare knew everything and remembered it all. Is there ever a release as jubilant as Friday's release from school? It is one of those single moments which is always new no matter how many times over and over it recurs.

Going to school is the necessary ingredient. It is the release from discipline that creates the ecstasy. The boys "hanging around," our description of the dropouts circa 1910, never knew the exciting experience of school's out, and they were the poorer for it.

Much has been made of how children dislike school. I never remember disliking it on Monday morning. By Thursday there seemed many other things I would enjoy doing more. All of us on the Lower East Side of New York were quite well aware of how important school was, what promises it held forth. But these promises were never immediate, and we all said "Praise be" at 3 P.M. on Fridays.

Our joy was greater than that of the Irish and Italians. Friday afternoon not only began our weekend but our great religious holiday—the Sabbath. It is hard to re-create the reverence in which the Orthodox Jews of fifty years ago held the Sabbath.

Let me say the Irish and Italian boys had Christmas once a year and once a year a celebration on a saint's feast day. We had the same exaltation once a week, every week.

The Lower East Side was then the most populous neighborhood in the world. Its streets were jammed with peddlers and neighborhood shoppers. Poor though we were, people were always shopping, always bustling along the concrete canyons. On Fridays, however, there came a wondrous stillness. The streets were patrolled then only by the Irish cops. The bearded men who held the young boys by the hand had made their way to the synagogue. Two blocks away from the synagogue that cop could hear the muffled chant of the cantor and the murmuring of prayers by the congregation.

Once the service was over, a boy came home to find his mother in her one silk dress with a white scarf over her head.

At the Sabbath feast, a father told his sons how all the sufferings of Jews through the ages were dedicated to this one moment, the celebration of the Sabbath, God's supreme gift.

The Sabbath was the most important event in life. Becoming an engineer or a doctor or a writer or a salesman was secondary to celebrating its arrival. Accomplishment was a bonus, as it were. Eventually, however, the bonus absorbed the joy of the Sabbath, which is perhaps as it should be.

A carrousel for Osaka

THE EL DORADO carrousel at Coney Island was the largest merry-go-round in the world. It mounted not only silver horses and velvet chariots but a four-ton organ. It was 62 feet in diameter. When I first rode the El Dorado in 1911, the first year of its operation, a ride cost one cent on the weekdays and two cents on Sunday. Hand-carved nymphs playing trumpets surrounded the perimeter. An esthetician could probably testify the El Dorado was the apogee of the baroque.

I took my wife for a ride on that merry-go-round, and I suppose I held each of my sons as they galloped in circles on pink pigs. I hesitate to say the El Dorado was to me what the "Rosebud" sled was to Citizen Kane. Yet I was touched the other day when I read the carrousel had been rescued from storage and was on its way to Osaka, Japan, where it will entertain still more thousands of the adventurous at the World's Fair there in 1970. I am sure the Japanese kids will love this merry-go-round as we Lower East Side immigrant boys did.

The thrill of Coney Island was that it was only a nickel away from Delancey Street. Its gaudy frills and honkytonk atmosphere never seemed jaded to us because we never had that many nickels. For thirty cents we could make a day out of Coney Island. Subway fare out and back was a dime. We would go swimming—bathing, we called it then—and we would spend another eight cents for an ear of corn which the vendor dipped into a vat of melted butter and a hot dog almost suffocated between the roll by forkfuls of sauerkraut. We rode the roller coaster, the merry-go-round, the bumper cars, and if we had any change left bought an ice-cream cone or a charlotte russe.

The boardwalk was filled with the strollers, and we would pose in front of the distorting mirrors which decorated the fun house. There was a nickelodeon filled with movie machines which resembled the modern parking meter. For a penny you could peer through the lens and twist the knob and see movies. That was, of course, long ago, in the days when the moon was something the cow jumped over and not a landing field for astronauts.

Coney Island was a changeless amusement park, an idea of fun as much as it was a place. But around the opening of the World's Fair in 1939, I remember the amusements began to change. There was a parachute jump which hoisted people 300 feet high and set them shooting down cables with silk billowing above. The last time I was there—perhaps thirty years ago—I spent a half hour watching people play bingo for prizes which ranged from kewpie dolls to electric toasters. A charlotte russe

cost twenty cents, although the beach was still filled with kids
who traveled on the subway wearing their bathing trunks underneath their clothes.

That the El Dorado merry-go-round is still revolving somewhere is a comforting thought. I hope the concessionaire makes
his profit, but I hope his prices are low enough for thousands of
kids who will come out of Osaka for a ride and stroll.

The Yiddish theater

The Yiddish theater along the Lower East Side of New
York City around the turn of the century and for twenty years
afterward was a sort of ever-continuing cross between a soap
opera and a university. It presented to its audience the conflicts
engendered in the process of becoming an American. It stated
the attitudes and counterattitudes of an immigrant *milieu*. But
this was a week-to-week process. Few plays lasted longer than
four nights. Their literary quality was, to say the least, suspect.

Jacob Latteiner, who wrote over one hundred plays, improvised
a whole play in one afternoon by the simple expedient of dressing himself in the costumes of the different characters and walking on in each role while the actors feverishly took notes. Of
Professor M. Hurwitz, another Yiddish playwright, actors used
to say they did not have to memorize their sides in any new
play, so alike were all his heroes and villains.

The themes of both these playwrights were realistic ones.
They always dealt with the conflict between the older, immigrant generation and the younger, assimilating generation. In
addition, the Yiddish theater often had weddings staged after
the show. Amateur night was initiated at Miner's Theatre.

The Yiddish theater was socialistic in character and owed its
profits to the motives of charity. Every performance was a
"benefit." On the Lower East Side you rarely heard the statement, "I'm going to the theater," but rather, "I'm going to a

benefit." Along with the prohibition "Post No Bills" and the important phrase "working papers," "benefit" was one of the first English words the Jewish immigrant learned.

My father, Reb Lebche, was president of the Mikulinczer Verein (Galicia), and he was in charge of hundreds of benefits for his society. Twice a year the Mikulinczer benefit was to provide dowries for unmarried girls in that Jewish community in the then Austro-Hungarian Empire.

A Mikulinczer benefit operated much the way a milk fund benefit operates today. The organization bought every seat in the house at a discount, sold the tickets to members and friends, and the net profit went to the designated cause.

My father always made a speech between the second and third acts. He owned a cutaway coat and a huge silk hat and was so articulate he made the women weep when he spoke.

Monday, Tuesday, Wednesday, and Thursday nights were invariably benefit nights. If the Mikulinczer Verein gave a benefit to help unmarried girls, so did the anarchists give up talking treason to hold a benefit for fellow members imprisoned in Siberia.

The cost of a ticket ranged between twenty-five cents and one dollar. On Friday, Saturday, and Sunday performances, however, the house could always sell out at $1.25—this despite the fact that two of these performances would fall on the Sabbath, Friday night and the Saturday matinee, a time when an Orthodox Jew will undertake no activity save walking to the *shule*.

The American ethic is a persuasive ethic, and the theaters, for better or for worse, were crowded with the Orthodox on the Sabbath. There were many whose consciences still gnawed them. Often they eased their consciences by heckling an actor whose role somehow desecrated the Sabbath. The audience would yell, "Smoking a cigar on the Sabbath, boo boo boo!" The actor would look startled at the hypocrites who should have been in *shule* at that very moment.

Physically, the Yiddish theater was located in several community centers, verein auditoriums, and lecture halls. Of the legitimate theaters, five were prominent—The People's Theatre, the Windsor, Miner's, the Thalia, and David Kessler's Second Avenue Theatre. The Thalia was the ritziest. It allowed no babies.

If the Thalia wasn't filled with mewling infants, it was still filled with shouting vendors. When the first-act curtain rang down, the aisles were filled with boys and men hawking ice cream, charlotte russes, and anarchist pamphlets. And sometimes they didn't wait for the curtain but surreptitiously started down the aisles while actors delivered their impassioned monologues. Most of the immigrants were young boys and girls whose parents had sent them on to America. On Saturday afternoons, the Thalia Theatre was filled with shop girls who had a good cry listening to Lucy Gherman sing "The Eibega Mama" (The Eternal Mother).

The curtains were always decorated with advertisements. Once, when Jacob Adler returned after an illness, he had a big red ad hung on the curtain at the People's Theatre which read, "The splendid eagle spreads his wings again."

The Yiddish audience was composed of the factory worker, peddler, shopkeeper, anarchist, socialist, rabbi, scholar, and journalist. And it served yet another function which has never been adequately explored. The shadkhan (professional matchmaker) used the Yiddish theater as the most convenient (and elevating) place for his couples to hold their first meeting. After preliminary discussion with each of the families he gave one ticket to the girl and the other to the boy. It gave the couple a chance to see each other without embarrassment or overcommitment. At the end of the evening they could say, one to the other, "I hope to see you again," without any definite invitation, and that was that, or the girl could invite the fellow to her home, which gave him still another chance to get out of it. But if he accepted, it indicated that a deal was on the way.

But the performance itself was only the beginning of the "Yiddish theater." It was a culture that involved round-the-clock arguments in the coffee houses, occupied pages of newsprint, and often divided families in fierce discussions over the relative merits of "the show" or the playwrights. Everybody was a critic, and the morning after a performance the fellow pressing pants in the factory would give his "review" of the opening the night before. Invariably he would say it was a *shmahta* (a rag)—a nothing. The interesting thing about these opinions was that the "reviewer" did not know that the *shmahta* was often an Ibsen, a Shaw, or a Sudermann play which the playwright had "oriented" to a sort of "Jewishness." But the intellectuals did not spare the playwrights, and Jacob Gordin, the most prolific of them, was also the most controversial figure in the Yiddish theater. After a Gordin opening the theatergoers waited for the inevitable blast from the editor of the *Forward*, Mr. Abe Cahan. His invective and satire was often a better "play" than Gordin had written. From there the coffee houses would take up the matter, and many a rolled-up newspaper came down on the head of a more effervescent Gordin (or Cahan) supporter.

But the actors were above criticism. People had their favorites, and where the big three were involved, Adler, Kessler, and Thomashefsky, there could be considerable argument, but all were highly respected. In fact, until their children discovered Ty Cobb and Christy Mathewson, the immigrants virtually made folk heroes out of the actors.

Thomashefsky was a sort of matinee idol, particularly after he appeared in tights in one of his musicals. He had gigantic thighs, which caused many a sigh among the immigrant women at a time when heft was still a mark of beauty. Adler was a source of great pride because of the recognition he had earned as an artist beyond the borders of the Yiddish world. When my father said "Yakob Adler," it sounded almost like a silent prayer.

Yet many of the experts believed that David Kessler was the greatest of them all. When he opened his Second Avenue Theatre with "God, Man and Devil," most of the important theatrical figures of Broadway were in attendance, and it was

Kessler who coached Enrico Caruso when the great Italian tenor was preparing his role as Eléazar in *La Juive*.

In public the actor would have two or three sets of disciples guarding his privacy, and the most honored place was the one closest to the actor himself. Bernard G. Richards, one of the stalwarts of Yiddish journalism, once wrote a sketch about the fortunate fellow who was so close to Adler that he was always known as *K'mat Adler*, meaning "Almost Adler."

By far the favorite playwright of the Lower East Side audience was William Shakespeare. I believe that eventually all of his plays were translated into Yiddish and adapted for the Jewish stage. Of course, these dramas were appreciably different from what they were when the Elizabethans first saw them at the Globe Theatre.

The Yiddish *Hamlet* (*The Yeshiva Bukher*) opened faithfully enough with the wedding feast. Claudius was no king, however, but a rabbi who occupied a position of prestige in a Russian village. Though Claudius was no murderer, he had metaphorically killed the king by wooing and winning Queen Gertrude. Young Hamlet arrives, fresh from his ordination as a rabbi, and turns the wedding feast into a funeral. The party degenerates into scenes of quarrels between mother and Hamlet, Ophelia and Hamlet, Polonius (a merchant) and Hamlet. The wicked Claudius conspires against Hamlet, convincing the villagers that he is a nihilist who does not believe in God. But Hamlet uncovers the plot, and the uncle is exiled to Siberia.

The most popular of all Shakespearean plays was the Yiddish *King Lear*. *King Lear* was a natural—a play about bad daughters and good daughters and the misery of an aged father. In the Yiddish *King Lear*, Goneril and Regan leave their father's house to marry Gentiles, while Cordelia stays faithfully by his side.

The popularity of the Yiddish theater began to decline along about 1930, when the children of the immigrants began to leave the Lower East Side for the open areas of Riverside Drive, the Bronx, and Westchester and Fairfield counties. A theater is only as popular as its language. As spoken Yiddish perceptively diminished, so did the theater decline.

It was one of the most productive of all theaters—and one of the most glamorous.

The performers who made the jump from the Yiddish to the American stage would make a respectable Who's Who of the American theater: Paul Muni, Edward G. Robinson, Luther and Stella Adler, Jacob Ben-Ami, Menasha Skulnik, Maurice Schwartz, Joseph Schildkraut, and many others, including my friends the Bernardis—Boris Bernardi, manager of the touring company of *Once Upon a Mattress*, and Herschel Bernardi, who played Lieutenant Jacoby on the *Peter Gunn* television series and who was also "Harry Golden" in the West Coast production of *Only in America*, by Jerry Lawrence and Bob Lee.

It was a world filled to overflowing with humor. There must be many of my contemporaries who remember the famous Grossman poster announcing a new *pyessa* ("piece"—a new show): "Samuel B. Grossman, Producer and Actor, presents *The Sorrowing Father*, a new play in Three Acts by Samuel B. Grossman; with Irving Grossman, Joseph Grossman, Helen Grossman, Music by B. S. Grossman. For benefits write to Treasurer Joseph Grossman."

Tickets to *Tobacco Road*

DURING THE depths of the Depression while I was a clerk in the Markwell Hotel, *Tobacco Road* was playing in the theater next door. When it first opened, *Tobacco Road* was nothing short of a flop but hung on to become eventually one of the longest-running plays in the American theater. At one point the producers were giving away free tickets for this show in the hopes that word of mouth might sustain the show. I got many of these tickets, and one morning, coming in on the commuting train from Red Bank, New Jersey, I gave two of these tickets to a rich neighbor who had a seat on the stock exchange.

Later in the day, he called me and asked if it was possible for me to get two more of these tickets. I said I would try and even asked him for the seat numbers. Sure enough, when I went next door to the theater, they had two empty seats beside the two I had given to the broker.

When I delivered these two tickets to my friend, he fell all over himself with gratitude. I assured him it was nothing, but he wouldn't have it. He insisted I join them for dinner, and he ordered all the courses. He couldn't do enough for me. He could have bought all those four tickets for eight dollars, but the fact that they had been obtained for him *gratis* was what thrilled and excited him. He bought forty dollars' worth of champagne to celebrate those eight-dollar tickets which he had received as a gift.

He even told me about some stock that was going to declare a special dividend in a couple of weeks. Had I bought that stock, I would today be measured conservatively to be worth about a half-million dollars. But if I had had the money to buy even one share of stock in those days, I would probably have bought into Wanamaker's Corner and be worth even more. Those two tickets are as close as I have ever come to a half-million, however.

Pretzels in the Polo Grounds

I'VE LOVED baseball all my life. All the immigrant boys on the Lower East Side loved it, too. In the summer I took turns with the other boys going to the Polo Grounds, which was 'way uptown then and today is no more, just a housing development.

Bock's Bakery was not far from our neighborhood. Mr. Bock made the pretzels for Harry Stevens, who owned the food and drink concessions at the ball park. We boys rotated delivering the pretzels from the East Side to the Polo Grounds. Mr. Bock paid us ten cents and gave us carfare up and back, and we carried two huge baskets of the pretzels to the concessionaire. But this errand got us in free to the Polo Grounds in the morning.

We spent two hours roaming around the caverns of the empty stadium, and then about noon the ballplayers came out and took their practice. I think the games used to start at three in the afternoon in those days, by which time, of course, the dime Mr. Bock had given us as well as the ten or fifteen cents our mothers passed out had been expended on hot dogs and Moxie, the cola of the day.

It was a long wait, but one of the pleasures was that we got to talk to the ballplayers when they took their noon workouts. Those of us who were well behaved often were admitted by the doorman to the clubhouse, and we were right up close to our heroes. I made pals with a New York Giant pitcher named Jeff Tesreau, a big fellow who for seven innings, the sportswriters said, was probably the best in the league. Later he became a coach at Dartmouth. Those were the days when Christy Mathewson and Jeff Tesreau were John McGraw's mainstays. Mr. Tesreau once came home with me to sample a Jewish meal and later took me to Fox's Theater on Fourteenth Street.

Mathewson, the greatest pitcher in baseball, was aloof, not a snob, but by nature a quiet and distant man. The rookies on the team called him mister, and only John McGraw and the veterans called him Matty. He was one of the first college graduates to become a big-leaguer. He broke the tradition that said this game was only for the sons of Pennsylvania miners or Southern sharecroppers.

I think what really makes baseball the great American pastime is the fact that of all our sports, it most easily lends itself to statistical assessment.

Look at the averages—the batting averages, the fielding averages, the team averages, the earned-run averages, and the changes in the daily standings. We are a nation addicted to quantity, and nothing symbolizes quantity like numbers. Baseball, with all its fractions and percentages, is poetry in figures

I still enjoy baseball, but I guess I identify the sport with those days of great fun when I delivered the pretzels to Mr. Stevens.

Tales of poverty

MANY YEARS ago my brother Jacob lost the two fingers of his right hand. I was eight years old when this accident happened, which makes it exactly fifty-nine years ago. Jack (for by this time we were Yankees and had metamorphosed Jacob into Jack) worked in a sweatshop on Mott Street, on the Lower East Side of New York. The factory made pocketbooks, and Jack operated the stamping machine which impressed cleats and clips and buckles into the leather. One afternoon his hand got caught in the machine.

I remember a policeman came to the house to tell us Jack had been taken to a hospital. In those days, as now, a policeman came to your house only to bring bad news. He asked neighbors where your family lived, and the neighbors knew it was bad news and were hesitant in telling him. They thought, of course, if they didn't tell him where you lived, the bad news would dissipate. But the policeman persevered and went on up the stairs, and one neighbor told another, so that when the policeman came out there was already a gathering crowd, apprehensive and curious.

Jack lost his fingers in the days before Governor Alfred E. Smith had made workmen's compensation part of the law of New York. I am not sure whether someone paid for Jack's hospitalization. I am sure no one paid for the lost wages, to say nothing of the fingers. In those days, too, people said, "He works for a wonderful firm, the boss paid all the doctor's bills."

Jack went back to work eventually—at an office-type job— but the interesting thing about the whole event is that a few years later I told my friends on Rivington Street that Jack lost his fingers in a shooting duel.

Jack's new job was as a clerk in a Broadway hotel (which I too was to become later), and this enabled me to embellish the story. I said a robber had come into the hotel one night and Jack had shot it out with him. Jack killed the robber, all right, but lost his fingers in the shooting match. What made the story credible to my friends was my telling them the robber had aimed for Jack's shooting hand. Bronco Billy was a movie star at the time, and he was always shooting the gun out of the villain's hand.

Such are the stories of poverty. Tragedies are always enlivened with a heavy dose of romance. When you get up in the world, you are not ashamed of having worked in a sweatshop and losing an argument with a stamping machine instead of a desperado. If Jack hadn't come up in the world, I suspect he too would have begun telling about the robber.

The poor are ashamed of their earliest beginnings, while the rich will exaggerate the hardships and wear their former poverty like a badge of honor.

Pushcart peddlers

THE PUSHCART peddlers sold just about everything, but the Italians stuck mostly to vegetables, fruit, fish, and other edibles. The Jewish pushcart peddlers went in more for apparel, umbrellas, and kitchen and household utensils.

The rent of a pushcart was ten cents a day. There were some traveling pushcarts, and the peddler would shout at the top of his voice in his native tongue, advertising his merchandise. Most of them, however, were permitted to have permanent stands on certain streets in Manhattan. It was necessary to get a pushcart license, but many of them evaded this requirement, and they were always in trouble.

During the administration of Mayor George B. McClellan, the police in New York were famous for their brutality and would use their clubs at the drop of a hat. The pushcart peddlers were fair game. The cops chased them from pillar to post, making wholesale arrests daily. They took them and their pushcarts to the police station and then took them to court before a judge. They were charged with peddling without a license or obstructing street corners, and the judge would fine them a dollar. Most of them stayed in jail till two in the afternoon to save the dollar fine, because they couldn't earn that much in those few hours or maybe even in a whole day. Most of the peddlers complained that while they were in court the cops ransacked their pushcarts.

There was a special pushcart for the sale of baked sweet potatoes, knishes, and chick-peas. It was equipped with a stove under four or five galvanized tin drawers in which the stuff was kept hot. Operating this kind of a pushcart took considerable skill. You had to be a fireman as well as a merchant. My uncle Berger, who eventually became wealthy in the hotel business, started out as a *haysa bubbes* (hot chick-peas) pushcart peddler. In his later years he always said that his first job in America was an "engineer," referring to the pushcart with the stove contraption.

Abuse of peddlers by the police was lessened considerably when Mayor Gaynor was elected. The first thing Mayor Gaynor did was to take the nightsticks away from the cops. Then he discontinued arrests for violations of city ordinances, and the police now had to issue summonses. This order played hell with hundreds of Irish immigrant cops who couldn't read and write. This is when that old joke was born about the cop who found a dead horse on Kosciusko Street; he got a rope and dragged the carcass around to Third Avenue so he could fill out his report.

Later on the peddlers became powerful politically, with a strong organization, and Mayor Jimmie Walker had to climb five flights of stairs to attend a bar mitzvah—that of the son of the president of the Pushcart Peddlers Association.

Then came La Guardia and the World's Fair. He said that

with people coming from all over the world the pushcarts would have to get off the streets. He built huge markets where the city charged a weekly rental of three to four dollars, and that practically eliminated the pushcarts.

It was very hard, but it also had its tremendous rewards in experience. From these pushcarts have grown the huge wholesale fruit and vegetable businesses. Some Italian pushcart peddlers became great importers of spaghetti and olive oil and other commodities from Italy. The Jewish peddlers became merchants, and now and then a former pushcart peddler has been introduced to an audience, justifiably, as a "merchant prince."

Free music lessons

ON RIVINGTON STREET is the University Settlement House. I went as a boy to the public baths in the basement and belonged to a debating club. I used its library and took music lessons there.

Thousands of children learned to play and to love music. Many of us only had meager talent, but what mattered is that we were cultivating a taste for one of the basic values of life.

The New York settlement houses are still there, though the neighborhoods are different. But they still teach music. Free music lessons were perhaps not the greatest gift America gave to the immigrant, but certainly they were one of the kindest.

The University Settlement House had a reunion recently. What was the menu? *Southern fried* chicken, of course.

Swimming in the ghetto

STANDING IN line early in the morning to get to use the swimming pool in the Rivington Street public bathhouse, cotton swimming trunks and a towel were all the credentials you needed to enter. Sometimes you waited as long as an hour before your turn. A speedy undressing, an obligatory shower, a plunge into the pool's cool green water, and fifteen minutes of pure joy with your gang. Then the gong as signal to get out of the pool . . . drying, dressing, wringing out the cotton trunks. The next contingent of kids was rushing to get in, and you went to the end of the line to get another fifteen minutes in that pool.

Levy and Rosalsky

IT IS a mark of affluence and status to have a person of prominence at your affair, to be there when they make the presentation to the *Man of the Year*.

Aaron J. Levy and Otto Rosalsky were among the first East Side boys to gain prominence in the open society, a big lawyer and a big judge. How many bar mitzvahs did Aaron J. Levy and Otto Rosalsky attend? You can count them by the hundred. The bar mitzvah was for a son of the head of the Pushcart Peddlers Association, the big wholesaler, someone else with influence in the congregation and in the voting precinct—and the invitation went to Aaron J. Levy or to Judge Otto Rosalsky. And they could hardly refuse. It meant something to them, not only in votes when they ran for public office, but in the councils of their respective political organizations—Aaron J. Levy in Tammany Hall and Otto Rosalsky in the Republican "Tammany Hall" under the leadership of Samuel Koenig. It was part of the game to shake hands with the thirteen-year-old boy after you asked someone to tell you his name.

The exotic capital

O'HENRY WAS one of the first writers to fall in love with New York City. It was an exotic capital to him. The city may no longer resemble the "Baghdad-on-Hudson" O'Henry described. Yet despite pollution and smog, countless thousands of young men and women still make their pilgrimages to it, thereby sustaining O'Henry's greater truth: that *the city* is still, to the young, the fabulous American dream of endless possibility.

My first dentist

IT IS a long way from paying fifty cents to have a tooth pulled to paying three thousand dollars to get a few teeth capped. This is quite a jump.

My friend David Krex of Mamaroneck, New York, reminds me of our dentist, Dr. Vetter, whose office was on Fifth Street on the Lower East Side. He was a kind old gent who depended more on touch than on sight. He always wore a Prince Albert coat, a wing collar, and an immaculately white shirt with wide starched cuffs. He spoke with a thick German accent, and he had a Kaiser beard like Emperor Franz Josef. He would tap every tooth in your mouth, and when you made a face, he knew he had hit the right one. Before you knew it, he dove into your mouth with the forceps—which had been concealed in the wide starched cuffs—and yanked out the tooth without injection or anesthesia. When you got home and began to rinse your mouth with the salt water, you always wondered whether he had pulled the right one.

The explorers

I APPLAUDED the decision to call the new bridge across New York Bay the Verrazano-Narrows Bridge.

I had been talking about Giovanni da Verrazano for over twenty years.

Verrazano's claim to exploration greatness was a result of his activities as a pirate. He had captured two French ships which had been dispatched by Cortez from Mexico, and the loot so impressed Francis I that the king commissioned Verrazano to explore the possibilities for French settlements in America, at the same time being ever on the alert for more treasure ships.

There has been some debate whether Verrazano actually entered New York Harbor, but his letter to Francis I dated January 8, 1524, is not only authentic but fully descriptive of that voyage. It was on this journey that Verrazano first sighted land near Cape Fear and spent two weeks on what is now the North Carolina coast and then continued his journey north to New York Harbor and eventually eastward to Narragansett Bay and Cape Breton.

In 1527 he embarked on another expedition, to Brazil. There he was captured by native Caribs, killed, and probably devoured in 1528.

I hope the next bridge in the New York area, or at the very least some important municipal project, will be named for Big Tim Sullivan, one of my favorite New Yorkers. He was also an explorer in his position of Tammany Hall sachem of the old Sixth Ward. And he had as much imagination as Giovanni da Verrazano, maybe more. Big Tim once had the ballots perfumed so he could tell whether or not his followers were voting the way they were paid to vote.

PART *3*

The Three Myths

Economics, animal crackers, and Einstein's letter

NOTHING IS as hard to understand as economic theories. This is because economists have managed to subtract all passion from the most interesting subject in the world—money.

The gross national product (or GNP) is just a phrase a Presidential candidate or Presidential Cabinet adviser tosses around.

Animal crackers will teach you about inflation faster than a fast-talking PhD. Animal crackers, about which Shirley Temple so lovingly once sang, used to cost a nickel. These days animal crackers are nineteen cents. They have moved from the necessity shelves in the supermarket into the luxury shelves, which are at a child's eye level so he will spot things he shouldn't have and throw a tantrum. That is how I understand inflation—by its total effect on the family.

One of the reasons poverty is still with us is that the unemployed are always represented by percentage points, not by their anguish. The poor are no longer referred to as poor, a word which has a certain Anglo-Saxon dignity and clarity. The poor are referred to as those with "marginal incomes" or as "welfare recipients," as though the Latinization of their plight makes it more bearable.

It is harder to understand what the economists mean when they describe the gold drain than it is to understand Einstein's Theory of Relativity. I say this because I wrote Albert Einstein once. I introduced myself as a Jewish journalist and asked if he would care to comment about his accomplishment for the benefit of my readers. Einstein replied that he could not explain his theory to either Jewish or Gentile readers, but if any of them wanted to stop off at the Institute for Advanced Study in Princeton, he could play it for them on his violin.

You should see the explanations I got as a Jewish journalist from the gold-drain experts.

The three myths

THE AMERICAN society, I have finally decided, is propelled by three myths, not one of which has any validity in real life. Nevertheless, we salute each of these myths as gospel truth whenever someone drags it before our eyes.

The first of these myths is that Spanish is an important language. In 1912, when I began my high school studies, my home room teacher touted Spanish. Trade with Latin America, he said pompously, was the coming thing, and the boy who spoke Spanish had a future. Spanish, he went on, was an easy language easily mastered, proficiency in which would gain me access into Harvard.

Fortunately for me, I cast aside this advice. Not so fortunately for some others, they took him at his word. Some of my classmates have retired from the post office, some are still making movies, and some made fortunes selling cheap dresses to fancy ladies who spoke Yiddish if they spoke any foreign language. None of them made a dime out of Spanish.

The headlines the other day informed me several Latin American countries wanted to know what had happened to Richard Nixon's campaign promises. They are holding their hands out, and Richard Nixon has put nothing in them. They forget they weren't able to vote. But the schools are still touting Spanish because Latin America is the coming continent. Rockefeller has trouble getting a night's sleep in Guatemala, so what makes our schools think a traveling Spanish-speaking salesman will have an easier time?

The next myth of meretricious proportions is that of the new car. Madison Avenue insists the whole town stands and gapes at the brand-new Electra or the Maverick or the Camaro.

The truth of the matter is that not only do all new cars look alike, but no one ever notices who is driving them. I have not personally owned a car for three years, and no one knows it unless I tell him.

The last of our myths is love. We believe that true love conquers time, space, and the neuroses.

If we could stop brainwashing ourselves about the prospects of love, Spanish, and the new car, we might get something done in the way of abolishing poverty.

I miss flying saucers

I MISS the flying saucers. I never saw a subject go away so fast from the front pages as they did. Even the hula hoop had a more dignified demise. Two years ago it seemed people were spotting the saucers here, there, and everywhere, and today —not a one to be seen.

I miss the saucers not because I thought they were there but because they made good copy. Richard Nixon's onward and upward climb to greatness, fame, and efficiency isn't interesting reading seven days a week. It's a slow progress anyway. But the saucers were absolute democracy. Cops in Des Moines saw them as well as Philadelphia lawyers. They picked up random motorists and manifested themselves to folks without cameras handy. The saucers were as interesting as spiritualism.

Fifty years ago I walked away from the mediums because I thought the dead were playing games with us. If I were going to talk to someone dead, I would rather talk to Georges Clemenceau, the Tiger of France, than to an Indian maiden who died in 1743, with whom I did speak in a séance in 1923. I was always suspicious of the dead because none of them ever spoke Yiddish.

This inhibition didn't exist with the saucers. They admitted no ethnic differentiations. They spun over the peaceful towns of Bethel, Vermont, and Pineville, North Carolina. I never myself understood why the saucer men would choose such out-of-the-way places. Washington, D.C., or New York would be my idea were I to come from Mars for a cursory exploration. But then we can't judge other worlds by ours.

What happened? I'll tell you what happened, the moon landings happened. Took all the romance out of outer space.

We have spent literally billions of dollars, and not one astronaut has sighted an unidentified flying object. This leads us to one of two conclusions: Either the astronauts sleep in orbit, or there are no UFO's.

Without UFO's what are columnists to do? What will become of the lunatic fringer? I always thought it was much more salutary for the health of the lunatics and the nation that they spent their time communicating with flying saucers than indulging in politics. And as I mentioned earlier, an editor makes much more sense discussing the existence or nonexistence of the Nixon Cabinet.

Violence on TV

ACCORDING TO Dr. William Stewart, Surgeon General of the Public Health Service, $1,000,000 is about to be spent on a survey to determine the effect of television violence on the young. He passed this information along to Senator John Pastore's subcommittee of the Commerce Committee. Senator Pastore is taking television to task for its bad taste and devotion to blood and thunder.

I wonder if any of the senators listening to the surgeon general were reminded of the $250,000 they did not particularly want to appropriate for another senatorial committee which was investigating hunger in the United States.

Does a study committee really need $1,000,000 to determine this effect? While I am no clinical psychologist or a Dr. Spock, I know the effect violence has on the young. When a kid sees violence on TV, he turns around and lets Daddy have one. This leaves the old man with three choices. He can throw the television set out the window, he can tolerate random blows, or he can let junior have five of the best right over the ear. This last goes a long way toward curbing juvenile aggression.

If the senators would listen to me, they would be freed from the unenviable task of trying to persuade TV network executives to finance segments of "Reasoning Together at the O.K. Corral." I have a feeling that tenement rats do more to destroy the family morale than the Noxzema girl who says, "Take it off, take it all off!" It took an awful lot of shaming before some of the senators voted the monies for a rent-control bill a few years ago. But $1,000,000 to find out why junior is full of hell is right up their alley.

The senators are asking whether the newscasts have to include such scenes as the Vietnamese police chief shooting a captured Vietcong through the head. The senators are not arguing it didn't happen; they are arguing whether we should know it or not. They are not even arguing that our knowing such crimes will inspire antiwar attitudes; they are arguing that this knowledge will teach us life is often pointless and cruel.

Television executives, of course, respond to Senate requests because they operate their stations under a federal license. These executives might point out in vain that Shakespeare manages more violence and terror in *Macbeth* than they could manage in five years of *Ironside* reruns. The argument will avail them naught. No senator can subpoena Shakespeare.

Senators who begin wondering what should or should not be shown make my blood run cold. Pretty soon they will get around to the big time, which is what should or should not be read. It is my contention that every television set has its own built-in censor: the knob.

The historical societies

GOOD NEWS!
I have been elected to the Mecklenburg Declaration Historical Society, with a whole house of its own, the bottom floor air-conditioned for the board of governors.

Until this moment I had always thought historical societies were self-governing bodies formed, say, in 1869 or 1871, whose members lived on with their trust into perpetuity.

Not so. Not so at all. Members are elected to fill vacancies for terms which expire from twenty to sixty years later. I fill the position of a professor emeritus whose term has expired now that he is seventy-eight, but he is far from expiration; in fact, he is going to Berkeley, California, to teach courses in metaphysical poetry, which he hopes will have some effect upon the rioters.

Our first meeting was a little sad. The chairman of the board of governors had to announce the treasurer had died. He hoped someone would volunteer for the interim appointment until the next elections, in 1975. Since I had run a business and still employ an accountant, I was quick to raise my hand. They didn't want me. The defunct treasurer hadn't really kept the books since 1943, and the board thought it might be wiser to appoint an older member who might recall some of the expenditures.

A word about the Mecklenburg Declaration. It preceded our Declaration of Independence by a few years. Unfortunately it was stored in a house out on Route 94, which is now the locus of a new development, and has never been recovered. But the folks swear to God it was written, and if the Redcoats hadn't paid a surprise visit to Charlotte, it would have made the city world famous.

There are unfortunately a lot of American cities with a coat of arms in the closet. Hartford, for example, boasts that the first constitution in the world was written within its confines in 1622. But the Redcoats showed up in 1628, and the patriots had to secret the charter in the famous Charter Oak, from which it was, alas, never recovered.

I heard a similar story when I lived in Monmouth County, New Jersey, and there's a story still circulating around the South about the plantation owner who figured out man was descended from the apes long before Darwin wrote his *Origin of Species*. This great thought was drowned out by the clattering of teacups during the small-talk hour on the old plantation.

I am proud, however, to sit on this board. It is nice to know some of the folks want to remember the real things. There are men who forget on what day World War II ended—August 28 —and a lot of men I talk to who complain about taxes being too high cannot remember when families used to chip in together to buy a bar of soap.

Lynching in America

THERE WERE always lynchings along the American frontier. The frontier was raw and dangerous, the people populating it violent and quick. But the number of frontiersmen summarily hanged was not in itself a sign of national weakness any more than the number of frontiersmen who succumbed to dysentery was. What does reveal a temperamental American weakness is the melancholy fact that when the frontier closed, lynching had an independent career.

Lynching, which is the killing or aggravated injury of a human being by the act or procurement of a mob, takes its name from Colonel Charles Lynch, an American Revolutionary soldier who helped found Lynchburg, Virginia. Colonel Lynch dispensed hard, fast justice to his tenant farmers and slaves in the courts he convened on his plantation.

As a popular word, "lynching" came into widespread use during the late 1830's. In 1834 aroused citizens of Vicksburg, Mississippi, formed vigilante committees to combat gambling, then flourishing in notorious houses along the riverfront. Well-organized raiding parties descended on these places, and all persons who were caught in the act of "dicing and gaming" were herded into the town square, where they were hanged without benefit of trial or hearings. As the notoriety of the incident spread, so did the word "lynching." The same fate that befell the Vicksburg gamblers was soon extended to abolitionists and escaped slaves. Thus "lynching" passed into the national vocabulary as a term roughly synonymous with "punishment." But it was not until after the Civil War that lynching found its chief victim— the American Negro, suddenly emerged in the unfamiliar role of free man.

Even before abolition, however, lynch mobs had taken a heavy toll of Negroes. And the white Southerner who marched with the mob had two ready explanations to defend his actions. In antebellum days he would say that lynching was necessary to counteract the threat of a slave revolt (this despite the fact that the only insurrection of any significance was that led by Nat Turner in 1831). After the Civil War, the Southerner said that mob action was the natural consequence of fear of Negro supremacy. When Rutherford B. Hayes recalled federal troops from the Confederacy, putting an end to Reconstruction, neither of these two explanations applied, even remotely, and the Southern apologist for lynching was forced to look elsewhere for a rationale. He found it in the Negro male's alleged sexual aggressiveness against white women, which proved to be a most effective appeal to the emotions and an infallible spur to violence. Schwerner, Goodman, and Cheney, Reverend Reeb and Mrs. Liuzzo lost their lives because their murderers thought that civil rights would lead to what Southerners dearly love to call mongrelization. The threat of miscegenation has been invoked not only in cases of intended or actual assault but also on numerous occasions when Negro males have been thought guilty of the crime of "ogling" or "leering."

Over five thousand Negroes have been lynched, half of them for alleged sexual crimes against white women. Even though 50 percent of lynch cases have been perpetrated on the basis of other transgressions, the terms used to describe the victim, such as "brute" and "beast," consistently evoke connotations of sexual aggressiveness.

Although lynching has been a constant in our culture for well over a century, it has not elicited an extensive literature. There are a number of sociological texts on the subject which describe specific lynchings and try to isolate generic causes. Such works often propose anti-lynching programs that emphasize education, religious instruction, and legislative action; they also stress the need for both Negroes and whites to reform. But the detached tone of these historical and sociological accounts minimizes the tragic and awful aspects of lynching, while at the same time they fail to suggest its endemic proportions.

An interesting sidelight on these texts is their correlation with antilynching legislation passed by Southern states. A surprisingly large and explicit body of such law has been written into the books by Dixie legislators, much of it dating back to the 1870's. Since few of these laws have ever been invoked to punish lynchers, the sociologists are right when they point out that these laws are no less than open invitations issued to mobs. For a half century Southerners have been able to prevent federal legislation against lynching by referring to their own antilynch laws, secure in the knowledge that no lynch mob has ever been identified under state laws, and in cases where individual lynchers have been brought to trial, no jury has ever convicted.

American fiction, too, lacks substantial comment on this subject. Few distinguished examples come to mind, and perhaps the best of these is a short story by William Faulkner called "Dry September." The story records the decent but ineffectual efforts of the town barber, Hawkshaw, to prevent the lynching of Negro Will Mayes by the bully John McLendon. "Dry September" ends with Miss Minnie Cooper's interior revelation in the midst of her hysteria that there was in fact no attack, no assault, no frightening encounter.

Another outstanding example, flawed but of great interest, is the fictionalized version of the Leo Frank case written by Ward Greene under the title *Death in the Deep South* (1936). Warner Brothers made a movie version of this novel in 1937 which was called *They Won't Forget*. It starred Claude Rains, Edward Norris, and Allyn Joslyn, and for what the information is worth, it introduced Lana Turner to the screen in the role of the ill-fated Mary Phagan. Greene was a close student of the Frank case, and he centered his attention on the district attorney, who undertook prosecution for political advancement, and on the journalist who inflamed the public in order to increase the sales and circulation of his newspaper. Leo Frank was a twenty-nine-year-old Jew, the superintendent of the National Pencil Company in Atlanta, Georgia. On Confederate Memorial Day, April 26, 1913, the murdered body of fourteen-year-old Mary Phagan was found in the basement of the pencil factory. Frank was arrested for the crime, tried, and in a courtroom besieged by mob fury and violence, convicted. When Governor John Slaton commuted the sentence to life imprisonment, not only did the Ku Klux Klan lynch Frank, but rioting Atlantans almost lynched Slaton.

Our literature has never encompassed the tragedy of lynching, not because our authors suffer from inherent limitations when confronted by the theme, but because the sadism of the mob, the attitudes and fears that band lynchers together, the torture they inflict and their reasons for inflicting them are essentially more dramatic and more interesting than the sufferings of the victim. The usual detective story, which enjoyed enormous popularity until very recently, when it was displaced by the spy thriller, operated on a similar principle: The murdered man was reduced to secondary interest, while great importance was given to the solution of the crime and the motives of the criminal. The victim is not important.

The Negro who suffered at the brutal hands of a lynch mob was almost invariably a cipher. Americans are prone to select their frequent heroes and martyrs capriciously, often for no good reason. We make no demand that hero or martyr either understand the causes of his hold on the public imagination or understand the forces that thrust him into prominence. In particular we suffer from a curious lack of interest in what went on in the minds of our various martyr-victims, what they were like. Truman Capote's recent novel *In Cold Blood* bears this out; when we are finished with the book, we know Perry and Dick intimately, Herb Clutter scarcely at all. Nor is this intended as fault-finding or serious criticism: Mr. Capote in his appeal to public taste in these matters has successfully achieved his intention.

Lynching usually takes one of two forms, of which the most common is death by hanging, hoisted up and down.

Mutilation often accompanies this. The victim is castrated, his ears cut off, his fingers separated joint by joint, his eyes gouged out. This is not so much to torture the victim as to wring from him a confession and words of repentance.

Another method is burning the victim alive. Here the purpose of the mob is usually to inflict grave suffering upon a victim who has already confessed his guilt or who has been adjudged guilty by the mob. Throughout the history of lynching, the stake has been almost as common a form of execution as the noose. Being burned alive, of course, is a more agonizing death, and it imposes greater anguish on relatives and friends, since there is no corpse to claim for burial. If there are any charred remains, they are plucked from the ashes by onlookers and kept or sold as souvenirs.

Burning a man alive is no unique American cruelty. Notwithstanding the numerous differences between New England and the Deep Southern states, these two share important traditions. While today there are Italians in Connecticut, Irish in Boston, Poles in Rhode Island, and Canucks in Maine, New England, like the South, had a homogeneous population until the 1900's. It is true that New England is urban and industrial and the South rural and agricultural, but it was in New England and in the South that the first English settlers planted their colonies. More than any other section of the country, these two have been most heavily influenced by English customs and Anglo-Saxon law. The fact that few lynchings have occurred in New England, as opposed to many in the South, is most likely the result of New England's early abolition of slavery. It is in fact one of the world's oldest punishments and possibly the oldest in point of continuity. The Romans, first to devise a systematic application of punishment to complement their legal code, burned Christians for heresy and mutiny. In medieval and Renaissance Europe, burning was thought to be an effective means of exorcising evil spirits from the living bodies of witches; burning a man in boiling water or oil was a common English penalty for intrigue. The Spanish Inquisition's *auto de fé* certainly surpassed in cruelty the violence perpetrated by lynch mobs in modern America.

Burning at the stake as a punishment in America dates back to the colonial period. Courts handed down this sentence to criminals found guilty of arson, insurrection, or murder by poison. Burning alive persisted as a penalty throughout the Western world until the advent of the Industrial Revolution, when it was officially abolished, along with public hangings. But the practice survives in modern electrocution and in execution by chlorine gas, which actually reduces the lungs to crisp cinders.

Men and women both have been hanged and burned in every state of the Union save these four: Connecticut, Rhode Island, Maine, and New Hampshire (Vermont citizens have lynched one white man since the Tuskegee Institute started keeping reliable records in 1882). Alabama, Florida, Georgia, Kentucky, Louisiana, Mississippi, Tennessee, and Texas have accounted for almost 4,000 of the 5,000 recorded lynchings in the United States. Georgia and Mississippi have had 530 and 578 respectively. The ratio of Negroes lynched to white men lynched has always been five to one.

In 1960 there were no lynchings in the United States. In 1961 there was one. Since then, however, at least twenty civil rights workers, white and Negro, have been murdered.

The public morality of America originally supported lynching as a necessary evil and occasionally encouraged it as a necessity. The best gauge of this morality has been the daily press. Newspapers often adopted a paternal attitude toward lynching, with the result that such newspapers shared an irresponsible paternity in its birth.

Such newspapers were irresponsible in always presuming that the lynch victim was patently guilty of the crime for which he was lynched. For several decades newspapers always reported a rapist had been hanged, never an "alleged" rapist; a murderer was burned, never a "supposed" murderer. Prejudgments like these helped encourage lynchings and created the illusion that no violence had been done to law and order. The sanctity of the law is an abstract sanctity, the ability to discern it a sophisticated ability. Naïve men and naïve communities are not easily aroused over injustices perpetrated against "murderers" and "rapists." Not only did the press and the journalists of the 1880–1920 era often prejudge the victim's guilt and declare justice satisfied; many of them also condoned the violence and the mob itself. In Alabama and Mississippi today, the local press always emphasizes that the murdered man got what was coming to him. When the general attitude of the press changed, there was a corresponding reduction in the frequency of lynchings. One of the man who helped to bring about this change was Ray Stannard Baker, editor of the nationally distributed *McClure's Magazine* (later Mr. Baker was to become the biographer of Woodrow Wilson). In January, 1906, Baker began publishing a series of eyewitness reports on the lynching phenomenon. "What Is a Lynching?" started off with the story, complete with photographs, of the burning of two illiterate Negroes in Alabama whom the mob had charged with rape.

Baker's view of the lynching phenomenon would fail to conform to modern liberal attitudes. He had absolutely no pity for the howling Negroes bound to the tree, but neither had he any sympathy for the gleeful mob that kept prodding the burning men with pointed staves.

What he did see clearly was the repercussions of a lynching. Whenever there was a lynching, an increase in crime and lawlessness followed—and it was an increase not in crimes committed by Negroes but in crimes committed by whites; and the increase occurred not in only a few of the communities that had tolerated a lynching but in all of them. In his series for McClure's Baker suggested that the rise in crime was the direct consequence of the feverish excitement engendered by the lynching party.

Baker understood, too, that the reason lynchings were hard to control was that the courts and the state legislators were slow to arrive at proper legal definitions (the definition used at the beginning of this study is Baker's, which he propounded with a consort of Southern lawyers).

Lastly, Baker began to see that lynching was neither deterrent nor punitive in its effect. It was, in reality, only a brutal indulgence. He listed some of the offenses by Negroes that had provoked lynchings in the year 1905: "bringing a lawsuit against a white man," "frightening school children," "trying to act like a white man," "seeking employment in a restaurant," and "expressing approval of the murder of a white man."

Ray Stannard Baker was a reasonable man who convincingly argued that lynching was not a rural condition of life to be tolerated but a national problem to be abolished. He was not alone in this position, for elsewhere too the mood was changing; but Baker represents rather an extreme reaction for his time. If his reports were gruesome, they were also enlightening. He went so far, in fact, as to urge antilynching legislation. He contended that the blame for a lynching lay with the entire community, not solely with the anonymous lynchers. In the event of a lynching, he asked that a tax be levied on all the citizens of the county, providing for no discrimination between those who were guilty and those who were blameless (in the sense of having not actually participated in the act). This tax was to be paid over to survivors of the lynched man as an indemnity. Since most communities exerted themselves in keeping the identity of the lynchers secret, Baker hoped a universally applied punishment would arouse the law-abiding, and once aroused, they would take measures to discourage the lynchers in their midst.

On the surface Baker's plan might appear to be workable, but of course it met with resistance from the start. No community ever paid willingly. Survivors of a lynched man had to take their case to the courts, where litigation dragged on and on; only in a few instances were indemnities collected. The federal government, however, has on several occasions paid indemnities to foreign countries on behalf of aliens lynched within the United States. Certainly Baker's idea had merit, at least in theory, even though it is repugnant to us to think of a tax as fit recompense for death by lynching.

Men like Baker were joined by the first vanguard of militant Negroes. I. B. Wells, the Negro editor of *Free Speech*, went to England when his journal was suppressed in the early 1900's and lectured widely there and later throughout Europe on lynching. He called for the establishment of an international committee to investigate this *American crime*. He was supported in his efforts by Booker T. Washington.

In 1906 a white mob spread terror and havoc for four days throughout the Negro section of Atlanta. A Negro professor of history and economics at Atlanta University named W. E. B. DuBois surveyed the devastation and founded an organization that might conceivably protect the rights of American Negroes. Thus began the Niagara Movement (so named because it was initiated at Niagara Falls, New York), which in 1909 became the National Association for the Advancement of Colored People.

Wells, DuBois, Washington, and others—these raised their voices and cried "Shame!" And the shame eventually became shock as Americans realized that forty years after they had done

away with slavery, the country still had a Negro problem of
international proportions.

Baker was succeeded by other journalists and reformers who
swallowed whole some of his misconceptions. It was Baker's
belief, for example, that only incorrigible Negro criminals were
lynched. Southerners had assured him that the self-respecting
Negro had nothing to fear and was always spared.

Largely because of the profound nature of Baker's influence,
such attitudes as these prevailed up until very recent times. As
late as 1933, historian Arthur Raper advised us in his *Tragedy
of Lynching*:

> Negroes can contribute much to the eradication of lynching by
> demonstrating the ability, character, and good citizenship of the
> race; by seeking individually and through their churches, lodges,
> schools and newspapers to allay the inter-racial fear and hostility;
> by consistently disavowing any disposition to condone crime and
> to shelter criminals; by reporting to officials and influential white
> friends when mob danger threatens; and by using their political
> influence whenever possible in the interest of honest and com-
> petent government.

This is not only unrealistic in the extreme but also a case of
accusing the victim of his own murder.

Despite this kind of confusion, the moral attention of the
nation began to focus on the phenomenon of lynching, and
this focus burned away some of the intransigence and led to
legislative action. The legislatures of lynch states—and these
states were by no means wholly within the South—passed new
laws. District attorneys and state attorneys general reactivated
old laws. The federal government no longer played a passive
role. So able an attorney general as Homer Cummings under
Franklin D. Roosevelt once confessed himself powerless to inter-
vene in a threatened lynching. But Democratic Senator Phil Hart
introduced an antilynching bill in the Senate which eventually
became Title 4 of the omnibus civil rights legislation of 1960. But
neither the Department of Justice nor the Federal Bureau of In-

vestigation needed this antilynching statute. The federal statutes against kidnapping and against the infringement of individual civil rights, the guarantees of the Constitution, were already sufficient. Attorneys General Herbert Brownell, Jr. and William P. Rogers both sent federal agents into the South on the occasion of a lynching. Their successors Robert F. Kennedy and Nicholas DeB. Katzenbach sent whole contingents of FBI investigators and federal marshals.

The reason lynching is no longer endemic in the South, save in Alabama and Mississippi, is not because of laws or humanitarian improvement. The nation began applying pressure to put an end to lynching not because some men were deprived of their rights and their lives but because other men were deprived of their property.

The lynch mob was always a mob of the propertyless, a mob of the disinherited. After destroying life, the mob destroyed property. The mob went from the place where they had hanged Leo Frank to a nearby drugstore and damaged it, and in Atlanta the mob that had pressed against the National Guardsmen defending Governor John Slaton after he had commuted Leo Frank's death sentence, once dispersed, charged through downtown Atlanta breaking windows and firing random shots through the dark hot streets.

Opposition to lynching came from Chamber of Commerce executives, bankers, insurance company presidents, and the cotton gin owners—the men with a vested interest in the community. Often they pleaded with lynch mobs to desist, and often they pleaded at great personal risk. All of them were well aware of the damage and destruction a lynch mob could wreak, and men with property were left with no redress or recompense for a loss so sustained.

Wilbur J. Cash recalls in *The Mind of the South* how, after a lynching, the big farmers and the factory owners formed a wagon ring around a town to chase back the fleeing, frightened Negroes. Every lynching saw a mass exodus of cheap labor and a mass exodus of credit debtors.

A lynching was more than a community aberration; it was also a blow against property. It was widespread in those very states which mounted the great Populist campaigns, the states which touch the east bank of the Mississippi River and the states below the Mason-Dixon line. The early reformers of lynching quickly detected a ratio between the frequency of lynchings and a low acre yield in cotton.

The lynching phenomenon abated not when the public and its elected and appointed leaders deplored it, nor when the states and the federal government promised to punish it—though both were controlling factors—but when the propertyless acquired property. Then a lynching was no longer to their advantage. The industrialization of the South, the economic reforms of the New Deal, and the boom years of World War II quieted the lynching fever until the issue of Negro civil rights again inflamed it.

Native-born Southerners like Lillian Smith and W. J. Cash have written that the entire racial problem floriates from the seed of sexual guilt. They have argued that every lynching is, in its way, a manifestation of the white man's guilt over his sexual exploitation of the Negro woman. In *Killers of the Dream*, Miss Smith says the white Southerner's inability to conceive of the gentlewoman as anything but a pedestal virgin makes him associate the vigor of life with the Negro female and with the Negro male. In his solitary but monumental book, *The Mind of the South*, W. J. Cash wrote of the white Southerner's "rape complex," a growing neurosis that convinces him the Negro will rape white women in vengeance for the advantage the white man took of the Negro woman.

Yet there is a narrower question upon which no Southern writer touches. What is it that led Americans to invent lynchings?

To argue that we are a frontier country is no answer, for Canada has no recorded lynching and Mexico but one. Lynching is a crime associated only with America, and we ought to know that American characteristic it reveals.

The Athenian Greeks forced the hemlock on Socrates, and the Florentines put Savonarola to the stake. History has a dismal record of injustices to sadden us. But only Americans tear down jails to hang or burn helpless and sometimes innocent men. What are the forces and the reasons responsible for this national affliction?

The grotesqueries of lynching are a direct result of the American belief that law and politics are synonymous. Everywhere else, law and politics are traditionally separate institutions. In the highly centralized governments of Europe, law is made for the people and is invoked by officials who are in no way answerable to them. Politicians, of course, must answer for political decisions, but Americans think a legal distinction and a political decision are nearly one and the same. Since Americans make laws, they presume wrongly they can unmake them. Since they determine what a judge can do, they presume they can do it themselves. The segregationist bawling his defiance of the Supreme Court thinks he can upset its judgments because he is under the misapprehension that the court is a political institution in the way a city council, say, is a political institution. When a mob of lynchers falls upon its victim, it is doing only what it wants the court to do and what the community is impatient to have done.

Despite all our piety, we are a violent country, ruthlessly brutal and ruthlessly materialistic; and we learn our lessons all too slowly. As a nation we may venerate many things, but law is not one of them.

That the Negro has to take to the streets and meet with violence there is an indication that what Americans do not like they sometimes refuse to accept. We shall not see the last of lynchings until we learn that the law is a way of securing freedom and liberty and that its restraints are the only guarantees of freedom and liberty.

Highway 85 and I

As LONG as I have lived in Charlotte I have always gone to the post office first to start on any journey. If it's a dinner invitation, I go to the post office and then proceed to my friend's home. If I am going to the Wheelers' after dinner, then I go back to the post office and proceed to the Wheelers'. If I have a speaking engagement in Utica, I go to the post office and then to the airport. And if I want a New York newspaper, I go to the post office because the out-of-town newsstand is across the street.

I never bother with Highway 85 north or south. The highway cleaved through Charlotte long enough ago as to be virtually obsolete today. A lot of motorists have met their deaths on Highway 85, but not one has died by going to the post office first. Highway 85 follows the collarbone of the city. It is less than 300 yards from my door. In town it calls itself Independence Boulevard. I never cross it except to venture to Leo's Delicatessen and the Independable Pool Palace.

What that highway was going to do for our town! It was going to bolster the entire city economy because the tourists from the North could get here in a hurry. Well, it gets the tourists in here and out of here faster than anyone ever suspected. When the folks came through Tryon Street, they'd stop now and then for a red light. Sometimes these same tourists would frequent our restaurants and even make a side trip to the Mint Museum, where they could buy miniature Confederate flags and mementos. A tourist who wants to can't get off 85. It is as though he has entered a wind tunnel, and there's no stopping until he reaches Miami.

Not far from where I lived was an Italian restaurant. An elderly man and his wife served lasagna and spaghetti, ziti and veal Parmigiana on checkered tablecloths. They always put a stack of Caruso records on their machine. When the concrete began to flow like lava, the realty values rose appreciably. No one can live on Highway 85—it's like trying to live in a closed garage with the car motor going—but Highway 85 had commercial possibilities. The Italian restaurant went the way of all commercial properties, and in its place is a shop where you get muffler replacements. Now a diner has to traverse Highway 85 to Gastonia if he wants white clam sauce, that or tolerate the Southern cuisine of fried chicken and fried steaks.

The engineers guaranteed that Highway 85 would make accessible all of Charlotte's culture. Ovens Auditorium was on 85, and the Coliseum, as well as the American Legion Memorial Stadium. Drive-in movies and bowling halls line its length. It's worth your life to park out there. The countryside becomes a sea of cars. I went out to the Coliseum to hear Richard Nixon and haven't been able to reclaim the car since. The police are still trying to clear the 25-acre lot. Some people just gave up trying to locate the old cars and bought new ones. The city will have to turn these abandoned cars in for scrap.

The woman's influence

I CALLED my neighbor and invited him to come over to my house to watch the World Series in living color. I told him I had a couple of quarts of beer, some liverwurst and pastrami and rye bread, and two Detroit baseball caps—everything we needed for a glorious afternoon. He said he didn't think he could make it—he hadn't cleared it with *her schedule*. What could her schedule be? The kids are in kindergarten. She should have her schedule, and he should watch the World Series.

My spies scattered here and there in the television networks tell me the big brass is considering dropping the televised football games on Thanksgiving Day. Too many obstinate wives are insisting hubby come to the turkey dinner in the middle of the second quarter.

The ladies are not only berating the man of the house for bringing home a large container of small curd cottage cheese when he knows she ordered a small container of large curd cottage cheese, but they are mounting a no-holds-barred antiviolence television campaign.

To my dismay, I find the women are also taking over the language. Last week, the wife of a friend told me, "Never kick a gift horse in the face," a metaphor which rivals Richard Nixon's "standing in the mainstream."

On lawyers

I HAVE heard it said that the lawyers who frequent the town hall searching deeds, marriage certificates, and ordinances passed by the Planning and Zoning Commission resemble nothing so much as a school of piranhas in a public swimming pool.

Card Sandburg in one of his poems asked, "Why does a hearse horse snicker hauling a lawyer's bones?"

In Sir Thomas More's *Utopia* there are no lawyers because the population "consider them as a sort of people whose profession it is to disguise matters."

The lawyers are getting the worst of it. For a while, the Madison Avenue advertising men took the brunt of our lynch fever. When they took off the football game to show the ads for *Heidi*, I thought they were goners, but they promised never to do it again, not even for *Cinderella*. No, I think the lawyers are still considered the archvillains of this society.

It is a bum rap. But we vilify lawyers because we are such a lawsuit-prone society.

In the last decade I have been sued three times. I settled each of these suits out of court, not because I was in the wrong but because the cost of the settlement was cheaper than the trial costs. In the old West, decent citizens had to worry about the bad men who rode in and shot up the town as the whim seized them. Decent citizens today worry who will run amok with a legal suit.

The universe awaits

AT THE very moment man is tramping around the moon, astrologers here on earth are having a field day, reaping a bonanza by dispensing computerized horoscopes, making the best-selling lists with their forecasts, even—in *Zolar's Magazine* —publishing a financial newsletter based on the configuration of the stars. No doubt the stars are configured, but it seems more likely man will influence them than that they will influence man.

There must a vast web of cultural dynamics, as the sociologists like to say, behind this newfound popularity. One thing the astrologers insist about their discipline, and that is that it is no short-lived vogue. It is a science, they pretend, as old as man himself. But the reasons for its revival I think are simple.

I think the chief reason why the folks want to fuss with elaborate charts which dictate and govern life and character is that no one takes such information seriously. We who do not subscribe to the astrological thesis think they take it seriously, but they really do not. I do not think the public is reading about its predestined career with tongue in cheek, but this time around the astrologers have given themselves a real wide area for hit or miss. Which only goes to prove man has made great progress since the days of the witch doctor who promised if he prayed rain came. If the rain didn't come, the aborigines sensibly boiled the witch doctor and got another.

Another reason for the spread of horoscopy is that it has dispensed with simplicity. Simplicity is terribly confusing. $E = mc^2$ is as simple an explanation as any ever offered, but it is incomprehensible to the majority of college graduates. "Sun favorable in 5th House August 1 to 22" is right up everybody's alley. Signs and signals make suckers of us all. Watching a third-base coach with a runner on first is like watching a man afflicted with a raging case of hives. Professional ballplayers say at best there are two or three men on a team who can pull off the hit and run, a fact known to infields throughout both leagues, but third-base coaches go through the signs and signals anyway. At what point the quarterback calls the automatic on the line of scrimmage is more important and thrilling to the football addicts than the touchdown pass. The astrologers have devised such a system of signs, signals, and symbols as to make an Aztec high priest pale.

Probably the last reason why reading the stars is displacing I Love Lucy and some of the more intelligent comic books is that with each passing month we realize we are not bound to live in a pleasant world. Events transpire in some obscure Middle Eastern duchy far beyond our power to control which affect sooner or later every movement we make. When we try to be reasonable, things only get worse. Astrology is personalized. It deals only with the "you" in all of us. Some go to great expense to discover in the past the family coat of arms. But there's a whole universe waiting to be related to you.

Send a salami

I AM an inveterate magazine reader. Magazines were cheap for me. I ran a personal journal, and almost every publisher will exchange his for yours.

As a matter of fact, one of the ways to determine which magazine is successful and which not is by the rapidity with which the subscription manager will cut you off. There are magazines in this world that it is virtually impossible to get rid of. The circulation manager may keep dunning you, but he simply doesn't confide in the subscription department, and the magazine comes on forever.

One of the most fascinating studies in this world is the way certain magazines attract certain advertisers. *The New Republic,* an articulate voice of the liberal position, has personals which read: "Live Reptiles: free list, Hiawatha Python, 750 E. Franklin, Mpls., Minn." And "Discover an intriguing fun approach to meeting alert, literate Jewish singles. No computers used. . . ."

Are they putting us on, do you suppose, or is it for real?

The New York Times Magazine sometimes seems more a catalogue of hosiery and lingerie manufacturers than a publication dedicating to explaining the issues. I have heard college students refer to the *Times* as the *Sunday Playboy.* These same students have told me it would be a better world if *Playboy* were published once a week instead of once a month. Off the point, perhaps, but I remember that *Playboy* published some of Carl Sandburg's last poems. Carl told me he was pleased by the check and more than pleased to write for an audience not one of whom believed in artificial insemination.

To read *The New Yorker* is to enter into a world absolutely devoted to boastful luxury. It amazes me that people really do buy all those things. I can believe the average American family will line up and proudly display their new oil burner to the neighbors, but that they would also display a $900-ceiling fixture somehow astounds me.

I am, of course, quite sensitive to advertising. I had to sell it for many years to the *Carolina Israelite.* I remember the absolute frustration of never landing an ad for liquor. The agencies always insisted the *Israelite* wasn't worth their while because Jews don't drink. I could have told them something about Jews, but I didn't want to speak ill of my subscribers.

I believe the *Israelite* for twenty-six years published the best ad in America. The ad sold Katz's Delicatessen in New York City. It always said, "Send a salami/To your boy in the Army." Worthy of Ogden Nash, don't you think?

Sojourn in the middle class

I venture out into the middle class only when it is absolutely necessary. My house insulates me perfectly. Margaret comes in at 8 A.M., prepares breakfast, tidies up, makes the lunch, and we wave good-bye. My secretary is here at 9 A.M., and she keeps us all in touch with the universe of publishers, newspaper syndicates, and lecture bureaus. After I walk my dog Gaon and his mate, Dubah (which means "Little Bear" in Hebrew), there's no other reason to involve myself in the giddy affairs of ordinary everyday living.

But Margaret had no scouring powder the other day. I volunteered to make the expedition to the supermarket. There I bought three canisters of Ajax, getting free Handi Wipes with each. Since they were marked two for forty-nine cents, I figured I owed seventy-four cents. I waited in the express line (five items or less) and displayed my purchase to the big hippie who was punching buttons on the register. By mistake he included among my three Ajaxes with their Handi Wipes a head of lettuce belonging to the lady behind me.

"That's mine," she said.

"You owe her twenty-nine cents," the clerk informed me.

I was about to hand over the change to this charming lady when I realized I didn't owe her twenty-nine cents.

"I only bought three cans of Ajax," I said, "I owe you seventy-four cents. Why do I owe her twenty-nine cents?"

"'Cause I rang it up on the register," said the clerk. Then he added, "You're right. She owes you twenty-nine cents."

"Why do I owe twenty-nine cents?" she asked.

The clerk started to explain. But she cut him off. "I know *that*. I understand. I thought the lettuce was nineteen cents."

He twirled the lettuce around to show her the twenty-nine cents inked on the cellophane.

"It says nineteen cents in the window," she insisted.

Later, arriving home with a head of lettuce I didn't need, my secretary informed me that a local VIP Democrat was on the telephone.

What he asked was, "Harry, do you know a Democratic piano tuner?"

"Do you mean a registered Democrat or a piano tuner who mixes with all classes of pianos?"

"Registered," he said.

"Why do you want a Democratic piano tuner?"

"We need a piano for the band at our Columbus Day Democratic Ball. If we rent one, it will cost twenty-five dollars. Ray Discepolo has an old piano in his garage. I thought if I could locate a Democratic piano tuner, he'd tune it for nothing, thereby saving the party twenty-five dollars."

I did not know any Democratic piano tuners.

"Well, at least," he asked, exasperated, "do you know anyone with a bust of Columbus? I want to take a publicity photo beside it to advertise our ball."

"Why don't you ask Discepolo?" I suggested.

"No good. He's from the north of Italy."

"I don't think I can help."

"That's the trouble with the party this election," he complained. "Everybody lets me down."

And we think people who live in ivory towers are foolish.

Tax-supported Shangri-La

EVERYTHING WE need by 1978 we should have had in 1953. We are a quarter of a century behind ourselves in education and housing. Since we chose not to build housing for the poor and still refuse the massive program we need, the white middle class fled the cities to the suburbs. The suburbanites had every right to flee, but they have no right to be so selfish now. Their flight was lavishly supported by federal credit; they could deduct interest payments from tax returns as well as local taxes from the federal returns. Their flight was facilitated by a $50-billion highway program which made their access to the city convenient. When the railroads began to falter, Congress passed an Urban Transportation Bill to shore up this other convenience.

As a matter of fact, this massive investment was cited by the McCone Committee as one of the underlying causes for the Watts riot. The shift of many good jobs from the center city to the suburbs is another reason why unemployment levels are so outrageously high in the city. My authority on this is the Department of Labor.

As a result of what can only be called federal charity, the white middle class has been able to build Shangri-Las with its tax dollars. They may not be able to live forever in their shaded and protected mountain retreats, but they live a good sight longer than the folks stuck in the ghettos below.

As a result of the middle-class shift to suburbia, those who remain behind in the slums and the backwoods receive less money for their schooling than those who have the most. The white middle class gets the "socialist" benefits from the welfare state, and the white and Negro poor get the circulars on free enterprise.

One of the easiest ways to correct this is for the suburbs, say, to pay for their own schooling out of the municipal tax dollars and forgo state and federal aid, passing it on to the city and the slums. Anytime a school can reduce a teacher-student ratio, it can educate more effectively, and the teacher-student ratio in our cities is ridiculous.

If we could soften attitudes, if we could convince Mississippians and Alabamans there is no such thing as a sovereign state, if we could convince the white middle class there is no such thing as an inviolate or homogeneous community, we'd make progress.

Alas! Not reason but law changes the hearts of men, Dwight D. Eisenhower to the contrary.

The suburbs won't blow up this summer; nice neighborhoods never do. But if the city blows up, where may I ask will the suburbanite work?

Making 'em nervous

USUALLY I disliked Hollywood cocktail parties. Invariably some one attempting to make casual conversation asks, "What studio are you with?" When I reply I am not with any studio, they say, "Oh," and move quickly away from me like vital businessmen do on airplanes when they see me reading a book.

But the last time was different. I got into an animated conversation with a psychiatrist who advises all the studios. He files succinct and precise reports on what makes people nervous. That is so the movie moguls will not make a picture which will fill the audience with anxiety.

Nudity no longer upsets the folks, nor does frank talk about subjects never mentioned. The American moviegoing public has matured to the degree it can bear the unhappiness of animals. Anything funny about money rattles 'em.

My psychiatrist explained he still treats patients who went into shock at the end of *The Treasure of the Sierra Madre* when all the gold blew away down the street. One of the movie moguls wanted to make a film accurately re-creating the famous Brink's robbery, but the psychiatrist dissuaded him. The immorality of the holdup wouldn't have bothered the audience but rather the fact that the Brink's money was never recovered. Some Feds found $100,000 of it behind a wall someplace, but there is another million cached someplace. It would never do.

Joseph Moriarity was a Jersey City bookie who stored a couple of million dollars in the trunk of his car before he went off for a brief stretch. Unfortunately someone accidentally discovered the horde, which didn't do Jersey City garages any good because everyone was out the next day tearing garages apart in the hopes of another lucky strike.

In the meantime the federal and state government started a wrangle which continues to this day as to whose money it is. Moriarity, not wanting more trouble than he has, keeps mum.

The sinking of the *Andrea Doria* is also a verboten topic. The Italian liner was freighted with gold and jewelry, all of which now lies beneath the sea. The tempting fact that the *Andrea Doria* is now full fathom five brings a cold sweat to the brow of many a man.

"Which reminds me," I asked. "What happened to the treasure in *Treasure Island?*"

"An imperfect story," he said dogmatically. "It'll never make it."

Ed Cahill, the golfer

I RECENTLY had occasion to talk to my good friend Ed Cahill, the Unitarian minister. Ed left Charlotte and environs eight years ago for a congregation in Pittsburgh. He was back to attend the ceremonies of Harry Golden Day in Charlotte sponsored by the University of North Carolina at Charlotte. Ed was a charter member of the embattled group in Charlotte which called itself by a variety of names. One year we were the Civil Rights Seminar, the next the Committee for Fair Municipal Practices, and finally the Human Relations Council. Ed and I remembered the early embattled fifties when these twelve members bent might and main to persuade the city to integrate the sole drinking fountain in the center of town and the restroom facilities. It took two years to win that fight. Those days are gone forever.

But we reminisced.

Before coming to Charlotte, Ed had a parish in a big city in Georgia. The group there thought it was time to integrate the library, and Ed set about agitating. One of the city powers-that-be told him they were integrating the libraries "gradually." Ed wanted to know just what that meant, since he had yet to see a Negro in a public library.

The official told him they had integrated the books.

"Just how do you integrate books?" Ed asked.

It seems the city had five mobile libraries, trailers filled with books which toured the neighborhoods. There were four for the white neighborhoods and one for the colored sections. Up until this time, the books had been segregated. There were books in these trailers only the white people could handle and read and books only the Negroes could handle and read. Now the libraries were transferring the books from one mobile unit to another without regard to what color hands opened them.

"But," said the official, putting his finger to his mouth in a plea for silence. "We don't want to hurry these things."

When the Freedom Riders invaded the Mississippi and Alabama towns, naturally Ed followed them. Never once was he stopped by a bully-boy sheriff or a cop. Now remember, priests, nuns, rabbis, ministers, and the mothers of governors were pulling overnight stints in Southern jails. I asked Ed what lucky star attended his journey.

He said it was not a lucky star at all. It was careful planning. He had bought a secondhand bag of golf clubs before leaving and prominently displayed the clubs in the back seat of his station wagon. Ed has a profound knowledge of human nature. No cop would think to stop a golfer. In fact, come to think of it, what golfer has ever made trouble?

When Ed ran for the Charlotte school board, the Human Relations Council backed his candidacy to the utmost. Ed ran on a platform promising to take the prayers and the Bibles out of the public schools and put the Negroes in. But politics, she is a dirty game, and the opposition candidates got together and issued a joint statement charging that Ed Cahill, as a Unitarian, did not believe in the divinity of Jesus. That was that for the school board. Ed got the votes of the Human Relations Council, me, and the vote of the CIO organizer.

The Beatles and prophecy

THE BEATLES were the panegyric subject of a magazine which I always call nameless except to say it isn't *Newsweek*.

What impressed the editors was that the nonmusical utterances of the Beatles "tend to take on the tone and weight of social prophecy." Mind you, *tend* to take on the tone and weight.

Eric Hoffer, the longshoreman turned writer, doesn't tend toward social insights, he has insights. Joe Namath doesn't tend to complete 56 percent of his passes, he does complete them.

I suppose these editors are remembering that when one of the Beatles announced they were more popular than Christ, this tended to take on the tone and weight of social prophecy. If there is another reason for this tendency, it is that no one ever asked Elvis Presley what he thought about Existentialism, the war in Vietnam, or the polychromatic scale.

The magazine, to be fair, buttresses its tribute with paeans of praise from the likes of Cass Elliot, John Sebastian, and Art Garfunkel, all of whom testify to the Beatles' preeminence. They remind me of Groucho Marx's joke. He asked once, "You think I'm crazy? Well, they thought Thomas Alva Edison was crazy. They thought Marconi was crazy. They even thought Joe M. Varilla was crazy." When someone confessed he had never heard of Joe M. Varilla, Groucho replied, "Joe M. Varilla? He really was crazy."

In short, I am not willing to trust my life and conduct to the likes of Art Garfunkel, John Sebastian, or Cass Elliot any more than I will trust life and conduct to Tommy Manville, Jr., Dick Haymes, or Joe M. Varilla.

Listen to the social prophecy the Beatles have to offer. Paul

McCartney says, "I don't recommend LSD. It can open a few doors, but it's not the answer. You get the answers yourself." Is that a statement we would want every high school principal to read after the Pledge of Allegiance?

Johann Sebastian Bach, after completing the score of *The Well-Tempered Clavier*, had only one social insight to offer. He told an adoring patroness, "Of course I like my wife. If I didn't like her, I wouldn't have the nine kids." That's the kind of social prophecy we should expect from musicians.

What is it then that recommends the Beatles? As a fifteen-year-old told an aspiring reporter from magazine nameless, "They're saying all the things I always wanted to say to my parents and their freaky friends."

One of my kids once took it upon himself at the dinner table to comment on the appearance of an aunt. He thought she looked freaky. The aunt took it gracefully enough, saying, "Well, he's just going through a stage."

"A stage is it?" asked my wife. "Well, the back of this hand is going to put him through four stages all at once."

Indeed it did. Haven't had a freaky friend since.

Unfortunate confrontations

THAT UNFORTUNATE confrontation many of us undergo has a gimlet-eyed fellow from the Bureau of Internal Revenue tapping his pencil impatiently, asking his questions with just a trace of disbelief cutting underneath his polite yet implacable interrogation.

"Just what is this six hundred dollars for entertaining?"

"A business expense."

"Business expense." Just the bald statement. Two taps of the pencil. He shuffles the papers. "How could this entertaining be a business expense if it was the day you came home from the hospital?"

Shrug.

I fortify myself for these ordeals by remembering other unfortunate confrontations, confrontations in which the dialogue virtually writes itself. I think of Edmund Wilson, certainly the most estimable of all our critics, trying to explain to the Internal Revenue why he neither paid nor filed his income tax for seven years. In his book *The Cold War and the Income Tax* Mr. Wilson argues cogently his explanation was reasonable enough, but nevertheless he surely paid for it.

I think of Gamal Nasser visiting Moscow after the Israelis had vanquished the Egyptians.

"What happened?" must have been Kosygin's first question.

"A surprise attack."

"Surprise? What did you think you were doing when you blockaded Aqaba? What did you think would happen when the United Nations pulled out? What did the Egyptians think when you promised to annihilate the Israelis?"

"Nevertheless, effendi, it was a surprise. The Israelis took us too literally."

"But the missile bases, Gamal. The missile bases. The Israelis captured a whole missile base."

"The explanation is beyond Allah Himself."

"Why don't you ask Allah for the money for the new jets?"

One always hopes he will do better in an unpleasant situation than Roger Blough of United States Steel did when he informed President Kennedy that the steel companies simply had to charge six cents more a ton.

Most of us survive that confrontation when a dear wife discovers lipstick on our collar or a blond hair on our lapel. It is at this point in life we say, "Don't think of lies. Think of attitudes!" If we survive this, as indeed Edmund Wilson survived to write more profound books, Nasser to wage bigger and more costly losing wars, Roger Blough to escalate the cost of steel, why we'll get by next April 15 with some of the poke still intact.

Games of yesteryear

In the course of writing my autobiography, I took the time to describe some of the games we played as boys on the Lower East Side of New York. We played "Johnny-on-the-pony," in which one side bent against the wall and the other side leaped on their backs and tried to shout "Johnny on the pony" three times without being shaken off. "Puss-n-cat" was played with a sawed-off broom handle and a piece of wood. The regular rules of baseball applied except we touched only two bases. Boxball was played in the squares of the sidewalk.

I had to describe these games and others more specifically in the book because my editor said, "There are people forty years old who never heard of these." One of my sons contributed a photographic essay to a national magazine on the games *he* played which are no longer in vogue: tag, leapfrog, hide and seek, and kick the can.

What games do kids play now? I know they have a soapbox derby sponsored by several organizations in town. I know this because in Charlotte, the speedway, so-called, goes down Elizabeth Avenue, right past my front door, where the soapbox derby officials station themselves. Every year these fellows give me a pith helmet made of plastic.

And towns also sponsor football and baseball leagues. I haven't seen a pick-up game with the kids choosing sides for years and years. I know they play basketball unattended by coaching adults because I see the hoops fastened to the garages. In fact, I drove up to a friend's house one afternoon as he poked his head out the window to yell at his oldest son, "If you don't learn to dribble that basketball, I'm going to take it away from you." Quite right, I thought. Quite right.

I never see a punching bag or boxing gloves. When I was first a father, boxing was popular. I always encouraged it not because

I thought they should learn to defend themselves but to learn a hard one in the nose doesn't hurt all that much.

I never see kids on roller skates, and I never see kids playing marbles. Roller-skate hockey became the rage in New York when the city covered over the cobblestones with asphalt or macadam. It was easier then because there were not as many cars to interrupt the game. When the Board of Education covered over the playground with asphalt to create more tennis courts, they dealt marbles a death blow. You could always tell a marble champ because he had a hole worn in his thumbnail, and the knuckles and joints on his shooting hand were oversized.

The kids are more attracted to organized sports today not because organizations are more fun or more sophisticated but because the parents insist they are. The parents want the kids in organized activities so that they have time for their own organized recreation.

Businessman's lunch

Lunch when I was a young man in Wall Street was the hot dog cart and a bottle of Dr. Brown's Cel-Ray. The business we discussed was John McGraw's Jints. Lunch was as long as it took to consume one hot dog and the pop, brush off our hands with a napkin, and walk back to the office. Luncheon varied if one of the peddlers came around with corn on the cob. It was buying an ear of corn on the cob that I first met Al Smith. He wasn't campaigning, he was just eating his lunch.

The businessman's lunch is an institution today. The only men I know who do not take an hour or a two-hour break for lunch are the men who own seats on the stock exchange and must be present on the floor lest sudden flurries wipe them out.

Whenever I go to New York to see a publisher, we always discuss our business at lunch. While I am always delighted to be treated, I wondered once to my editor, Bill Targ, why we never discussed contracts and the like in the Putnam office.

"Don't you know," he said seriously, "you can't get anything done in an office? The printers are always calling to say they will be late, the sales department wants to change the titles of books, the publisher for reasons of his own wants to call a sudden conference. No," he said, "the office inhibits thought and work."

My publisher always takes me to lunch either at the Algonquin or the dining room at the Plaza. He never considers the Playboy Club or Sardi's or the Four Seasons; it's either the Algonquin or the Plaza. Since the business luncheon is an institution, I have discovered the men who perpetuate it follow several patterns without deviation. First they choose restaurants in which few women dine. That is because there is rarely any waiting for a table. A woman will wait for a table just to admire the tasteful menu, but a man will not wait at all.

The men frequent the same restaurant because they like the food and because they don't want to be surprised by it. I have yet to hear the maître d'hôtel describe the specialty that my host didn't recommend it. When mock turtle soup makes its first appearance on the menu with a change of chefs, it's as though you hit the businessmen over the head with a sledgehammer, so stunned are they.

The last reason for the popularity of the businessman's lunch is that people do not tend to argue over food. In the Orthodox homes of the Lower East Side, the evening meal was the most important event of the day. The entire family gathered, and the father said a prayer. I doubt this custom is unique among Jews. Carl Sandburg told me the immigrant families from Sweden also sat together, and the mother blessed the bread.

People who have to consult a lawyer almost invariably avoid the dining table. They make do with coffee in a paper cup and a roast beef sandwich wrapped in wax paper by the delicatessen.

Beggars

CHARLOTTE, NORTH CAROLINA, my hometown, prides itself on being a major American city. Its population is well over two hundred thousand, and in most respects if not all, it is a major city. To me, a major city is any town where you can get a shoeshine easily and buy a newspaper at any time of day.

One of the things Charlotte does not have is beggars. No police campaign has ever cleared them out. There is certainly as much need here as elsewhere, but in Charlotte there are no panhandlers or professional mendicants.

There are men who are on their way from one place to another who stop, ring the doorbell, and ask for an odd job to make some money. They will clean the gutters of leaves or mow the lawn or shovel coal, which is a fair enough exchange for a meal or a buck, but I have never seen the beggar who wanted the dime out of charity.

No city in the world has more beggars than New York. Many of them, of course, are fakes. I have seen them tapping their white canes through the crowded subway car, their eyes shielded by sunglasses, a printed placard hung round their necks. Near the Algonquin Hotel in midtown Manhattan sits a beggar I have seen on every one of my trips. He has a little dolly on which he crouches with wooden legs. There's a fellow with the same dolly and the same kind of legs over near Grand Central who parks beside the newsstand in the morning and early afternoon. Then there are the young hippie beggars in Greenwich Village, a real innovation. Eighteen- and twenty-year-old beggars in the richest city in the world!

I do not doubt that San Francisco has beggars, but I never see them. I do see them in Chicago, but not in Dallas.

I have come to the conclusion that beggars inhabit the cities which promise great expectations. Now the middle class in Charlotte is prosperous, probably as prosperous as any middle class anywhere. But these folks haven't come to Charlotte to be composers or actors or writers or even millionaires, though indeed they become these things, some of them to their surprise. But the folks do go to New York and Chicago and San Francisco filled with the hopes of adventure and high accomplishment. The expectant don't become the beggars, but it is as if their expectations must trail human litter and debris in its wake.

An American tourist who pauses on any street corner in Marseilles is besieged by an army of beggars, and in the Middle East, in Turkey, in Thailand, giving alms for the sake of Allah or Buddha admits a man to heaven. Beggars there make no bones about the duty they perform. But our beggars here are theatrical, and I've often wondered if they go home at night and wash up and tell the little woman how tough a day it was.

Vote of confidence

WHEN I resigned from the Student Nonviolent Coordinating Committee, the black power organization, I received almost one hundred letters from arch-segregationists who said they didn't know what SNCC stood for, but if I was against it, it had to be good.

The four-year campaign

THE CAMPAIGN between Nixon and Humphrey was duller than most, once they got themselves nominated, that is. Anyone who worked in it thought it was going to last forever. Why we now so eagerly carry forward speculation about 1972 is beyond me. Why should every campaign be a four-year campaign?

I think the answer is television. Nothing lends itself to television like politics, and no one wants to lend himself as quickly as a politician.

Years ago, a four-year term was just that—four years. But today four years is just around the corner, and our politics resemble a soap opera:

> Will Dick prevail in Vietnam?
> What about Muskie in Maine?
> Is Senator McCarthy's threat a power ploy?
> Can Hubert make a comeback?
> What is Fred Harris really like?
> Tune in tomorrow.

The Israelis do not seem overly concerned about who will succeed Golda Meir, nor are the British forever staring into a crystal ball about Harold Wilson's successor, nor are the Italians worried about the identity of the next Pope.

But we Americans are an impatient people. We cannot wait for the years or the seasons to catch up to themselves. Nowhere is this more evident than in the jolly Yuletide season or national politics. The Christmas shopping season starts the day after Columbus Day, and the morning Richard Nixon woke up as President-elect everyone started to speculate on the Democratic nominee in '72.

Aztec country

THE AZTECS had a refined civilization, but it was all superstructure, no real foundation. Their God was a sensuous God of sun and rain who wanted satiation from the blood of young maidens. No doubt the Aztecs felt reverent about their God, and no doubt He served them in many ways, but He neglected to tell them about the wheel. When a handful of conquistadors came, they conquered the Aztecs with a minimum of effort and a maximum of bluff. The Aztecs simply did not have enough worth fighting for.

Nathanael West, the American novelist, said of California that the people all came there to die. They came because it was warm and because living required less effort in California or Florida or similar places than it did elsewhere. And indeed this opinion was refined not too long ago by S. J. Perelman, who said California was the land of the living dead. I call it Aztec country. Tables rattle there every night as ectoplasm materializes. Rosicrucian crosses line the highways, stretching for miles. The gun clubs proliferate, all populated by hysterics who fear an immediate Communist invasion, the John Birchers sing their hymns of hate round the clock. It is indeed the land of the superstructure, "no foundation, all the way down the line."

The message

A SOCIALLY prominent matron invited her doctor to dinner. She asked RSVP. The doctor was prompt in his reply, but the matron couldn't make out his scrawl. Was he or was he not coming? Her dear hubby came to the rescue. He said he would take the doctor's reply to the local druggist, who had years of experience deciphering the longhand of many doctors.

The druggist read the scrawl, bent down, and put a big black bottle of medicine on the counter: "That will be three eighty, please."

My grandson's car

IN ORDER to popularize its new two-thousand-dollar sports car, the Ford Motor Company offered a plastic scale model of the Maverick. My daughter-in-law, the proud mother of an

eighteen-month-old son, immediately sent off for it. The little
boy goes into ecstasies over anything on wheels. Promptly the
model arrived. The first time my grandson wheeled his new car
across the floor, the little plastic bumper fell off. My daughter-
in-law wrote a letter to Ralph Nader.

The Hudson Dusters

ONE REMEMBERS the Hudson Dusters, a gang of toughs
who hung out in Greenwich Village. The Dusters terrified the
Bronx. They were the scourge of the Palisades. The police precincts always had their eye out for the appearance of the Dusters.
What happened to the Dusters was that the Bohemians began
to move into Greenwich Village. These poets and artists and
writers thought the Dusters were charming fellows. The Bohemians used to recite their poetry aloud at Duster meetings
whether the Dusters wanted to hear or not. Eugene O'Neill
found their conversation stimulating. When the Dusters realized
none of these painters and writers and poets was afraid of them,
sullenly the gang broke up, and the Dusters all found gainful
employment.

Jeremiahs

THE CITIZENS of Shawneetown, Illinois, have recently
apologized for its bank officials, who in 1830 turned down a
request for three hundred dollars made to them by the City of
Chicago. The Shawneetown bankers thought Chicago was too
far away ever to become much of a city. The population of
Shawneetown today is not 1 percent of Chicago's, although it
was the first town in Illinois to have a bank. All of which goes
to prove bankers are no Jeremiahs either.

Educational hazard

I DID not know the Taft Youth and Adult Center existed —one of the most worthwhile projects in the entire educational system. Up in the Bronx the Taft faculty conducts a night school for thousands of working people, men and women, who leave their homes a few nights a week to study drawing, painting, sculpture, and watercolor, as well as advertising, bookkeeping, business English, the operation of business machines, stenography, auto maintenance, ceramics, leathercraft, radio repair, and television repair. There are also the humanities, English and dramatics, short story writing, the dance, ballet, a course in citizenship, and another course in health and hygiene. Competent teachers head these classes, and there are four such centers in Greater New York.

There's one sad note which I must record. The attendance has dropped off in the last year or two. I was told confidentially that many housewives are afraid to leave the house at night.

Revelation in confinement

I HAVE purchased a new hi-fi stereophonic set. It was a lot of trouble. Not the money, mind you. I saved up for that. It was a lot of trouble convincing a salesman I had a space exactly three by three by four in which to store the apparatus.

He told me all America is making space. All America is assembling hi-fi kits.

I told him I wanted one I could carry out of here.

It was touch and go. But I won.

Not everyone is so lucky. One of my friends assembled a huge set all by himself. He put in every little transistor and tuned all the woofs and wasted a year of nighttimes. One night in fact his wife absentmindedly locked him in his cellar. He had neither key for the two exits. He might still be there except he has that practical turn of mind that got him before a workbench anyway. He went to the fuse box and twisted out an SOS on one of the sockets, and she came to and let him out. I can't help feeling that perhaps he realized a lot of things had gone out of the marriage. He wasn't missed. Nowadays, they play their home-made hi-fi all the time, accompanied by a terrible melancholy.

The clergy and cigarettes

THE BIBLE Belt has changed. When the General Assembly of the Southern Presbyterian Church met in West Virginia, it considered passing an anti-cigarette statement because of the new finding on tobacco and lung cancer. The statement never passed. Why? Because so many Presbyterians are tobacco farmers. (And it was so recorded in the minutes.)

Naming the high school

ON ONE of the last occasions I saw Mrs. Roosevelt, she told me how the Carl Sandburg School in San Bruno (California) got its name.

The first name proposed for this new school was the Eleanor Roosevelt School. But the school board at the time was composed of three Republicans and two Democrats, and voting on strictly party lines, Eleanor Roosevelt lost, three to two. One of the Democrats then proposed they name the new school after Carl Sandburg, who was still living.

"What party is he in?" asked one of the Republicans.

The Democrat replied, "I don't know his affiliation, but he is the biographer of Lincoln, the first Republican President."

This was enough. The school board voted three to two for Carl Sandburg, one of the Democrats, a lady from the South, voting against, and one of the Republicans, who wanted to name the school after somebody dead, also dissenting.

The Eyetalian from Bridgeport

MY GOOD friend Miss M., who works for the New American Library and is probably the best copy editor in publishing, goes often to cocktail parties, teas, and receptions for her authors and important publishers. The word precedes her; she's an ITALIAN, and the men gather around her like bees around honey. They have visions, I suppose, of a Neapolitan orgy. Then Miss M. tells them she's an Italian from Bridgeport, Connecticut, and they drop her like a hot potato.

If Sophia Loren were an Italian girl from Norwalk, she'd just be another gal putting on weight from too much pasta.

Make no mistake about it.

Teachers' revolution

THE SCHOOLTEACHERS are getting smart. At the monthly PTA meeting the more experienced teachers advise the new ones, "Keep talking until the bell rings. Do not allow a lull in the proceedings. The moment a parent rises to say something, interrupt. Say, 'By the way, there's another point I must make now.' Just keep chattering."

The teachers are learning. Recently a parent asked a teacher, "And how is my little Lloyd doing?" and the teacher said, "Oh, playing the fool as usual."

There's more guts in the li'l ole brick schoolhouse, less intimidation. The teachers are professionals. Doctors and lawyers don't take any guff—why should teachers?

Sacramento's wisdom

THE CITY council in Sacramento, California, decided that the century-old Plaza Park in the heart of downtown Sacramento should make way for a parking lot. "The first step," said one of the city fathers, "is to get rid of the bums," so the tables and the benches where old men played pinochle and argued with their friends were to be removed. The city council was promptly stunned by the outraged protests of citizens.

It seems the citizens enjoyed rest and recreation in their own busy lives by watching the old gentlemen enjoy themselves without the steaming pressure of modern life. The tables stay. Good for Sacramento.

Laughable pledge

WE HAVE heard the Southern politician pledge his constituents he will defend white womanhood to the death, while white womanhood simply sighs over the follies of white Southern manhood.

Marx never knew

YOU HAVE created the greatest middle class in world history. You have proved beyond any doubt something which escaped Karl Marx.

Karl Marx did not know how short is the distance between

a hungry man and a convertible, a set of golf clubs, and a home in the suburbs. He did not know how even after a single generation of distance from the stockyards and the coal pits, that once-hungry man parades with the flag of the Confederacy, and his favorite literature is no longer *How to Become a Citizen* but *Gone With the Wind.*

PART 4

Civil Rights and the Terror of the Deep

Why I am an optimist

I AM an optimist about America because we are witnessing a great miracle.

The South has eliminated within fifteen years a social pattern which existed for over one hundred years, which is a miracle.

Fifteen years ago Dr. Ralph Bunche couldn't get a room at the Hotel Charlotte, but a year ago the hotel had a sign on its marquee, "Welcome Delegates of the NAACP."

For one hundred years the Southerner was watching the bus to see that a Negro moved from the front seat to the back seat. Now he's stopped watching the bus and he's selling insurance and building high-rise office buildings and the money is rolling in. I always knew the big victor in the civil rights movement would be the white Southerner. There has been integration in such cities as Charlotte, Atlanta, Richmond, and Chattanooga, and the streets are paved with gold. The Southerner has not only overthrown a great spiritual burden, but has enhanced the economic greatness of his cities. All of this makes me an an optimist about America.

The terror of the deep

HOLLYWOOD USED to make marvelous movies about the giant gorilla which menaced all of civilization because of his huge size and his propensities for tossing white virgins on high. Sometimes the writers made the gorilla into a monster shrimp, awakened from its long underwater slumbers by a hydrogen explosion. The shrimp would also menace civilization, swimming toward the city, intent on chewing up the whole population. It was thrilling to see these menaces knocking over trolleys, stamping on automobiles, flicking artillery shells aside.

But I could recommend to an idea-starved producer the real terror of the deep. That is the school bus, particularly if it is loaded with disadvantaged, underprivileged children from out of town, i.e., "colored" children.

The men are absolutely heroic: They will try to stop it with their bare hands.

The bus is the symbol of invasion. What makes its approach frightening is the realization that the airplanes could stop King Kong, electrocution could stop The Thing from Outer Space; the population can eventually devour the giant shrimp. But what stops that bus?

The folks try logic first. They yell at the bus. They keep saying, "We are a homogenous community. Do not adulterate us."

Inexorably the bus keeps moving. The folks keep yelling other things, like, "You won't be happy here. You're happier with your own." The bus has no ears.

Here is where the movie becomes innovative. In the genre of horror movies, the threat is defeated because the people organize. Scientists produce new weapons or the military deploys strategically or the mesmerists unite and hypnotize the devil out of the giant shrimp.

In this movie, however, the people panic. They run around tearing their hair. They drop their realty values. Some stampede to the nearest restaurant to get baseball bats. Others vote for George Wallace. Some flee to another suburb only to be forced to flee again. Some of them lock up the schools. Ominously the school bus waits.

Anarchy. Of course, it's only a movie, a brief scenario of a movie at that. It's only make-believe.

Tin Pan Alley and the South

THE JEWISH boys on the Lower East Side of New York did more to romanticize the South than a hundred Margaret Mitchells and *Gone With the Winds*.

> Swanee, how I love you,
> My dear ole Swanee

was written by Irving Caesar with George Gershwin.

"Carolina Moon" and "Waitin' for the Robert E. Lee" by Wolfie Gilbert, and "I'm Alabamy Bound" and "Chattanooga Choo-choo" and hundreds of others, such as, above all, "That's What I Like About the South."

The reason for this was that the idea was to become an American as quickly as possible, and the Jewish boys of Tin Pan Alley thought of the South as the most American section of the country. And they put it in their songs and in their lyrics.

The future of civil rights

THE GREAT problem concerning the American city is not new; it really began in the early 1880's when America's frontier tradition gave way to its immigrant tradition.

At the turn of the century I lived in a seething, overcrowded, unsanitary ghetto, admidst three other ghettos—Little Italy, Polishtown, and the Irish Hell's Kitchen.

Remembering those ghettos, I think that while the books of James Baldwin and Claude Brown may be literature, they are irrelevant. Some of the poverty I saw among the immigrant Jews of the Lower East Side of New York and among the Italians in Little Italy would make James Baldwin and Claude Brown part of the station-wagon set. The Irish were not so bad off because they had the language; immediately they could occupy the service positions. As a matter of fact, the moment after an Irishman got off the boat he filled out three applications—fireman, motorman, and policeman.

What is relevant to the basic question of whether Americans can live together constructively in the midst of a revolution in technology and a revolution in human aspirations is that *we* could get out and the Negroes cannot.

We knew and had proof positive that if we studied hard and kept going to school and reading books we could enter the American open society. It was a guarantee. The immigrant mother who couldn't speak English told her children, "This is America, the school is free, the library is free, the college is free," and then the phrase we all heard nearly every day—"In America you can become—an anything."

Why do our cities now sit on smoldering volcanoes, despite the vast government administered by some of the kindest and most dedicated people in the world? Why did Tammany Hall and private philanthropy with less funds accomplish in the Jewish, Irish, Italian, and Polish ghettos in 1905 what the present government has found so difficult to accomplish in 1969 with huge funds and noble administrators?

The reason is that earlier the philanthropists and politicians did not contend with caste. Caste goes deep in the human consciousness. So deep that it makes a machinist in Cicero, Illinois, where the average wage is $2.84 an hour, cheer a politician from a state where the average wage is $1.72 an hour. Caste makes one set of Americans determined not to grant equity to another set of Americans.

In our own ghettos, at the turn of this century, as seething and as poverty-stricken as Watts and Harlem today, we had another advantage: We had separate but equal poverty. We had nothing, and the Irish had nothing, and the Italians had nothing, and the Poles had nothing, and the Hungarians had nothing. No one resented Andrew Carnegie or J. P. Morgan. But then along came the vast programs of social legislation which created the greatest middle class the world has ever seen. Now the middle class is so vast that the basic drive today is no longer for money, but to maintain caste.

Where wages are low and the wonders of middle-class life are absent, the poor whites cheer the politicians who make them plantation owners retroactively.

For the past century we proved that we had the power to annul the Negro's simple human dignity. One thing we must get clear in our minds forever—whatever besides his color is distinctive about the Negro was made so by the pressures of the American environment.

In the North the Negro's protest is to participate in the wonders of American middle-class or near-middle-class life. His protest centers on employment and housing.

But let us bear in mind that the struggle of the Negro in the North is not as simple as the struggle of the several ethnic immigrant groups, some of which made it in a single generation. The Negro cannot change his name to hide his origins, cannot move from one place to another to achieve anonymity. So he must have law every step of the way—national "open housing" and eventually a national FEPC. This would not only lift a great burden from the American people but would usher in a wave of economic prosperity such as we've never known before.

We must smile at those who say that law cannot do it. They would negate the foundation of the Anglo-Saxon ethos. The Southerners themselves came to the Constitutional Convention, Tennent, Gadsden, and Pinckney, demanding a provision for religious freedom. The Presbyterians had gone underground with their first seminary, and the Methodists built their first churches with a fireplace so that when the Anglican sheriff came around to arrest them they could hide their prayer books and say they were visiting the sick. In arguing for law guaranteeing religious freedom, the Reverend Tennent paid his tribute to the great libertarians of the day, but he said, "The hearts of men

doth change." Today in the Deep South there are Negroes working in cotton mills performing white men's jobs for the first time
in history, and these white men, mind you, were those who were
the fiercest in their resistance to integration. The Negroes are
there because of the Kennedy equal opportunity directive. If you
discriminate, you lose your government contract, and even the
poor whites of the Carolinas, Georgia, and Alabama said,
"Bring them in."

The Negro lawyers who have walked in and out of the American courtroom for the past thirty years, attempting to liberate
themselves, liberated the white man first.

Tammany Hall taught us that we didn't have to marry each
other or even say hello to each other; but if we voted together,
each of us would achieve equity. If the white American wage
earner and the Negro voted together, the basic question would
be purely academic; the answer would come from the thousands
of voting precincts. The grandeur of America is that we are a
politically oriented society.

But a political coalition of white wage earners and Negroes
appears to be a long way off.

I believe we should seriously consider an "indemnity." Here
the word "indemnity" should be in quotation marks. The war
to keep the Negro securely locked away has been lost. The Negro
has won. He deserves back pay. We had him locked away during the greatest wealth-producing period in the history of the
world. Such a period will never come again.

Moses must have been a great sociologist. Even over three
thousand years ago he could have walked from Egypt to the
land of Canaan in thirty days. But Moses kept the Israelites in
the wilderness forty years. He did not want to enter the Promised
Land with those who had tipped their hats and stepped off the
sidewalk and bowed low to their masters. He wanted to enter
the Promised Land with those who had grown up in the wilderness. We must say to ourselves, in having lost this war, that
we will provide an adequate living for those who became adults
in the segregated society and who may not be able to compete

in the industrial world of today, and that we will provide at least one hundred billion dollars over a ten-year period for education and housing, including a vast network of vocational schools and neighborhood houses. This is an "indemnity" paid not to a foreign power but to ourselves. If we only get ten W. C. Handys out of it, it will have repaid us a thousandfold.

To talk about the "welfare state" and "handout psychology" is evil. No individual or civilization or people or nation ever made it without a push, without help. As late as the middle of the nineteenth century America solicited funds from thrifty French peasants to build the railroads. Is there a corporation president or a college boy or a bank clerk who was not helped somewhere along the line?

And the greatest help of all is the opportunity to exchange ideas with the surrounding society. Just think of the evil we inflicted upon the Negro when we cut him off from this opportunity. Chief Justice Fred M. Vinson, who really smashed legally enforced racial segregation in America, set the pattern for the entire Negro revolution in his decision *Sweatt v. Painter*. He enunciated that man is more than body and mind; he is also spirit. Deny a Negro law student the right to exchange ideas with his future colleagues and you not only deny him an equal education, but you dehumanize him as well.

The Jews were in the ghettos of Europe for a thousand years, and they survived. They produced notable scholars and Talmudists. The family religion kept them together. But it was only after Jews entered the open society at the beginning of the nineteenth century and had the opportunity to exchange ideas with the rest of Western society that they produced Heine and Mendelssohn and Disraeli and Einstein and Jonas Salk and a few million others who have enriched the world.

Julius Caesar reports that many of the Anglo-Saxons had some degree of tribal law, but life was primitive in England, Scotland, Ireland, and Wales at the time that Greece had filled the world with intellectual splendor and glory. And Rome had already established the structure of city government, and her engineers had already built roads, dams, and aqueducts.

So what happened to produce Shakespeare, Milton, and Winston Churchill? First the Romans and then the Jewish merchants from Antioch came, and then the Danes, the Normans, the Spaniards, the Illyrians. And the Island Kingdom entered its period of Gloriana.

Never in world history has there been so noble an advance by any people as by the American Negro. One of their great men, Frederick Douglass, wrote that he educated himself by crouching below the windowsill of the manor house when the mother read to her children. He crouched for as long as she kept reading, day after day.

The Negro has conducted the greatest experiment in establishing the sacredness of the individual in world history. His revolution has not been to alter a single existing institution. He did not want to burn the Bastille or get rid of the tax on tea. What he has been telling us is that the American institutions are so desirable that he wants in on them. He is in the position, however, that he needs this push, and in our complex world the only way this push can come is for this nation to give him back pay; at least one hundred billion dollars for welfare, education, vocational training, and housing and "open housing" would be the greatest investment ever made. This is not as overwhelming as it sounds. The annual cost of the war against poverty, in the process of being dismantled, was only two billion dollars. So we haven't even scratched the surface, and those who talk of a "welfare state" must have in mind the three billion dollars we spend on dogs every year. The recommendation of legislation for this urban Marshall Plan of at least one hundred billion dollars would be a good beginning to help solve the urban problem of the enclaves of poverty—the white, Negro, and Spanish ghettos of America. The passage of such legislation would give the entire world a spiritual lift. Silver miners in Peru, Kaffirs in Africa, Buddhist monks in Vietnam, peasants in Rumania, Russia, and China would look on in wonder. And America itself would have ensured its perpetuation for centuries to come.

Negro anti-Semitism

Time MAGAZINE ran a cover story on the confrontation between Jew and Negro. As usual in these matters, *Time* was scrupulously correct in its assessment. Jews in New York City, along with many of the municipal authorities, were outraged by an anti-Semitic editorial which introduced an exhibition at the Metropolitan Museum entitled "Harlem on My Mind." Recently, I resigned from SNCC when its leadership condemned Jews and Israel. The bitter irony of this confrontation is that the first white allies the Negroes had were Jews. Rather than pity the breach, let me try to understand it.

The confrontation, the anti-Semitism, reached newsworthy proportions in New York City. While the great majority of cops with whom the Negro would come in contact are either Protestant or Catholic, the overwhelming preponderance of teachers and social workers is Jewish. Negroes are not pressuring to be enlisted on police rolls; the thrust of the civil rights movement has been toward the schools and the social services. One of the many manifestations of this thrust has been the concept of decentralization. Local boards want autonomy to choose teachers and curricula. This sounds reasonable. But a Jewish principal who has served in a school for twenty years may not think this is reasonable at all. His union certainly does not think it is reasonable, and his union has a predominately Jewish membership.

This is an oversimplification, of course. There are other reasons, two of which are important.

One of these is that the Jew is the weakest link in what is popularly called the "White Establishment," or what Karl Marx called the "superstructure." One of the tactics the Negro sit-ins employed when they went out to integrate the Southern department stores was to picket the Jewish-owned store if there was one in their city. The Jewish storeowner in the South was more vulnerable, and the Negroes knew the chances that he was a profound champion of white supremacy were slim. For the same reason, the textile unions of the South always struck the Jewish-owned plant first. Few Jews can long bear strikers picketing their plant while they sing, "Onward, Christian Soldiers."

The instinct, however, played the Negroes false in New York City, which is a Jewish city. The Jewish schoolteachers are not going to abandon their tenure any more than railroad firemen are going to abandon diesels.

The last substantial reason for the confrontation I suspect was the Negro-Jewish alliance itself. The most vociferous of the Negro anti-Semites are the ones who command not only constituencies, but also positions of power, responsibility, and influence. In short, they are the intellectual, articulate, perhaps college-educated Negroes, the Negroes who would know Jews best, the ones who think they can do it all alone and resent those who lent aid in the past. I suspect Rap Brown or Stokely Carmichael can get as mad at Lillian Smith, the first Southern woman to publish Negro writings and verse, as they can at Albert Shanker, the head of the teachers' union. Today, W. E. B. Du Bois is a more significant figure to many Negroes than Booker T. Washington. Booker T. Washington was up from slavery. W. E. B. Du Bois was a militant.

The pertinent question

THE TROUBLE with the civil rights movement is that, when given a specific example, most people would deny the rights guaranteed in our Constitution and its amendments. When it is presented as an abstract principle, most would support the right. This is natural, for when it is presented as an abstract principle, the average man can identify himself with the victim who is being denied his right. When a concrete example is offered, he most often finds that he is not the victim but the oppressor. He arches his back at that. What comes into play then is the human instinct to hate those whom one has wronged.

Suppose a Gallup poll in the 1830's had asked factory workers in Manchester and Welsh miners and sheep herders in the Hebrides this question: "Do you want the Catholics to have the right to vote?" We can well imagine the response. But the prime minister knew better. His question was, How can England deny the vote to people living their lives on British soil? How indeed can such a situation be tolerated?

We are not as sophisticated as Parliament. We made each of our citizens oppressor-conscious. "Do you want your child to be bussed to a school for a more balanced student body?" The interesting thing about this is that some eighty thousand children were being bussed to school in New York with never a word. It became an issue only when it involved the Negro child. "Do you want a Negro to move into your neighborhood?" And so on and on, instead of asking the only pertinent question, the Lord Macaulay question: "How can the United States of America countenance an idea such as second-class citizenship for a segment of its population?"

For an expanded DAR

I HAVE recently become a board member of SCAWDAR, a nonprofit organization which does not, at this time, particularly need contributions.

SCAWDAR is dedicated to the proposition that at least sixteen Negro women ought to become members of the Daughters of the American Revolution, another nonprofit organization. These Negro women are lineal descendants of Crispus Attucks. Anyone who knows his American history knows that Crispus

Attucks was the first Patriot killed in the American Revolution.

Attucks was a runaway slave who had made his home in Boston. On the night of March 5, 1770, he joined a group of unarmed Patriots who were incensed at the British troops stationed in the city to enforce the notorious Townshend Acts. They were demonstrating against these troops when the British opened fire on these unarmed men. Crispus Attucks was one of the three men killed instantly; two others died of wounds later.

The funeral, which started at Boston's famed Faneuil Hall, was an event which let the colonists give vent to their hatred of tyranny. And a monument was erected at the site where the massacre took place. It commends Crispus Attucks and his four comrades in martyrdom with these sentiments:

> Long as in Freedom's cause
> the wise contend
> dear to your Country shall
> your fame extend

The bylaws of the Daughters of the American Revolution specifically decree as eligible for membership in the Continental Congress all the descendants (female) of Revolutionary soldiers.

SCAWDAR has so far certified one hundred and sixty-four female descendants of good old Crispus Attucks. There are probably many more, since it is a matter of record that at his death Attucks was survived by five nephews and seven nieces. It has taken SCAWDAR (which stands for the Society for Crispus Attucks Women to Join DAR) many years to locate these Attucks descendants. Now the work will accelerate because the Crispus Attucks women, several of them resident in Boston, are also lending a hand.

Perhaps in two years the DAR convention will be asked to certify the Attucks women for membership. SCAWDAR charges no dues, nor does it solicit donations. The money for the research is privately donated. The report, which it will eventually forward to the hierarchy of the DAR, will not involve any DAR expense.

Segregation and the schools

WHEN I read a criticism of the schools, I say to myself, much of it is valid—particularly that coming from such eminent students as Dr. Conant and Admiral Rickover—but I think what is lacking in this criticism is the one basic premise—that this civilization is the first in the history of man that has attempted to educate the entire mass of the population.

When you think of it in these terms, the criticism falls into proper place, and you can accept that which is valid, because no civilization has ever tried this experiment. Not even our sister democracies today have this. But I tend to differ with the idea that your challenges are more important today than, or even as important as, your challenges have been in the past.

This is nothing new, that the classroom and teacher occupy the most important part, the most important position of the human fabric.

I happen to know that in the late forties the Negroes were debating whether to mount their protests on health. They had good arguments—six times as many Negro children die in infancy as whites; five Negro women die in childbirth to each white woman. Tuberculosis is the fourteenth cause of death among whites; it is the second cause among Negroes.

Some of them figured there would be less opposition to this, there would be no bitterness. But wiser heads said, "Oh, no, it will never do; the pattern of segregation would remain; you would be entering another phase of paternalism, of letting the Negro pregnant woman come into the hospital."

We are a school-oriented society. The wiser heads said, "Once you break segregation in the public schools of America, the whole fabric of segregation everywhere will collapse." And this is essentially sound, because it is happening.

I spoke to a mill worker in Greensboro, where they had hired several Negroes to do white men's jobs for the first time in history. Mind you, Negroes are now among those who are strongest in their resistance to integration with the poor whites.

I said to this worker, "How do you feel about it?" He said, angrily, "Hell, they're going to school with my kids, ain't they?"

Of course—what is working beside them? "They're going to school with my kids."

In the schoolhouse we have the heart of the whole society.

The commitment is the result of six Supreme Court decisions and five Acts of Congress, but more than that, there is a commitment of an idea whose time has come, and no one can stop that. Man has always institutionalized those forces which tend to what the Greeks call the good life. Sometimes it takes them one thousand years to do it, as it did to institutionalize the military and the police force; it is only one hundred and twenty-five years since we institutionalized public education.

We had bitter struggles to institutionalize the eight-hour day in labor-management relations. The old-timers will tell those who worry about the Negro protests that this has been a pink tea party compared to other protests in this attempt to institutionalize the forces for the good life.

I remember as a boy that white Protestant Anglo-Saxon ladies chained themselves to a fire hydrant in front of the home of Senator O'Gorman, who was against women's suffrage. I remember some of these ladies were dragged over the street to the paddy wagon.

I don't have to remind the old-timers of the terrific freedom rides and sit-ins and violence of the labor struggle from 1880 to 1930, of the Molly Maguires and Pinkertons, the assassination of the governor of Idaho, the Haymarket, the bombing of the Los Angeles *Times*. In Harlan, Kentucky, the blood ran thick down the streets.

This is a very great and wonderful revolution. Twenty-two

million people under the greatest provocation have hardly made any serious mistakes. We now have a few hitchhikers getting in. This is also a pattern of social upheaval—hitchhikers who have given the segregationists something that they waited for for a long time.

The teachers do not have it as tough as they had it sixty years ago; it is only the demagogues with the myths who have created the idea that it is tougher. The teachers have not lost their dedication. They are not less talented than they were sixty years ago when they took 11,000,000 immigrants, 9,000,000 of whom could not speak a word of English, and turned them into American citizens within a single generation. It was the greatest miracle of human relations in our history. I watched them do it.

We were no different from the Southerners confronted with a social upheaval. I remember that in my classroom there were nothing but Jewish boys, sons of immigrants or immigrants themselves. We were a completely homogeneous society, with all the comforts that this brings.

The teacher talked Yiddish to you once in a while; the principal spoke Yiddish to your mother. Then suddenly, one day, the Italians began to move across the Bowery and there were strangers in the room and it was no longer as comfortable; the principal no longer spoke Yiddish to your mother; he used an interpreter now. This was a "public" school—it was not "our" school; there were strangers there.

But what happened to that class is now, I notice, happening to the South where desegregation has been complied with, as in my city, and in Richmond, the capital of the Confederacy, and Atlanta. Your educational status will go down for a while, of course, just as it went down when this boy who could not speak English came into the class. Of course it went down, but those who say that the level of education suffers with the Negroes coming in are unwittingly uttering a very evil statement.

What they are actually saying is that the results of racial segregation shall be used as the excuse to perpetuate it. This is evil. Put a child in a basement where he can't hear for ten years and take him out. Put him in fifth grade and say, "Go on back to the basement, you cannot keep up with us." This is an evil thing.

The U.S. Office of Education had some dramatic evidence of what we are talking about. It was a study by the Surgeon General in 1965 which showed that when tested for induction into the armed forces, eighteen-year-olds from the South fared far worse than those of any other region of the country; an average of fifteen Negroes out of every twenty failed; an average of six whites out of every twenty failed.

South Carolina's eighteen-year-olds—Strom Thurmond's South Carolina—counting both Negroes and whites had the poorest record of all the fifty states. More than half the South Carolinians, 54.6 percent white, mind you, failed the armed forces test. The white man in segregation is held captive as much as the Negro.

I would like to make one point that I think teachers should think about, because this is a big problem. You must remember that the Negro is challenging separate but equal. He never said, "We demand integration," he challenged "equal." That is all he challenged—"It ain't equal."

The Sweatt case began when Mr. Sweatt challenged "equal." He said, "My Negro law school in Texas has 11,000 volumes in the library; the University of Texas Law School at Austin has 274,000 volumes in its library. It's not equal.

"In my Negro law school we have seven instructors; only three of them have master's degrees. At the University of Texas Law School there are eleven instructors, all of whom have PhD degrees. I don't call that equal."

It was Justice Fred M. Vinson who smashed it. The Warren court decision was a 20,000-to-1 shot, if you gambled. There was no other way to go. The furrows had been dug very deeply, four times, by the Vinson court.

The judge in the Sweatt case said, "The facilities have nothing to do with it. If you gave the Negro law school gold doorknobs, private PhD's for each student, segregation of itself is unequal education, hence unconstitutional."

It was at that moment that the Negroes themselves began to sue on the whole Vinson idea: segregation. If you have a Negro law school—suppose you gave each one a private PhD—but separate, you are denying them the right of education: to exchange ideas with their future colleagues.

While Earl Warren was still governor of California, it was the Kentuckian, Vinson, who set the new direction for the social revolution. While the Negroes were still suing for "equal" in the Sweatt and McLaurin cases, Justice Vinson said "separate" was immoral. This was the big moment in the civil rights movement of America's mid-twentieth century.

The Vinson Court was stating a philosophical truth in deciding that the Negro law school in Texas was not equal to the University of Texas at Austin.

Enunciated here was the truth that a man is more than body and mind. He is also spirit.

Wishing Gentiles prosperity

WE JEWS are a mere handful. A corner of Africa or a single province in China or in Indonesia would overwhelm us in numbers.

We do not have the atomic bomb or standing armies. We work in clothing factories and operate retail stores and manufacture ladies' garments and chemicals, operate on the sick, work in laboratories, write plays and books and many songs, and conduct orchestras. And vast numbers among us are concerned with but one idea—to get into the Gentile country club.

But we find that in England the Nazi groups parade the streets with placards proclaiming the threat of the Jews. And in Paris Roger Peyrefitte writes a popular book telling how the Jews are all-powerful, and among the Jews he lists are President

Johnson, the late President Kennedy, Queen Elizabeth of England, former President de Gaulle of France, Generalissimo Franco of Spain, Fidel Castro of Cuba, and former West German Chancellor Adenauer. He even lists as a Jew the notorious anti-Semite of the Inquisition, Torquemada. In Hamburg some neo-Nazis decorate Jewish gravestones with the swastika. In Kansas City, Los Angeles, Birmingham, and Chicago, anti-Semitic pamphlets are handed out: "Buy Christian." In Montana in a place called Crotlandt two Jewish students are annoyed and harassed on and off the grounds of the schoolhouse.

What is remarkable about all of this is that only about twenty-five years ago, 6,000,000 Jews, one-third the Jewish population of the earth, were slaughtered in the Nazi death camps. One would have thought that the mere memory of this vast massacre would have provided sufficient mental orgasms for the anti-Semites. But it is never enough.

I have had no illusions about the end of anti-Semitism. There is no real cure. If all the Jews disappeared tomorrow, the anti-Semites would still have the gravestones. After they had destroyed all the gravestones, they would still have the bodies to dig up. It is endless.

Our only hope is to maintain vigilance, particularly in the democracies, to resist with all our might any attempt to destroy or subvert the democratic institutions which protect us, and to pray daily for the good health and the prosperity of the Gentiles. We are in danger only when the Gentile suffers some bad luck.

On black power

STOKELY CARMICHAEL and the New Left helped elect Richard M. Nixon and a few "white backlash" governors, congressmen, and sheriffs.

"Black power" not only helped elect these politicians but also encouraged the unreasonable fear of the civilian Police Review

Board in New York and helped bring the entire civil rights movement to a halt with the alienation of the white liberals and the Jews.

There are people who dispute this. There are reasonable people, liberals, who say how could Stokely Carmichael with about one hundred and seventy-five followers do all of this? They say, after all, "black power" means nothing more than "political power."

But "black power" is not what the Negro leaders say it is. Nor is it what the *Village Voice* or the *New York Review of Books* says it is. "Black power" is what the white segregationists say it is. That "black power" may be nonsense is irrelevant. What is relevant is that hundreds of thousands of whites who did not think it decent to speak out against civil rights during the past ten years have now found their tongues.

Stokely Carmichael has handed them a weapon.

Many whites were frustrated early in the civil rights movement. These people feared the unfamiliar, feared the Negroes' competition for jobs, feared the Negroes' intrusion into their neighborhoods. But they could not fight back, not the decent people. How could they fight a group of Negroes kneeling on the sidewalk in front of Woolworth's praying to be allowed to eat hot dogs at the snack bar? How could they fight a Negro protest which was using Christianity as a weapon for social justice?

But along came Stokely Carmichael with black power, and all these many thousands exclaimed, "Now you're talking. Now we understand you."

Mr. Carmichael spoke the language of the Ku Kluxer. The only difference is that any three Ku Kluxers know more about that kind of "power" than all the 22,000,000 Negroes put together.

The danger is far from over even if Stokely Carmichael loses all one hundred and seventy-five of his followers. With the advent of black power, we face polarization. This could lead to a quarter of a century of cold war, white and black. With polarization comes the elimination of protest, sit-in, parades, forward movement.

Law and the hearts of men

TOO OFTEN we have heard that the law cannot do it. No less an American presence than Dwight D. Eisenhower once told a press conference, "Laws cannot change the hearts of men."

Thomas Hobbes held that man's life is solitary, poor, nasty, brutish, and short. He might have added very little changes the hearts of men. Law might not change their hearts. But it changes their practice.

Consider the equal opportunity directive issued by President John F. Kennedy in 1963. The plant superintendent called in the foremen and announced, "We are hiring three Negroes for the carding room tomorrow."

"The hell you are!" they said. "What about the toilets? What about the lunchroom? What about the water fountains?"

"If we don't hire the three Negroes, we don't get a contract for four hundred thousand dozen pairs of socks for the Pentagon."

"Bring them in," said the workers.

Some years ago, Senator Eastland warned Attorney General Robert Kennedy, "We don't care what the Supreme Court rules. Their decision is the law of the case, not the law of the land. You want Negroes to vote? Sue us for every Negro, every voting registrar in the South."

After talking it over with Burke Marshall, head of the Justice Department's Civil Rights Division, and John Doar, Robert Kennedy wrote a memo on a yellow pad which read, "Get the road maps and go."

They didn't need a thoracic specialist to change hearts; they only needed the law. Justice Department officers and FBI men walked down dusty roads in Mississippi, Alabama, and Louisiana, stopping at tar-paper shacks, asking Negroes, "Did you try to register? What happened?"

They won their suits. Judge Minor Wisdom in ruling for the government in one of these suits said, "The wall of segregation must come down."

The victory is not complete, but Negroes vote in unprecedented numbers today. They did it all at once. There was nothing wrong with "gradualism"—it was a brilliant concept—except there was no such animal. The riots don't occur gradually—they explode all at once. If we are to put the cap on them, we can't do it gradually. Perhaps we will have to rely on the law rather than on our charity or goodwill.

But I know since the civil rights movement began in the early 1950's there hasn't been a single solitary voluntary act on the part of any Southern state. Whatever progress has been made was made through the pressure of the law.

The third society

SEVERAL YEARS ago, former Mayor Stan Brookshire of Charlotte, along with several wealthy businessmen, invited the Negro leaders to lunch. Each of the white men took several Negro guests to one of the posh restaurants. Some went to the City Club, some to the Epicurean, some to the Hearth and Embers. Everyone was served. The example was set. Integration, at least in the restaurants of this Southern city, was a *fait accompli* that noon.

I have always suspected the cruel joke about "taking a nigger to lunch" was inspired by this simple yet effective action. For many years a Negro who wanted to dine at a good restaurant had to travel to the Dogwood Room at the Charlotte airport. He was served there because the airport was built with federal monies. The civil rights bills which were enacted in the mid-sixties enabled Negroes in theory to dine where they chose. But until Mayor Brookshire organized his little party, it was theory, not practice.

Dr. Sterling W. Brown, the president of the National Council of Christians and Jews, has described a "third society" consisting of those whites and Negroes who believe that integration is not only feasible but desirable.

According to Dr. Brown, the third society is the forgotten society.

I have to count myself a member of this society.

I know there are black militants who would just as soon kill whites as look at them. These militants simply do not have the franchise the Ku Klux Klan has. It seems to me that the folks who do not want to join the third society do not want to worry about the Klan; they only have time to worry about the Black Panthers or Olympic sprinters who wear black gloves.

They have no time to worry about the unsanitary conditions that necessarily obtain in a tar-paper shack because the depreciation of suburban realty values is the most crucial worry in their world.

They are the people who insist they want to eat lunch in a homogeneous atmosphere, like rare goldfish who can only live in milk.

The Christian academies

INTERPOSITION DID not work; nullification did not work; even the closing of the schools did not work. But there are Tarheels who will not give up. In a recent year, die-hard segregationists financed the opening of almost fifty new "Christian academies" for the instruction of white children.

These are private schools whose purpose is to offer "quality education." In reality, they are renovated barns, small frame houses, old quonset huts, sometimes even a dilapidated school building long deserted by mice. Tuition runs from two hundred and fifty to seven hundred dollars a year. The labor needed to paint the walls, refinish old desks, landscape the yard, and construct the playground is all contributed by the parents. At Twelve Oaks Academy in Shelby, North Carolina, a school not yet approved by the state, the headmaster teaches psychology, English, biology, and physical science. Another teaches chemistry, French, and history, and a third teaches all elementary grades.

North Carolina moderates and informed educators are caught up in a dilemma. These private schools are draining support from the public school system. Bond issues are easily defeated at the polls. Budgetary requests are denied, and state funds appropriated on the basis of student enrollment are less than boards of education anticipated.

It is even sadder for the children attending these Christian academies. Southern colleges do not lower their standards no matter how parents clamor for a show of their patriotism. The South already has 3,000,000 illiterates. The Christian academies are bound to improve on this.

Is the *Times* Jewish?

I HAVE been reading Gay Talese's wonderful book *The Kingdom and the Power*, which is both a history and a commentary on the world's greatest newspaper, the New York *Times*.

What interests me particularly about the *Times* is its desire not to be thought of as a Jewish paper. Adolph Ochs, who bought the foundering paper in 1896 and started the *Times'* rise to preeminence, succeeded because he also spawned a Jewish dynasty to manage the *Times*.

"Balancing both sides, careful not to offend, the *Times* wishes to be accepted and respected for what it is," writes Talese, "a good citizens' newspaper, law-abiding and loyal, solidly in support of the best interests in the nation." For that reason, says Mr. Talese, the reporters on the *Times* feel the need to handle with delicacy and caution any story about Jews or of special interest to Jews.

I have news for the *Times*. When some advisers told Winston Churchill about the tide of rising anti-Semitism in America during the late 1930's, he thought the *Times* should expose the hatemongers. "After all," he said, "the *Times* is a Jewish newspaper."

Half the population of Charlotte, North Carolina, surely one of the most sophisticated cities in the South, still believes that anything that comes out of New York City is Jewish inspired, dominated and financed. New York is where all the Jews live, they tell you, and anything that is published where Jews live is Jewish, *a fortiori*. Charles Bloch, a Jewish lawyer of Macon, Georgia, is the segregationist philosopher of the state. He led the Georgia delegation out of the 1948 convention because of its integrationist platform. So the anti-Semite Roy Harris of Savannah ran a headline in his paper, "Jews Mongrelize the South," and I wrote him, "You say the Jews are mongrelizing the South, but you don't say, 'except Charlie Bloch.'"

The *Times'* concern for its ethnic image Talese believes goes back to the harsh criticism voiced about Jews by George Ochs-Oakes, the brother of Adolph Ochs and the father of John Oakes, present editor of the editorial page. George Ochs-Oakes thought the Galicianer Jews who were the immigrants of the 1880's and 1890's were inspiring anti-Semites. These Old World Jews were clannish and superstitious; they made of their Judaism more than a religion. George had some unpleasant things to say about these Jews. The *Times* is still sorry for his intemperance.

Well, you can tell that to Sweeney, as the New York *Daily News* used to advertise. First of all, George Ochs-Oakes was wrong. The anti-Semite couldn't care less what else the Jew might profess in assimilation as long as the Jew professes Judaism or his father did. It is the greatest newspaper in the world. That should be sufficient to carry it along and rid it of the worry of its Jewishness.

The boy adults

THE JEWISH boy of my era, like the peasant boy and the boy of the lower economic classes of all eras and of all nationalities, was turned loose on the world almost immediately after he was weaned. A Jewish boy became a member of the congregation at thirteen, but he had savored much of the adult world for six years before that. He listened to all the talk and often participated in the decisions of the family.

What would have happened to me and to every Jewish, Irish, Italian, and Polish boy of my generation had we suddenly announced to our mothers, "We ain't happy"? No mother would have comprehended such a statement. If finally one mother did understand what the boy meant, she would have taken whatever she was cooking and dumped it over the kid's head.

Conceivably there was a mother who said, "My son is unhappy because he has to use crutches," but she would have been, at that, an ultrasensitive mother.

All the boys I knew—and I mean *all*—made their own decisions. At fourteen or fifteen a boy told his parents, "I think I'll go to law school," or "I intend to stay in the hat factory and become a salesman."

Today's fictional hero can make no decision or can make only wrong ones. I think that is because our novelists do not recognize that the bourgeoisie has dealt itself a new hand.

The American nightmares are about collective bargaining, calories, and Communism, probably in that order, with body odor not far behind.

The Jewish bourgeoisie is, of course, doubly exposed. That is the Jew's burden. He is a capitalist and a Jew, a radical and a Jew, a banker and a Jew. This double exposure is all-important, and it forever contributes to his sense of alienation. In the affluent society, the Jew has as many dilemmas as the Gentile, but he has several additional worries. Will he get into the country club? Will he be accepted as a Little League manager?

Or maybe I've been traveling around another planet for the past sixty-six years.

Who has lost touch?

ABOUT 1960, I began lecturing at colleges throughout the country. The American college is the modern Maecenas. It supports not only the poets but the public speakers. Always my subject was the civil rights movement. I talked about the South, about the emergence of the Negro leadership in the struggle, about the need for federal legislation in the matter of homes, jobs, and schools. I would be exaggerating if I said I was "hailed," but I was recognized as a liberal who was demanding equity for fellow citizens. Invariably the sympathy of college audiences was with me.

Almost ten years later, these same sentiments provoke the hecklers at the colleges, and often I am hard pressed to finish the speech.

I have just finished a tour of five colleges in the California educational complex, and at each of these schools my views were challenged by black militants and by white dissidents. Nor were my sentiments challenged in any question-and-answer period or over the clinking of tea cups but before I finished what I wanted to say.

These students said I was a "reactionary." To which I can only say, "Hah!" They said I was a bonded member of the Establishment.

The black militants want separate dormitories, separate courses in black culture, separate departments. I had to tell them they were crazy. The NAACP, Philip Randolph, the ministers, the teachers, the white liberals fought for almost fifty years to have the Negro integrated into the mainstream of American life. There were Negroes and whites in the South who fought Jim Crow tooth and nail, and here these militants want it reestablished, as though their control of it makes it in any way different. As for African culture, why, the slavers denuded Africa of millions of people, and that is why it has no culture.

The white dissidents are angrier. They want to know why I cannot understand and sympathize with the revolution of the young. I told them that my idea of a revolutionist is Régis Debray, who is about to spend the next thirty years in a South American prison for his ideals. But do not tell me a kid who runs into the dean's office, pokes the man in the nose, burns his papers, and refuses to evacuate the building unless he is granted amnesty is a revolutionist. A revolutionist is a man who is prepared to have others take him at his word.

If I didn't have a good sense of personal equilibrium, I would think I had lost touch. But it isn't I who have lost touch. Anyone who insists Harry Golden is a reactionary has lost touch.

Cemetery segregation

CITY COUNCILMAN Fred Alexander's proposal to remove the fence between the Negro and white sections of the municipally owned cemetery was defeated by the Charlotte City Council.

Opponents of Alexander's proposal argued that there had always been a fence. One part of the cemetery was for whites and one part was for Negroes, they pointed out. Why not let folks alone?

Mr. Alexander cautioned the council that it is precisely this meaningless intransigence which results in what mayors and police chiefs euphemistically call a "long hot summer." There is neither integration nor segregation in a grave, just the dead.

Most of the souls have departed for points north and south, some whites sharing heaven with blacks, some hell.

In Georgia I saw an animal cemetery. The color of the *owner* of the dog was the determining factor in which section of the cemetery the dog would find its final resting place. A black dog owned by a white man was somewhat curiously buried in the white-dog section; a white dog owned by a Negro was even more curiously buried in the colored-dog section.

Do we hate war?

AN OLD ghetto proverb holds that a man says he hates war while he rubs his hands.

We Americans have always insisted we hate war. Dwight D. Eisenhower ended the Korean War, and Richard Nixon will probably end the Vietnam War. But I am not sure both these men acted because of a basic antipathy toward war. I rather suspect we ended the Korean War and will end the Vietnam War because we have discovered war is so frightfully expensive. Had he purchased anything for the vast sums of money he spent, Johnson would have been the unanimous choice of the electorate. The Tet offensive made Americans turn their backs on him. They turned their backs not because he had waged a war which was cruel but because he waged a war which was pointless.

The central myth we entertain in our history texts and patriotic pamphlets is that America is the great neutral. Our pacifism is supposed to be proved by the fact that only civilians manage our war apparatus. Lincoln, Wilson, and Roosevelt were politicians elevated to greatness when they took charge of a nation faced with the exigencies of war.

It is also true that each of our wars has made a soldier into the President. The Revolutionary War made George Washington; the War of 1812, Andrew Jackson; the Mexican War, Zachary Taylor; the Civil War, Ulysses S. Grant; the Spanish-

American War, Theodore Roosevelt; World War I, Herbert Hoover (who was Woodrow Wilson's food administrator in Belgium); and World War II, Dwight D. Eisenhower.

"War is hell," said an American general, not meaning we shouldn't venture into it. We glorify soldiers, and glorifying soldiers is not far from glorifying war.

Should Richard Nixon's administration find a "just and honorable peace," I would still hesitate before I declared America would never make the same mistake in Asia again.

If we get a bargain rate in Asia, the troops will be back. Despite the Berlin uprising and the Hungarian Revolution, despite the Wall and the Czech invasion, we have avoided a direct confrontation in Europe. I do not think this avoidance means we are peaceful but that we are thrifty.

The student riots

I am filled with admiration for the rootin'-tootin' tactics of Samuel I. Hayakawa, the semanticist turned university president, at San Francisco State College. I have asked many teachers and many students about the meaning of the new disorders, and I have had a great many answers. Basically, I believe these riots are inspired by an especially strong anti-intellectual disposition. Most of the professors I talked to insisted the bulk of the student protestors were always the C— or D students, although they are often led by an articulate and facile minority. The students who storm the dean's office have been there on many another occasion.

I believe Dr. Margaret Mead supports this point in her excellent study "The Wider Significance of the Columbia Upheaval," which appeared in the fall, 1968, issue of *Columbia Forum*. Dr. Mead's point is that the student riot at Columbia was related to other events transpiring in New York City, in the nation, and in the world.

"Higher education," writes Dr. Mead, "is no longer a privilege or even a right. It is an arduous requirement laid on young people by the standards of employment in the society."

This is the key: A college education is a financial necessity for the members of the middle and upper-middle classes, which is roughly almost everybody.

The trouble comes when the students realize that not only do they have to put in four years in which they do not participate in the working world as adults, but the university also has some minimal standards they must meet.

For the anti-intellectual, four years of passing grades just to qualify for a trainee position with a major corporation is an impossibly strenuous demand.

Hence the riots. The first demand of the students at Columbia for quelling their disturbances was amnesty, which was the last thing any authority could grant. It may well be immature to declare, "I will suffer for my principles," but it is a quixotic immaturity—not a desperately selfish immaturity like saying, "I want to raise hell and desecrate buildings as long as you won't hold me to account."

Of these students, Dr. Mead concludes: "When they begin to make socially responsible demands, they will almost immediately acquire the education in real life which they complain the university denies them."

Songmy

ON THE morning that the story of the massacre of the people of Songmy broke in the international press, wholly coincidentally I was talking to a professor at Israel's Hebrew University who is a holocaust specialist. Studies of the Nazi extermination of the Jews have engaged the attention of a growing faculty of Israeli historians. When I confided in this gentleman that I could hardly believe Americans capable of such brutality, he said, quite simply, "I believe it. I have had to believe it of the Germans, the Ukrainians, the Hungarians, and the Poles. I had better believe it of the Egyptians. Why should we refuse to believe it of the Americans?"

The truth, of course, was that I didn't want to believe it. We incline to think genocide and mass murder has to be organized on the German plan—that to kill large groups of innocent people a nation or an army needs a special apparatus, skilled in killing, that its personnel be scientific and remorseless. But the Mongols could kill whole peoples in the thirteenth century. Killing people isn't hard. One needs little planning.

The victims at Songmy counted for something. The Egyptians have killed almost a half-million Libyans, and this devastation goes unreported. The Nigerians have decimated the Biafrans, and this goes for the most part unlamented.

What makes Songmy doubly shameful is the attitude of the Saigon government, which stated flatly that there had been no massacre. Instead, Saigon came up with the evidence that the Vietcong had murdered three thousand Vietnamese in the Tet offensive, as though one crime mitigated another.

Surprising, too, was the guarded sympathy I heard from an Israeli, not for the act, but for the American nation and ideal, which he said still represents the last best hope of man.

What I didn't read, however, was a comment from an authoritative military source in Israel which pronounced the obvious: The massacre at Songmy did absolutely nothing to advance American strategy or tactics. In their madness, these limited, unimaginative soldiers may have wanted to prove the meaninglessness of it all.

The young and the old

BY NOW everyone knows the story: The parents of an eight-year-old Jewish boy send him from Paris to the French countryside to save him from the Nazis. He lives with a family, one of whose members is an old man named Pepe, an anti-Semite. But in the end the old man and the boy exchange the precious gift of love.

Or does everyone know the story? It isn't a war story. It takes place during the war, yes, but the war is incidental to the old man and the young boy. When the war ends, the old man knows the boy will go home. That saddens him.

I wonder if it is really a Jewish story. Pepe doesn't like Jews. Many of his opinions are outrageous. He never in fact learns that his young companion is Jewish. But he does come to love best that which he imagines he hates worst.

Because the young boy is Jewish and therefore knows what Jews are, he can tease the old man about his prejudices, a mischievous boy teasing an old grump.

The young boy does not change Pepe's life because he is Jewish—he changes Pepe's life because he is young.

Pepe teaches him things about the countryside, lessons he would never have learned in Paris. As Pepe enriches the young boy's life, so does the young boy enrich Pepe's. They show each other different sides of life. There is one secret between them, and that is that the boy is a Jew.

The young boy keeps the secret. The story is why. I think he keeps it because he does not want the old man to be ashamed of himself, to be disappointed in himself. Pepe is capable of vast love, and that is reason enough to keep the secret from him. Probably the young boy knows that Pepe wouldn't be much of an anti-Semite anyway, not when the chips are down, not when love is at stake.

This then is the story of the reciprocal reverence between the young and the old. It is an ancient story, a story told over and over.

From Mount Nebo, Moses finally sees the Promised Land, but it is Joshua who must lead the Israelites into it. Garrulous Socrates, the gadfly of the city, is condemned to death by the Athenians for asking impious questions, but those questions inspire the young Plato to invent philosophy and turn the world upside down. In Samuel Butler's *The Way of All Flesh*, young Ernest Pontifex must *not* go the way of his selfish and hypocritical father, the Reverend Theobald Pontifex.

The old must set an example. It is only from examples that the young learn, so it had better be a good example. Curiously, the old set the example because often the young teach them the most valuable of all lessons. Life does not go on forever, but the young think it does. They think there is all the time in the world for love and promise and meaning. And of course they are right.

Hippies of the past

THE HOUSE OF REPRESENTATIVES served notice to the kids that if they decide to invade the President's office, the federal loan goes down the drain.

When I was young there were no loans at all for college, let alone federal monies, which explains perhaps why there were no hippies forty and fifty and sixty years ago. In those days, to our disadvantage maybe, all of us used to shape up.

It was hard being different. My best friend was an Irishman named John Duff, who was passionately devoted to sports. John wanted to become a sportswriter, but his parents prevailed upon him to go to law school. But at that, he was the manager of the Columbia baseball college team which boasted Lou Gehrig as the first baseman. In his law years, John always represented athletes and boxing promoters and never missed a Yankee home game.

One of the moments I remember was when he told me he had been to see a professional football game.

"On a *Sunday?*" I asked incredulously.

Milton Esterosky was another fellow bound on being different. Milton, like the rest of us, lived in a tenement, but every Saturday in the spring and the summer, Milton went fishing.

He used to dress up in what we called then "white ducks" with newly cleaned white shoes and a blue blazer, and he took the subway up to the far reaches of the Bronx and fished in either the Hudson River or the Bronx pond.

Literally, we thought Milton was crazy. He would go off, two pieces of matzahs and cheese in a paper bag, a pole with a reel over his shoulder, bright and gleaming in his ducks and shoes. If Congress had passed a law against him, we would have said Congress was right.

We admired the fellow who wrote poetry, however. We even listened to it. Anyone who could play the piano was our champ.

There were gangs in those days. There were Italian gangs, Jewish gangs, Irish gangs; everybody was in a gang except the Chinese. But no one had a "turf." We just threw milk bottles loaded with sand at each other, and those who survived went back to grammar school the next day.

The long hair and the beard seem to give the boys more courage these days. I wonder, however, when they go for that first job, won't they shave? We who were Itzak became Irving, and we who were Moshe became Maurice when it was time for that first job.

Communion on the way

NEW YORK CITY has long had a program of taking Negro slum kids to all the museums and opera houses and theaters in the hope that this exposure will bring hope to the hopeless.

The bussing from slums into summer schools and pools is motivated by much the same inspiration.

Summer pilot programs can be the handwriting on the sidewalk, as it were.

The idea of the affluent providing opportunity to the poor by sharing facilities is new. Only grudgingly do the affluent consent to taxes which are spent on welfare and slum removal. Those

taxes are stay-out-of-sight money. I have no doubt that the prospect of intercommunion between city and suburban school systems will be called unconstitutional. But I have no doubt that
intercommunion will probably bless all of us sooner or later.

The making of chaplains

UNTIL THE Civil War there were no Jewish chaplains in
the United States Army, although Jews had served in the Continental Army, fought against the British in 1812, gone off to
the Black Hawk War and the Mexican War. In 1861 Congress
passed a bill commissioning chaplains as long as they were
"regularly ordained ministers of some Christian denomination."

Outrage was expressed not only by Jews. A Christian editor
of the Philadelphia *Dispatch* argued, "Our law-makers appear
to have forgotten that there are Americans in existence who,
though not Christians, are their peers in all respects, and en-
dowed with equal privileges and immunities."

Rabbi A. Fischel of Temple Shearith Israel in New York
circulated a petition among his parishioners alleging the law was
totally unfair, discriminatory, and unconstitutional.

Simon Cameron, the Secretary of War, replied that the law
was the law.

The Jews wrote back and said their patriotism was unexcelled.
Two thousand of them had enlisted from New York alone, and
all were in need of spiritual consolation.

The Jews turned to their good friend Abraham Lincoln.
Henry Hart addressed a letter to him apologizing for intruding
upon his duties but pleading on behalf of his "coreligionists who,
expending their life blood in the noble cause of country, are
still, when racked by pain and suffering, debarred from the privilege of the ministrations of spiritual advisers of their faith. . . .

"May we not earnestly solicit you to confer on the Reverend
Dr. Arnold Fischel, a capable and respected minister of our

faith, duly ordained, whose testimonial, as required by law, was duly forwarded to your Excellency . . . the appointment of chaplain to the hospitals in and around Washington, so that the pain of our brethren may be assuaged and their mental agony soothed?"

Lincoln promised to do what he could and informed Fischel he "would try to have a new law broad enough to cover what is desired by you in behalf of the Israelites."

Lincoln, according to the report from the Civil War Centennial of the American Jewish Archives, was good as his word. In 1862, the bill was amended to exclude the discriminatory clause.

I think about this when I read of young folks burning their draft cards.

The poverty stalemate

AT THE turn of the century, the Negroes in North Carolina became bricklayers. Southern pine is too soft for siding, and mass-produced bricks from local ovens became the conventional material for houses. Because the Negroes were bricklayers, white men shunned the profession. Not until World War II, when the whites discovered that bricklayers on government contracts were making as much as editors or teachers, did any white lift a hod. Then, of course, they pushed the Negro out.

A similar circumstance has overtaken the poverty program in North Carolina. Poor whites in the rural areas refuse to participate in any of the programs; they deny themselves much-needed aid because these programs are integrated. As a result of this, the preponderance of welfare is black, and the whites sullenly refer to "the nigger poverty program" and stay clear.

Since the Reconstruction, the black man in North Carolina is the poor man. White men chopped and tied tobacco for twenty-five cents a day, their children working away in the hot fields with them, but these workers never believed they were poor as the Negroes were poor. White men had hope. The hope never led them anyplace, but still they believed it distinguished them from the black man. In these rural areas poor white men did enjoy a certain social equality with the big plantation owners and the rich farmers. To apply for aid from an integrated federal agency would forever doom that equality.

James K. Batten of the Charlotte *Observer* reported on the status of the poverty program in North Carolina. We have more poor than any other state, 234,000 families, and 66 percent of these families are white, according to the 1960 census. Yet only a small fraction join any poverty program.

Negroes are quick to take advantage of whatever help they can get. But as the white segregationist will remark, "Niggers ain't got a hell of a lot of pride to swallow."

In Craven County, North Carolina, there are 5,132 poor families—people who live in tar-paper shacks and are functionally or wholly illiterate. Two thousand seven hundred and twenty-two of these families are white, and 2,360 are Negro. James Godwin, the director of the Craven Operation Progress, believes the whites simply refuse to acknowledge their plight. How to reach them baffles Godwin.

Compounding the problem are the local booster clubs, which never tire of singing the praises of these poverty-ridden towns. The white establishment is quickly annoyed when a poverty agency moves in.

Batten did find some whites who did participate; one of them, a fifty-eight-year-old mother, told him her daughter was a member of the Neighborhood Youth Corps. The young girl earned $12.50 a week doing odd jobs at the nearby Farm Life High School. The money enabled her to stay in high school. A high school diploma is the only ticket out of dreary Craven County. When Batten asked this girl's mother what the neighbors thought, the woman said, "They hain't throwed off on me. I've always treated colored people right, but I've always been taught to go with my color. But if you're poor you can't help it."

It is true these poor whites are victimizing themselves, and our pity won't help them.

Social progress doesn't always banish problems. I remember a taxi driver in Charlotte condemning Roosevelt intemperately. When I asked him why he was so mad at F.D.R., he told me he had just delivered a Negro preacher to his home. "He paid me with a five-dollar bill," the driver said. "Now when did you ever see a nigger with a five-dollar bill before Roosevelt?"

The threat from below

ALMOST ALWAYS, the middle class feels threatened from below.

One has to wonder about this fear after reading Homer Bigart's articles on hunger in America in the New York *Times*. The Negroes in the Mississippi Delta and in the ramshackle Florida trailer camps are not threatening anyone. They are fighting a losing battle against starvation. Their children grow to adulthood—if lucky—retarded because they suffer from malnutrition and from the lack of stimulation in the home. These people are too weak and demoralized to demand a square meal from the government.

No one with either a grain of sense or a notion of history ever expected the middle class to have a heart, but one would expect them to know whence to expect threats. Threats never come from below; they come from above. The professionally employed Negro who wants to move into a white neighborhood is actively encouraged and abetted by giant institutions like General Motors and Youngstown Steel and probably Sears Roebuck. General Motors wants to sell each of them an auto, Youngstown wants to move its kitchen cabinets, and Sears Roebuck will send a catalogue to a black man or to a red, white, and blue man if he spends over twenty dollars a year in mail orders. Probably each of these giants would like to sell goods to the hungry Delta

Negroes in Mississippi. General Motors, Youngstown, and Sears are always enthusiastic about raising the standard of living and increasing the gross national product.

Industry would just as soon do away with the middle class and have one vast buying class. Industrialists are lucky in that they have so far escaped detection. The middle class is mad first at Christians, whether or not they wear a collar, and next at elective officials. The higher the office, the madder the middle class gets. Lastly, the middle class is mad at the native-born Negro citizens who either want their rights or expect hominy or grits for the next few days to keep the family alive.

Effect of the assassinations

THE STRUGGLE for civil rights was made infinitely longer by the assassinations of Martin Luther King and Robert Kennedy.

I did not know Martin Luther King well. I met him several times, usually at meetings where we spoke to raise money for the Freedom Riders or the NAACP Legal Defense Fund, and I talked with him on the occasion of the March on Washington in 1963.

When Bobby Kennedy, who was my friend, and for whom I spoke to all the B'nai B'rith in California, was murdered two months later, I realized the maniacs themselves may have been accidental, but their purpose was not. The deaths of King and Kennedy changed the terrains where the armies contended.

Martin Luther King and Robert Kennedy were equally important heroes. They were heroes to whom white and black could relate.

King's singular contribution was to prove that Christianity still had its uses. He was able to portray the civil rights movement as a moral drama. Americans always have trouble with moral difficulties.

The difficulty in maintaining a dialogue with the new militants is, first, that we insist they speak our language, which they choose not to or cannot do, and, second, that they keep telling us we are not nice people, which we indeed are not, though we don't want to hear it.

The only white man who could speak this language was Robert Kennedy, one of the few white men I ever met who could think black. Kennedy shared much with Martin Luther King. He too saw the issue as a moral issue. He once exclaimed to Governor Ross Barnett of Mississippi, who sent state troopers to deny James Meredith entry to the university, "But it's wrong!"

Where Martin Luther King chose religion as the vehicle which would unify black and white, Kennedy chose politics, elective office, pressure groups, lobbies. He won the California primary, in one instance, because he was able to recruit hundreds of Mexican farm workers and weld them into political cells, telephoning Mexican friends and neighbors, ringing doorbells, handing out foreign-language pamphlets. They worked for him because they knew he would deliver as he promised. In California, Kennedy set up the nucleus of a powerful minority bloc. Had he lived to become President, perhaps he would have so organized the country with nuclei intent on achieving law and justice in order to secure law and order. It will not happen that way now.

With Martin Luther King gone, equity for all will not come through a religious crusade; with Kennedy gone, it will not come through political innovation.

The bridges were washed away that spring.

The undetected flaw

HERE IS a true story. It was on an intelligence test for Negro children as part of an antipoverty project. One of the pictures on the paper was of a window with a crack in it. "What's wrong with this picture?" was the question. And none of the Negro children gave the answer. A crack in a window was not a "wrong" to them. They had cardboard for windows, or rags, or they had no windows at all, and thus we succeeded in this past century to strip these people of human dignity.

The true aristocracy

CHARLESTON IS a place of absolute gentility and mannered living. Despite the defeat of the Confederacy, one still remembers the crinoline hoopskirts and the officers who wore butternut-gray and yellow sashes. And the chandeliers still sway to the tunes that come floating back from the ancient, glorious, and chivalrous time.

If there is such a thing as a "legitimate" segregationist, he lives in Charleston. Folks there are born to the purple, and while the stately mansion, mint julep, and field hands have given way to cotton and tobacco warehouses and batteries of insurance clerks, the flavor is still there. This was the town that produced America's true aristocracy, and people there are still polite—except for one glaring inconsistency.

In Charleston the women's restrooms are labeled either "Ladies—White" or "Female—Colored." But is this really enough for Charleston? We can understand that it is adequate for the newly arrived middle-class folks of Birmingham and Jackson, but Charleston needs much more. Aren't some folks disturbed when the wives and daughters of mill workers use "Ladies—White"?

To be consistent Charleston should have Class A, B, C, and D restrooms under appropriate signs: "Who was her father— White," "What school did she go to—White," etc., and "NAACP—Female—Colored," "Has she paid her poll tax—

Colored," and so on down the list so the folks can really be classified.

No one here but us chickens

THERE'S AN elegantly stratified dining place out there in Nevada owned by a Chinese couple. The cashier is an Anglo-Saxon, and the waitresses are all Mexicans. The bus girls are Navajo Indians, and the janitor is an exchange student from India.

With all that color on the board, the day a Negro family entered to wine and dine, the Chinese proprietor ran at them, flapping his apron as if the family were a flock of geese, shrieking, "No cullah here, no cullah."

A true short story

WHILE I was visiting Munich, I met an American corporal who told me that next door to him lived an American sergeant and his family who hailed from the Deep South.

When the government school started, this sergeant learned one of the teachers was a Negro, and he was quite upset about the whole prospect. He had a hard time finding out who this teacher was, and after two days of futile asking about the base, he put the question to his six-year-old son: "Is your teacher colored?"

The boy replied, "I don't remember. I'll look and see tomorrow."

They got rhythm

IT'S THE year 2015, and, of course, the Negroes have "taken over" the Presidency, the Cabinet, and a majority in each of the houses of Congress.

There is an important meeting of the Cabinet, and they are sitting there worrying about the fate of the world while a janitor busies himself with his broom and dustpan. The janitor is very happy, because he's humming to himself as he sweeps up the old cigarette butts and discarded paper.

After watching this contented and skillful soul at work for some time, the Secretary of Defense leans over to the President and says, "I tell you one thing, these Jews may not be smart, but they are happy and they certainly got rhythm."

Letter from a Southern lady

KATHERINE McVEY, a Southern lady who now lives in Alhambra, California, wrote me, "We know there is not a pure-blood Negro in this country... there is also not a pure white in the South, and probably not in the U.S. since they (and we) moved around so much.

"Our fine, aristocratic slaveholding gentlemen forebears bred up a storm of quadroons and octoroons who, immediately after slavery was abolished began to 'pass.' They all married white men and the South is made up of their descendants and relatives of their descendants. My mother knew hundreds of them and let it be said to her eternal glory she never gave one of them away. One of them married our small town banker. There were millions of these women at the time, there must be scores of millions by now.

"I wrote all these things to Gov. Wallace and pointed out

his own Negro characteristics. Among other things I said, 'All the women in my family have been members of the DAR and I will match my family tree against yours any day, but we had a sister who had a slight curl and my late husband had a slight curl in his hair. We know where it came from for there is no other place in the world it could have come from. Since we are all cousins, why not let's be friends and not set the dogs on our poor relatives?'

"He has since had his hair cut and the curl doesn't show."

PART 5

Language, the Library, and the Lost Vegetable Garden

There is no substitute

It has become a cliché to say something is wrong with our school system. I admit that I approach my own criticism with timidity. Yet the criticism I make is valid because I can prove it mathematically. I have checked this with authorities in ten of our state universities. There are literally thousands of our boys and girls, graduated from high school, who cannot write a simple declarative English sentence.

Even the word seems to have disappeared—composition. I do not know what they call it today.

There is only one way to *composition*—reading.

Young people write for advice about a writer, and I answer that there's only one way—reading. A child learns to speak because it hears; a writer learns to write because he reads.

There is no other way.

"Don't teach me the answers," said the first great philosopher, Socrates. "Just find me the questions. If I know the questions, I will make it a better world."

The discovery of *the question* is the great bonus reading confers.

When you read, you are really thinking with minds of genius, of experience, of courage.

Reading properly helps you become a self-thinker.

No one ever did a considerable piece of work in this world who was not a self-thinker.

The people who helped encourage our anti-intellectualism are the same people who resent self-thinkers. History shows that the best government was conceived by the self-thinkers, the literary men.

Benjamin Franklin was probably the number one philosopher of his time. Thomas Jefferson read everything of consequence. Alexander Hamilton was an intellectual, and so was James Madison. John F. Kennedy was a reader who made notations in his books, as every self-thinker does. So was Woodrow Wilson. Across the Atlantic, the greatest accomplishments were made by the literary men—Disraeli, Gladstone, Balfour, and Churchill.

Alexander the Great went looking for the literary man, and when he found Diogenes at Corinth, he said, "Were I not Alexander, I would wish to be Diogenes."

Caesar was a literary man. His *Commentaries* were not excelled until Winston Churchill.

Napoleon was a literary man, probably one of the great readers of his time. Wherever he went, he tried to spend as much time as possible with learned men. Lord Rosebery in his biography of Napoleon says that the conqueror had a library of eight hundred volumes on the field with him at Waterloo.

There is no substitute for reading, which leads to composition.

The student who says, I intend to go into electronics, law, or business, and therefore Shakespeare, Plutarch, Hugo, and Emerson are a waste of time, is terribly short-sighted. Who were the great lawyers of our civilization? Choate, Darrow, Leibowitz, and others who could address the court and jury with page and verse from the Bible, Shakespeare, and Omar Khayyám. The salesman, insurance man, merchant, and physicist must have the means of self-expression and some knowledge of the uses of the past, or they face a life of mediocrity. There is no other way. There is no substitute.

Penicillin of my youth

THE CHICKEN soup makers of the world quarreled with the ruling of the Department of Agriculture. The department had insisted that chicken soup be at least 2 percent chicken. The soup makers took it right up to the Supreme Court. But the Court said, "Yeah, if you're going to make chicken soup, 2 percent of the soup has got to be chicken."

Before I leap to a dissertation on chicken soup, the panacea of the Lower East Side, the penicillin of my youth, let me remark that this ruling has opened up new fields to the scholars and pedants. This is not the first time the Supreme Court has taken chicken with its session. The Supreme Court ruled over thirty years ago that Roosevelt's NRA was unconstitutional. The case which made the law involved a butcher who was selling chicken. Chicken in fact almost did in the Common Market. There was a vicious dispute between France (who else?) and Belgium, I believe, over what was common and what was marketable, as far as chickens go.

My mother always included the chicken feet. She said the feet produced the gelatin. We have to figure the feet are more than 2 percent of the chicken, so things have really gone downhill since I was a boy. She put a hen into three and a half quarts of water, added carrots, celery, parsley, salt, onions, and dill, and, after bringing the soup to boil, cooked it over a medium heat for one and one-half hours. It sounds simple enough. But I have yet to see anyone duplicate that soup.

Chicken soup cured any indisposition for which you did not have to be hospitalized. Colds, bronchitis, laryngitis, broken bones, concussions, bad cuts—chicken soup was the remedy.

Of course in those days a broiler was a luxury. Farmers saved the chickens for their eggs. Today, I understand, it is hard to find soup chickens. Apparently it is harder than we imagine, judging from that 2 percent. Whether a canny housewife can make chicken soup from a broiler is something I shall leave to the modern in-a-jiffy cookbook editors.

There are as many ways of preparing chicken as there are of preparing soup. The Spaniards prepare chicken à la Valenciana, but they don't need their Supreme Court to instruct them to use 100 percent of the chicken. The Italians commit 100 percent of the chicken to chicken cacciatore. Nor do the Yugoslavs stint on the chicken making chicken paprika.

No one expects a whole chicken in one of those two-for-twenty-nine-cent cans. But 2 percent? What do they expect to heal with 2 percent? How much love is that? No one will ever get the boys out of the pool hall with 2 percent chicken soup.

The Constitution

WE ARE the first country in the world brought into being by a piece of paper, which is one of the facts to which we don't give enough prominence in celebrating Independence Day. The piece of paper is still in Washington under glass but unread unless one is a state, federal, or Supreme Court judge. The Constitution consists of a preamble, seven articles, and a series of some twenty-odd amendments, the first ten of which are called the Bill of Rights.

It was conceived, written, and promulgated by a patriotic band of intellectuals, men who had taken over a farmyard rebellion and made it into a mercantile revolution. Washington, Jefferson, Adams, Franklin, Mason, Monroe, and Madison put together a country out of some abstract notions about rights, religion, and governing agencies. Not until the Bolsheviks put together the Soviet Union in 1917 did any other country try to build so idealistic a national structure (and the Bolsheviks succeeded finally because they shot up the opposition).

I have read the Magna Carta in England, through which King John granted certain political and civil rights to English earls and bishops in 1215 at Runnymede. For the life of me I cannot repeat a word of it. It no longer has an organic texture; and, in fact, Parliament is now considering abolishing some of the Magna Carta's anachronisms. The granting of the Magna Carta was a historical, not a continuing, event like the Constitution.

The important fact about the United States Constitution was that even if the Revolution had failed, even if King George had suppressed the colonists, many of the provisions in the Constitution would still have become law.

Liberty, Equality, and Fraternity have not always coexisted in France, but free speech and a free press were here to stay even if America were still governed by an English King and Parliament.

There is a wide streak of anti-intellectualism in the American character which many of us deplore. The Fourth of July would be a good time to remember just what intellectuals can do when they put their minds to it.

Taking a nap

EVERYBODY KNOWS who the Cartwrights are. They are the central figures of a continuing Sunday night TV series called *Bonanza*. *Bonanza* is dedicated to recounting the derring-do of these Cartwrights, who number father Ben, sons Hoss and Little Joe, and cook Hop Sing. They live on a spread called the Ponderosa in Nevada in the year 1859.

Last Sunday I watched the Cartwrights rid the old West of assorted nuisances. I was afforded a priceless, once-in-a-lifetime experience, one of the gems supreme in the history of taped television. Ben Cartwright, beleaguered by bad guys, harassed by a plot riding off in nine directions at once, told Hoss to escort one of the Ponderosa's lady guests to safety.

"I was sorta figurin' on takin' a little nap," said Hoss, "but okay."

This is 1859, mind you, when the desperate Apache still infested the foothills and the rustlers made bold at every roundup. Still, not only did Hoss know what a little nap was, he was figurin' on takin' one. Some cowboy! The last of my boyhood dreams has been dissipated. On the Lower East Side of New York City, we immigrants never imagined cowboys slept in beds, let alone took naps on couches.

Personally, I have myself been thinking of taking a little nap ever since I got my first job in 1916. I hope Hoss Cartwright gets around to his little nap sooner than I have gotten around to mine.

Hoss's willingness to forego the restorative powers of a little nap is as poignant a dramatic moment as John Wayne's when, as Genghis Khan, he told a startled Susan Hayward, "Yer beyoodiful in yer wrath," or Tony Curtis' when, as Sinbad the Sailor, he told a straightfaced starlet, "Yonda lies de palace of de Caliph, my fodder."

I have never been approached to write anything for television. Often I have indulged paranoiac speculations wondering if television producers had it in for me. Last Sunday's *Bonanza* made me face a truth about myself. I cannot write for television because I could never imagine those basic little touches which reveal the true humanity of heroes like Hoss Cartwright. I might have had him kiss his horse from time to time. I might have had him order milk at the Gold Dollar Saloon. But I would never be imaginative enough to think of him taking a nap, let alone give up taking a nap.

It's talking about naps that makes those millions out there in viewerland stop yawning. Hoss's sacrifice shamed me, home before my television set, surrounded by Babylonian indulgences.

Lincoln and Seward

THE CHIEF contender against Abraham Lincoln at the Republican convention of 1860 was William H. Seward. Seward, in fact, was favored to win the nomination. When he did not, he went home in bitterness to Auburn, New York, vowing to refuse all offices Lincoln might offer. "I must be the head or nowhere," said Seward, and he meant it.

But Lincoln had no intention of punishing Seward. He knew the man's ability. Lincoln went to Auburn: It was no easy trip. There were no Pullman or sleeping cars yet, and it took two days to go from Chicago to Buffalo, and from Buffalo to Auburn was another day's journey.

Lincoln stepped down from the train at the Auburn station unattended, carrying his carpetbag, a homemade affair with the initials A. L. embroidered on the side. Seward and his two sons met the Republican nominee. The boys laughed at this gangling, dusty man, rough and uncouth.

A carriage waited, but Lincoln refused it, saying, "Boys, let's walk." It was a long walk to Seward's house, but when they reached it, Lincoln not only offered Seward the post of Secretary of State, but Seward accepted with alacrity and enthusiasm. He served the sixteenth President with loyalty and devotion.

Too many languages

A CORRESPONDENT writes me about his homeland, New Guinea. He says what keeps this country primitive is not its inhabitants' inability to converse with the world but their inability to converse with each other. New Guinea has over seven hundred languages. The island, second largest in the world, has remained static all these centuries because no one language has ever become predominant.

Primitive cultures remain primitive not because they have no language but because they have too many languages. Ethiopia has over seventy languages. Some other African nations have virtually a different language for every tribe. The civil war which rages in Nigeria between the Ibos and the Hausas could be settled if the two tribes would elect a common language. Among civilized people, the immigrants to America, for instance, country determines language; among semicivilized people, language determines country.

India, which is sophisticated and has a long cultural history, counts Hindi as its official tongue, but this is only a nominal designation. Languages proliferate in India, and each language fires the breast of the patriotic nationalist. Indian universities are often discouraged because of the variety of languages which the faculty confronts.

Irwin Edman, a Columbia professor in cooler and calmer days when students went to university to attend classes, once opined that English was only French poorly spelled. Economists claim that English is the language of the dollar. Whether English will succeed as the language for one world is dubious. George Bernard Shaw thought the trouble with English was that it had letters and diphthongs for which there were no sounds.

Shaw, in fact, left a sum of money in his will to develop a new alphabet. He wanted a separate letter for every sound.

This is but a start. At least if English were spelled the way it is spoken, it would be an easier language for others to appreciate.

A widely covered speech

JAMES M. ROCHE, chairman of the General Motors Corporation, is a tall, white-haired, bespectacled executive. Anybody who is chairman of General Motors, believe you me, has something to say, and no one knows it better than the mayor of Chicago, Richard Daley, who invited Mr. Roche to say his piece at the annual Mayor's Prayer Breakfast.

When Mayor Daley is not wondering who will be the President of the United States or instructing his police for riots or upholding them after a raid he is praying publicly.

All the newspapers in Chicago sent reporters, but to this day no one but Mr. Roche knows what he said.

Chicago's liberal newspaper, the *Sun-Times*, headlined, "Supply Jobs to Needy, Business Urged." According to this paper, Mr. Roche insisted that "business and industry must supply jobs to keep the peace in the streets." The story went on to say that "the G.M. Board Chairman echoed a theme of President Johnson's withdrawal speech in appealing for unity of purpose as a nation." "Current domestic problems," Roche said, "are as important for the future of our children as any war we have ever fought."

The conservative paper, the *Tribune* (what else?), came down hard on Mr. Roche's demand for "strict enforcement of law and order." "Without law and order," the paper quotes Mr. Roche, "society becomes a jungle—no one can justify riots. The causes cannot be fixed overnight, but we must start. The country cannot support those who are unproductive, those who take arms against the society that supports them, or those who cripple productivity through long strikes." Other businessmen joined in a hearty "Amen" at this, but then remember, it was a prayer breakfast. Spurred on by their fervor, Mr. Roche maintained, "Long strikes for unreasonable demands are a luxury we cannot afford if we are to maintain world leadership." Down at the bottom of the story the reporter summarized Mr. Roche's hope that industry would supply jobs to the needy.

Chicago's middle-of-the-road newspaper, the *Daily News*, headlined, "Build Youth Values, Mayors Urged." In this story, Mr. Roche was making a pitch for a return in building character in young people. The reporter seized on Mr. Roche's observation, "Something important is missing in today's youth.

They have not been imbued with a true sense of values, with a respect for authority, a sense of personal responsibility, the value of self-discipline."

While I am quite sure Mr. Roche tries to be all things to all stockholders, he is probably not at pains to be all things to all men. Yet he appears to have delivered three different speeches—if you believe everything you read. It could be a hoopskirt speech. A hoopskirt speech is one which covers everything and touches nothing.

The Southern censors

THERE'S A sheriff in Rutherford County, North Carolina, who sees red when he sees "Adults Only" on the movie marquee. Sheriff Damon Huskey recently closed up the Midway Drive-in Theater for showing the film A *Piece of Her Action*, which he said was a "nasty, filthy movie." The sheriff, in fact, took the movie to jail along with the theater owner, Mrs. Susan Dantzic, although it slipped his mind to arrest any of the audience who wanted their money back.

Sheriff Huskey promises no one in Rutherford County is going to see a movie labeled R (restricted to persons over sixteen) or X (restricted to persons over eighteen) as long as he is in office. He rests on his statutory authority. Mrs. Dantzic with the aid of the American Civil Liberties Union tests this ruling by suit in federal court.

What always amazes me about Southern sheriffs is that not one has ever urged a school board to assign Shakespeare's *Macbeth* to high school students instead of *Silas Marner*, nor have they ever petitioned for the inclusion of Herman Melville in the local library. But Damon is a demon when it comes to clearing pornography and nastiness and filth out of Rutherford County. I have never heard a Southern sheriff express any concern over the fifteen-year-old virgins the farmboys drag into the barn. That is not covered in the statutes, probably because so many of our Southern legislators once dragged fifteen-year-old virgins into the barn.

Moonshine is the third biggest industry in our state. I have few doubts that a dozen stills bottle white lightning in Rutherford County itself. North Carolina is second in the nation in car thefts because title is easier here to come by than anyplace else. But Southern sheriffs rarely express any more concern over stolen cars than they do over the virgins, less'n, as we say down heah, it's their car.

They concentrate on movies. But the important question is: Do they clean up the county?

The answer is no. They lose in court. Some years ago, Charlotte prosecutors tried to close up the Visulite, a movie house right up the block from me, for showing a film whose action took place in a nudist camp. The owner sued and won.

For months the lines to the Visulite stretched around the block, with constituents waiting to be defiled. The profits were so enormous the owner installed Cinemascope, renovated the theater, and put in new seats. Then he booked Charleton Heston in the movie about Michelangelo, and a patron could shoot deer in the theater, it was so empty.

How I became a vegetable man

THE SCHOOLTEACHERS used to send the immigrant boys and girls up to the De Milt Dispensary on Twenty-third Street. The dispensary gave free inoculations, eyeglasses, and a dental checkup to the poor. I can remember the dentist there telling every one of his small patients to eat more vegetables. The trouble with vegetables was that in the winter the Lower East Side and the vegetables were perfect strangers.

My mother did not know how to can vegetables to preserve them. Had she been instructed in the process, she still wouldn't have believed in it. She boiled what vegetables were available from the stalls—carrots, potatoes, cabbage, and turnips. However, my teeth held out until my sixties.

I would guess that America is probably the greatest vegetable-eating nation in the world. Certainly we grow the greatest variety of vegetables, although it is possible the French prepare them with greater delicacy. We believe in vegetables. What other people in the world would follow the adventures of Popeye, who conquers all when he eats his spinach? Who else carves a jack-o'-lantern out of a pumpkin?

South America, I believe, gave the world the tomato, but North America gave it tomato juice. To this day, I can recall when I had my first glass. It was in the home of a friend who was an "uptown Jew," meaning his parents had both been born in America and were already part of the middle class. When I told my mother about the adventure of tomato juice, she wondered if my friend's mother was really a Jewish mother. Tomato juice, she wondered, was it kosher?

While I am not the most widely traveled of men, still I have been around the world. No vegetable I have ever been served can be compared with corn on the cob. That was a vegetable the Lower East Side took to its heart. Vendors used to patrol the streets pushing a little steam wagon. They would take the ear of corn, punch it onto the end of a stake, and dip it into a vat of melted butter. It cost a nickel.

My mother's supreme concoction, of course, was borscht, the national dish of the Russian Jews. I doubt seriously that the dentist at the De Milt Dispensary would consider the vast amount of borscht we ladled a sufficient guarantee we would never have cavities. Borscht is made from beetroots and sour cream. No one has yet suggested that sour cream is a substitute for fluorides or vitamins.

It is my experience that any woman can cook a roast or a steak. There really aren't a great many culinary tricks to perform with meats. The real test of a good cook is whether her vegetables are always appetizing. One of the French critics once commented that you could distinguish a great painter by the art he put in his background. So you can tell a great cook by her vegetables.

I really found out about vegetables when I bought a house in Charlotte in which I lived and published my newspaper, the *Carolina Israelite*. In this neighborhood the houses are all set near the sidewalk, which provides an immense backyard. Mine almost reached downtown. A backyard to me is like the nape of my neck, something I never expect to see. But my neighbor, Mr. Biggers, presented himself on my porch and asked, if I wasn't going to use the backyard for a parking lot, could he set out vegetables in it? When I asked him what was wrong with *his* backyard, he said that was where he grew his roses. Go ahead and use it, I said.

Mr. Biggers had grown up on a farm and had farmed in his youth. My backyard looked better than any roadstand you ever passed. I told Mr. Biggers he had a green thumb because I was under the impression Carolina red clay wasn't good for anything, and he said there was no secret to farming if you had a hose.

In appreciation, Mr. Biggers used to give me a bushel of fresh vegetables every week or so. And Mrs. Biggers brought me over some of her specialties. It was just like working shares. At first, I wasn't interested. I kept the corn because I knew how to shuck it and boil it, but the other produce I distributed to the staff.

It was Mrs. Biggers' cooking which hooked me. I had never had a bean salad with vinegar and onions mixed in with it before. It became a staple at the *Israelite*.

Then she would boil beans, and as they cooled, she would brown some flour in a frying pan. She would stir this into the residue of the water and garnish this sauce with squares of bacon. Lo! It was a meal in itself. She gave me whole tureens of steaming hot peas surrounding mushrooms, butter swimming over the whole. When I told her it was delicious, she said modestly, "The mushrooms were store-bought."

I became adventurous and went on to collard greens.

Mr. Biggers died some years ago. Mrs. Biggers moved away, and I bought the house from her. The vegetable garden has gone to seed. But the roses still bloom every spring, even though their appearance is a mystery to gardeners, since I never cut them back. I wish we had the vegetable garden again.

The library

Two INSTITUTIONS turned millions of immigrants into Americans within a single generation—the greatest miracle of human relations in the past century. These two institutions were the free public school and the free public library.

It's hard to communicate to a present-day audience what the public library meant to immigrants. The librarian was a sexless saint. I remember in the ghetto branch of the New York Public Library there was a washstand in a booth off the main entrance. You washed your hands before you went to the shelves. This was no insult. Indeed it was a compliment, a tribute to the men and women who came out of their sweatshops to stop at the library on the way home, a tribute to boys and girls who sold newspapers or played in the street and who went into the library to spend an hour before supper. If you were under fifteen years of age, the librarian would actually ask you to show your hands and you turned them over and she either said, "Go ahead," or "Go wash them."

Immigrant mothers like my mother, who couldn't speak a word of English, went into that library, held up their fingers to indicate the number of children at home. The librarian issued cards, and the mother handed them out to her children. She said, "Go, learn, study, read." This was part of the process of becoming an American.

If we draw up a balance sheet of America's fixed assets, we

would say that the public library is one of our most precious possessions.

The top of the world

THEODORE WHITE's *The Making of the President* 1968 is as eminently readable as its predecessors. White is an astute political reporter. He is not an innovator trying to predict the new trajectory of national politics but a historian trying to offer simple explanations. He is often subjective. In this book he almost apologizes for coming to respect President Richard Nixon.

White's books are successful because they are about the top of the world. *The Making of the President* describes the one political subject in which everyone manifests some interest. With the exception of *Advise and Consent*, I cannot remember a trade book on politics which has enjoyed the same popularity that White enjoys with his series. Though there are millions of Americans actively engaged in politics, in PTA elections, planning and zoning disputes, and municipal elections, they don't want to read about it. One of the ways not to succeed in publishing is to issue books on politics. Politics is boring unless one knows the gossip about the politicians. One of the biggest splashes the Republicans in North Carolina ever made was when they discovered that their probable candidate for the gubernatorial nomination was leading a double life with one woman in Virginia and another in North Carolina. (I always thought it was a political mistake of catastrophic proportions for the Republican State Committee to insist on his resignation.)

Books about writers and publishers also are largely unsuccessful because writing is essentially a dull profession.

Theodore White himself wrote a modestly successful book about publishing called *The View from the Fortieth Floor*. What was exciting about that book was the same thing that was unexciting about *Youngblood Hawke* by Herman Wouk. Publishing is small potatoes. Once in a decade, if lucky, a publishing house issues a book which earns a million dollars. An IBM third vice-president spends or earns for his company a million dollars every day before lunch.

In the last ten years I'll bet I have read over a dozen books re-creating the modern labor movement and the careers of top labor leaders, but these books have dropped, to borrow Hume's expression, stillborn from the press. Very, very few people are on strike today. To gain any attention labor leaders have to talk about packages that total millions and millions of dollars. Liston Pope's descriptions of the Loray Strike in Gastonia, North Carolina, *Millhands and Preachers*, is a literary milestone. John Steinbeck's *In Dubious Battle* is a great novel. But I haven't talked to anyone who has read them in years.

Strikes, politics, publishing, and let's add poker are my idea of things not to write about.

The movies

I STARTED at the beginning. I have been going to movies for fifty-five years. I watched Louise Fazenda and Bronco Billy Anderson and saw them succeeded by Rudolph Valentino and Pola Negri and saw them succeeded by James Cagney and Jean Harlow and them by Rock Hudson and Sophia Loren.

One of the truths I have learned through this lifelong experience is that movies were never meant to be edifying.

What the movies always guarantee is relaxation through anonymity. That is why the movie I saw last night, whatever it was, did not annoy me. Over my lifetime I have seen only one truly bad movie, and that was *The Five Little Peppers Grow Up*.

One of the fondest memories I have is that of the late Sir Cedric Hardwicke, of all people, that brilliant English actor, in a movie with the title *The Invisible Man Returns*. Why Sir Cedric Hardwicke was miscast I have no idea unless it was that Claude Rains had refused to return after inaugurating this improbable series. Sir Cedric spent the narrative chasing the Invisible Man and finally had him cornered with a loaded .45 above a coal chute. He took careful aim with his automatic.

Up in the balcony, someone shouted, "For heaven's sake, don't shoot him. Shoot me."

Everybody laughed. And as we piled out of the movie when THE END flashed, the whole audience realized we had had a moment of enjoyment.

Nothing relaxes a man like a movie. Often, in the middle of the working day, I leave my desk and perambulate over to the Visulite Theatre up the street from my office. I do not look at the posters, don't even worry what's playing. When the cashier says, "The movie has already started, sir," I reply, "Don't worry, dearie, I'll catch on."

That's what the movies are for.

The party needed me

OVER ONE hundred serious thinkers were invited to Princeton University for a week of investigating the woes of the United States *vis-à-vis* the modern world and the twentieth century. These colloquia were sponsored by the International Association for Cultural Freedom, headquarters in Paris, France, as our soldiers like to say, and the joint sponsor was the Institute for Advanced Study, Princeton.

In attendance were Jean-Jacques Servan-Schreiber, author of *The American Challenge*; John Kenneth Galbraith; Lillian Hellman; Arthur Schlesinger, Jr.; the exiled Greek political leader Andreas Papandreou; and countless other brains. I call them "brains" because they condemned the inaccuracy of reporters who called them "intellectuals."

The most significant oversight of this convention was that I was not invited. Admittedly, I was in Iowa the week of their convention, but laying the twentieth century to rest is important, and I might have been persuaded to cancel my other commitments. Further, I would have announced myself as an intellectual. I have been called a lot worse. Whenever a Supreme Court ruling annoys the South, the segregationists sneer Washington is populated by "inna-lect-you-alls."

According to the metropolitan papers, one of the issues which consumed the delegates was each others' credentials. These symposia are not different from the party of the aristocratic dowager. The aristocratic dowager will invite the young countess with a past so that all the guests can turn on her rather than themselves. The intellectuals needed one good square for stimulation, someone who has written for *Life* magazine or confesses to reading detective stories. This is precisely what I could have offered, plus my vast reservoir of wit and charm.

But they went ahead and had the party without me. And notice something? The woes of America *vis-à-vis* the twentieth century and the modern world are still with us.

PART 6

National Soap Opera

The East Side and Theodore Roosevelt

THE FIRST election I remember was that of 1912. That campaign, too, involved three candidates—Theodore Roosevelt on the Progressive or Bull Moose ticket, Republican President Howard Taft, and Democratic Governor Woodrow Wilson. What generated my interest was not the three candidates. For all I knew at that age, there probably had always been three candidates. I was terribly concerned over the election because Oscar Straus, the great Jewish philanthropist and diplomat, was running for governor of New York.

He lost, but it wasn't the immigrant Jews who denied him victory. They were at the polls early in the morning, for the first time dodging the Tammany sachems.

Oscar Straus was the first Secretary of Commerce and Labor in Theodore Roosevelt's Cabinet. At a dinner celebrating his appointment, President Theodore Roosevelt told the assemblage, "When Congress authorized the Cabinet appointment, one name flashed in my mind. That name was Oscar Straus."

Applause.

The next speaker was Jacob Schiff, the famous banker and a Republican power.

Schiff, also a Jew noted for his philanthropy, was deaf and on this occasion had forgotten his hearing horn.

He told everyone, "I was in my office when President Roosevelt talked to me. He said the Congress had approved a new Cabinet post. He asked what Jew I thought could fill it. I said Oscar Straus."

The Lower East Side took Theodore Roosevelt's loss hard. Roosevelt was the President during the peak years of immigration, and thousands of Jews like my father said, "Tudder Roosevelt made me a citizen," because Roosevelt's signature was on the citizenship papers.

The Lower East Side is still an immigrant neighborhood, but now the tenements are filled with Puerto Ricans and Negroes.

If I had a wish for the country it is that one day these immigrants put Richard Nixon's picture on the wall as the old immigrants did with Theodore Roosevelt's.

George Wallace

IT SEEMS to me I have met George Wallace somewhere before. The scowl, the laugh that reminds one of the victorious Neanderthal, the disguised act of the combative underdog. Of course. He is the American demagogue that the constituency throws up every other decade or so. He is Huey Long and Joe McCarthy tailored for the crises of the sixties and the seventies. Like Huey Long and Joe, he is threatening ugly portents. Joe McCarthy wanted to purge the State Department, then the Army, finally the White House of subversives and traitors; George Wallace wants to run over demonstrators in his auto.

Huey talked about the rich and promised to make every man a king; McCarthy talked about the Communists and promised to make every man secure; Wallace talks about the Negro and promises to make every school and factory lily white.

But there is something more—an absolute anti-intellectualism, an absolute demand that the marginal population reject everything that men of reason have accomplished.

"They look down their noses at you and me," says George

Wallace, and he means by "they" the people who teach school or edit newspapers or serve in government.

Joe McCarthy's prime targets were teachers, government officials, and book writers, but only teachers, government officials, and book writers who lived on either the East or West coasts. The Midwest was Joe's bailiwick, and he left its populace alone. Huey Long talked Klan in the northern parishes of Louisiana and anti-Klan in the southern. He flooded the state with free textbooks and paid two dollars a yard for highways which private contractors could build for sixty-seven cents. He kept promising the "flop hats" and the "pea pickers" he was going to make a revolution for them.

In 1968, and probably again in 1972, Wallace promises an administration dedicated to states' rights. To understand exactly what he proposes, simply read that "people's wrongs." Anyone who has passed fourth-grade civics knows there hasn't been a sovereign state since 1789. Certainly Mr. Wallace has no intention of letting states coin their own money or impose their own tariffs. Under his administration, states' rights would let welfare agencies exclude Negro appplicants and voting registrars close doors on Negro registrants. This is essentially what is happening now except that the Attorneys General for the past three administrations make Southern officials nervous with their pesky questions and investigations.

By no means would ex-Governor Wallace deprive either Mississippi or Alabama of the Federal monies which inundate the states from morning till night. In fact, Mississippi and Alabama might well be termed federal preserves in terms of farm subsidies, soil banks, space projects, welfare, and Social Security payments.

All American demagogues affect a vulgarity which may or may not be natural.

The demagogue's key to the sixties and seventies is closing the schools and running over dissent, as the key to the fifties was to rid the American commonwealth of any critics who insisted a complex world surrounded us, and the key to the thirties was to abolish the great business institutions and "share the wealth."

The thrust of the demagogue's argument is really that no American will ever have to share anything, either his schools or his neighborhood with Negroes, his world with conflicting ideology, or his invincible ignorance with those who would better his position.

The last secret

I HAVE written that the ultimate secret the adultress exchanges with her seducer is the true amount of money her husband makes.

The climax of any political campaign is always the candidate's revelation of his net worth. This disclosure is attended with all the breathless anticipation of a new Pope's first encyclical. To know a man's net worth is in some mystic glittering way to believe we have dominion over him, like the primitive savages' belief that to know a man's name was to own him.

It is infinitely easier for a union to organize men who know how much they are all paid per hour than it is to organize an office where no one knows how much his desk colleague earns. Handing out the office pay check on Friday involves a stricter security than a CIA memorandum to a general with an "Eyes Only" classification.

Yet there are few surprises in store for us when, in our own devious way, we do learn our colleagues' net worth. The last surprise I had was when Lyndon B. Johnson revealed he had more money than the late Jack Kennedy.

I doubt that I get any jollies out of knowing the worth of Spiro or Ed, Hubert or Dick. I remember editorializing in 1960 that if Pat Nixon was worried about going back to teaching, I would gladly trade my income for the next five years with Nixon's for the next two, and I can only say now I am sorry they didn't take me up on it.

If nothing else, this unrivaled honesty of the candidates ought to spur some of the kids on. While office holders never tire of telling us how they love the country, flag, and constituency, it is also obvious they are on to a good thing. A Tammany sachem once told a City College of New York classroom that there were two types of men in politics: those who had money and wanted to keep it and those who had none and wanted to make it.

Let me wonder how cooperative a candidate would prove if, say, his net worth was eight thousand dollars. Could we trust such a man in office? Maybe the secrets of the budget would stagger him and he would flap, as the teenagers like to put it. Would his opponent argue, "If a man can't make one hundred thousand dollars in these times, he doesn't deserve office"?

Nixon and his options

ONE OF the fortunate aspects about each administration is that sooner or later it enriches our language. While John Fitzgerald Kennedy called his administration the "New Frontier," the word bequeathed us was "charisma." I am not sure that is an enrichment, however. Franklin D. Roosevelt got elected four times, and he never heard of "charisma."

Lyndon Johnson called his administration the "Great Society," but we remember him best for the "credibility gap." Victory was always around the corner to Lyndon B.

Herbert Hoover gave us the word "Hoovervilles."

What will Richard Nixon give us? My guess is that he has dusted off the word "options," and by the time he is through, "options" is going to be much like the aristocrat who jumped on a horse and rode off in nine directions at once.

When critics worried that the antiballistic missile program was not only costly but inefficient and absurd, I thought the

President had one of two alternatives (two alternatives I believe is the limit).

He could either abandon the program or implement it. But I did not reckon with the options. We are going to have the ABM, but it will be modified so as to enrage neither the Russians nor pinch-penny senators. What options will pacify the folks who live next door to these sites is not yet public knowledge but I suppose will be made known in due time.

The option that has to command our attention is the one the President will elect to end the Middle East impasse between the Arabs and the Israelis. The Israelis have promised not to return the captured territories until the Arabs effect a just and lasting peace, and the Arabs promise they will never sit down with the Israelis.

Anyone who could shoulder an option between these two conflicting attitudes is a real option man.

The key precincts

WHAT I want to know is, What happens to all those "key" precincts after the election? Do those key precincts just melt back into the amorphous whole, the folks therein unaware they have informed the entire electorate about who is and who is not going to win? A sad waste. On election night, those key precincts are invaluable to Howard K. Smith, to Chet and Dave, to Walter Cronkite.

"With one percent of the New York vote reported, our key precinct indicates Humphrey will carry the state."

"With twenty-one percent of the Illinois vote reported, Nixon will win, no matter what Richard Daley does with the absentee ballots."

It must be that the powers do not tell the folks they are living in a key precinct. What I could get done if I knew I lived in a key precinct. It's about time we got rid of the grass roots and went to where the action is. Watching grass grow is like watching Ivy League football.

If I lived in a key precinct, I'd get them organized.

The first thing we'd do is put the Electoral College down the drain—blurg, blurg, blurg, blurg. From there we'd move against the seniority system in the House and Senate. I see no reason why these old rascals from constituencies which have never seen an automatic voting machine should be perpetuated as chairmen of important committees. I say give the young rascals from the key precincts a chance. Our election officials might just as well listen to the voters from the key precincts as to lobbyists from the National Rifle Association.

It is a frustrating experience to realize your very residence might emanate with the power to tell ABC, NBC, and CBS what to do and say.

Years and years ago there used to be only one key precinct, and that was the State of Maine. Maine held its election for Presidential electors in September until the feds got the Down Easters in line with the rest of us. Politicians always said, "As goes Maine, so goes the nation." These were the years of the Republican hegemony. Along came Franklin D. Roosevelt, which led Jim Farley to remark, "As goes Maine, so goes Vermont."

I have seen the Chamber of Commerce throw itself into a frenzy of hope that one of the national magazines may designate the old town one of the "All-American Cities." Imagine the frenzy of the town boosters if one of the networks pointed its finger and said, "Bangor or Charlotte or Dubuque, you are a key precinct. You are not a mediocre burg filled with gas stations, supermarkets, and septic tank cleaners all afloat on a sea of blacktop. No siree."

Such a statement might reinvigorate civic pride and stop the folks from fussing too much about the new roads which cut through their property.

The reformers' victory

WHEN RICHARD NIXON was finally elected, all of the dissident Democrats who set out to reform the party by denying the Presidency to Hubert Humphrey could breathe more easily. They went back to making money and enjoying leisure. In four more years, they would have another chance. They can agitate for whatever reform it is that tickles their little hearts. Yes siree, the reformers not only taught the regulars a lesson, the reformers even knocked off a couple of congressmen who supported Johnson.

But if I were a Negro boy waking up in a ghetto, the realization that Spiro T. Agnew was Vice President of the United States might well dismay me.

I suspect the realization probably dismays Richard Nixon, too, but he and the electorate have spoken, as it were.

If 1968 proved nothing else, it did prove the permanence of the party structure. Those of us who believe in the party structure, who believe splinter groups like the Wallace effort are divisive rather than constructive politics, have one man to thank for this effort. That man is Hubert Humphrey.

Eugene McCarthy and Chicago and the Vietnam War had literally rent the Democratic Party. Hubert Humphrey and Edmund Muskie saved it and not only saved it from oblivion but almost made it a winner.

Sixteen years before, Adlai Stevenson also saved the Democratic Party. In the face of the Eisenhower popularity, the Democratic Party would have absolutely disintegrated had it not had Adlai Stevenson. It would never have come back to win in 1960.

The Democrats may not win in 1972. The dissidents may wake up again and decide they want to strangle all of the "bosses" who go to precinct meetings the year round, address envelopes, and pass out free coffee on behalf of campaigning constables.

As for Richard Nixon, I drink a toast that he will accomplish all that he promised: that we will have full employment without inflation, that he will restore our prestige abroad, that he will win an honorable and advantageous peace in Vietnam, that he will bring the private sector's wealth to bear on the problems of poverty, that we will have law and order with justice. If he does two of these things by 1972, he has a Republican vote for life.

Way down deep, I think the folks made Nixon President so that David Eisenhower could marry Julie Nixon in the White House.

The conservative straight line

GOVERNOR RONALD REAGAN of California and former Governor George Wallace of Alabama castigate the federal government as though it were a foreign power. And they talk much about the American Way of Life.

The conservatives believe that history goes up in a straight line, without turning or deviation.

Senator Strom Thurmond of South Carolina says if the federal government advances financial aid to American education, it will destroy private initiative. He says this on the very day the federal government is pouring millions into South Carolina for roads, airports, welfare, and farm subsidies.

The South indeed and California have been federal preserves these past thirty years, like Yellowstone National Park. They pick up the checks daily, the cotton check, the veteran's check, the checks for roads, airports, army camps, urban renewal, aircraft building, shipbuilding, and school lunches. And as they pick up each check they say, "The government's getting too big."

Another thing these conservatives are saying is that we are placing an intolerable burden upon our children. Well, we are ensuring that our children and grandchildren may pay taxes, just as our grandparents ensured we would. They may be high taxes, but what wonders will be left the next generation in science, technology, and medicine alone are difficult to imagine.

When I was a boy, this government owed no money; every year it announced surpluses. Yet despite these surpluses, there were millions of people scraping together the pennies to buy a cake of ice once a week. I do not speak here of ghetto people; I speak of farmers and factory workers, blacksmiths, grocery clerks, and millions of others in the fields, mines, and cotton mills.

In those days any American could rattle off the names of the rich men—Rockefeller, Harriman, J. P. Morgan, Carnegie. Today our national debt is high, and no American can count the number of millionaires in Los Angeles or Houston, indeed, in Providence or Charlotte.

These conservatives on the platform offer the simple solutions, and there are no solutions; there are only questions. In his House Divided speech, Abraham Lincoln said, "If we could first know where we are, and whither we are tending, we could better judge what to do, and how to do it."

Tammany will come back

THE NEW breed, the men like Nelson Rockefeller and John Lindsay, transformed politics. These men are not only well informed on every issue to come before them, they are skilled in exploiting all of the communication media, at interpreting polls. They have made it a whole new ball game—and for the most part, a rich man's ball game. The new breed did Tammany no good. Considering that both Nelson Rockefeller and

John Lindsay are New Yorkers, one could say Tammany is out of luck this decade.

But Tammany will come back. Ah! How I loved Tammany. When the immigrants got off the boat, there were the Tammany men waiting for them. The Irishmen got applications for the police and fire departments, the Italians for sanitation and building trades, and the Jew got a peddler's license.

Every year Tammany took all the Lower East Side kids on a boat-ride picnic to Bear Mountain up the Hudson. As the celebration date drew near, all the Jewish mothers began worrying about poison ivy. "Watch out for the poison ivy" became a choral chant along the Lower East Side. Michael Ahearn, the Tammany sachem, worried about poison ivy, too. "It could cost us votes," he said dourly.

Tammany always posted spies in the marriage bureau. The district leader had his wedding present at the bride's home before she shook the rice from her veil.

They were always the first there for the funeral. Two Tammany men who represented different districts once had a bare-knuckle fist fight on the sidewalk over a body, each wanting to claim it for the funeral. The sachems were even more precipitous. One of them sent a hearse before the defunct was defunct.

A cousin of mine was a Tammany counter. The night before an election a mysterious hand always threw an envelope with a one-hundred-dollar bill over the transom with my cousin's name written on it. He was also given a ring which had a setting but no stone. A piece of charcoal was where the stone should be. Cousin was supposed to use the ring to void Socialist ballots. If the X for the Socialist candidate was one-millionth of an inch below the square—mark it void. The X for a Socialist had to be perfectly centered.

If the Socialists ran strong, Tammany men switched off the lights. The sachems fixed the election by simply throwing the ballots into either the East or Hudson River. The knowledgeable always said William Randolph Hearst's margin of victory lay at the bottom of the Pike Street slip. But, of course, this was in the days when William Randolph Hearst was a Socialist campaigning for public ownership of the public utilities, for the abolition of child labor, and for an eight-hour working day.

While Tammany pulled some raw tricks, let it also be remembered that Tammany put more coal in the cellars of the poor than all that Scranton, Pennsylvania, ever mined.

The Fifth Amendment

ABOUT EIGHTEEN years ago Herbert Brownell, then President Dwight D. Eisenhower's Attorney General, suggested that the Congress repeal the Fifth Amendment of the Constitution, which protects witnesses from testifying against themselves. Mr. Brownell said those fourteen words—"I refuse to testify on the grounds that it may tend to incriminate me"—were letting subversives run wild. Congress did not act on Mr. Brownell's suggestion, and for one reason or another the country is still unsubverted.

More recently Thomas E. Dewey, three times governor of New York and twice the Republican candidate for the Presidency, also urged abolition of the Fifth. Unless the Fifth were abolished, Dewey warned, the criminal element, perhaps the Mafia itself, would take over the country.

The argument that the country is threatened because it guarantees civil and individual rights is specious. But I am perfectly willing to consider other reasons for abolishing the Fifth Amendment. I do not believe the quality of life in America would be radically changed if the Fifth were abolished. At the same time, I do not believe abolition would stop the riots in the cities nor that it would curb the Mafia. The truth of the matter is that, much as the Mafia needs it, we need it, especially if we want to bet a sure shot or borrow ten thousand dollars over the weekend.

The Fifth Amendment was not conceived by the Founding

Fathers to protect either Communists or criminals. The framers of the Constitution included the Fifth Amendment because they believed it was cruel and inhumane to make a man testify against himself. They believed this because at one time in the sad, empirical history of the Western world, torture was applied to make a defendant testify.

It is my contention that the Fifth Amendment does not prohibit testimony but prohibits torture. As long as we were assured that no American court would torture a defendant, I think we could live without the Fifth Amendment.

That assurance is the rub. Adolf Hitler in this century persuaded the Germans it was a reasonable and sanitary practice to sterilize the insane and the retarded. Once he gained assent, it wasn't hard to pass a law that it was just as healthy and sanitary to kill Jews and gypsies and Russians and the whole world.

It is also the custom that a defendant need not testify and that from his refusal the jury may not infer either guilt or innocence. I see the logic in the rule that if you are charged you must stand trial, but I do not see a logic in any theory that if you are charged, you yourself must answer. The state has an elaborate apparatus to establish that it may have a case; the individual does not.

I have said we can probably live without the Fifth Amendment. I believe we can live more easily with it.

Republicans of the South

PARADOXICALLY, THE "white backlash" had less to do with the 1968 Republican victories in the South than elsewhere in the country.

Where the resistance to Negro civil rights is still strong, as in rural and small-town Georgia, both the Republican and the Democratic candidates for governor canceled out the issue by saying, "I am more 'white backlash' than you."

The big story of the South was missed entirely. In Tennessee the four Southerners, two Republicans and two Democrats, running for governor and U.S. senator appealed directly for the Negro vote: "Let us march together with our Negro brethren."

The Republican Party will get stronger in the South. Within the next ten years it will elect councilmen, sheriffs, commissioners, governors, and senators. These Republicans had been registered as Democrats because of white racial solidarity, of which the Southern Democrats were the champions.

Once the Negro moved from the back of the bus to a front seat, the Republicans-registered-as-Democrats said, "As long as they can't keep the Negro in his place anymore, I may as well vote my convictions."

This "radical solidarity" will eventually destroy the Southern Democratic Party as we have known it, because it paid no attention to the precincts. There was no loyalty whatsoever. The precinct worker throughout the South asked one question, "How much is he paying?" and after the precinct worker accepted the assignment, the next question was "What's he running for?"

But there is a silver lining for the Democrats. Without racial segregation, the old Democratic Party of the South will go the way of the Whigs. With both candidates running on a "conservative" platform, the Republican voter will now turn to the "real" conservative instead of the "amateur." And the only chance the Southern Democrats will have, indeed the only choice, will be to become part of the National Democratic Party—at last.

Presidential popularity

THE PRESIDENTIAL popularity polls seem to me an institutional form of gossip. The Nielsen ratings can devastate a television show, but that is gossip regarding junk. I doubt the polls can devastate the Presidency.

Abraham Lincoln was the most unpopular of American Presidents. He did not take office with a majority of the electorate, and if the Union had not won at Gettsyburg, perhaps the Copperheads would have unseated him. The *Literary Digest* informed the country that Roosevelt was doomed to defeat in 1936, but he won in the most significant landslide ever recorded in American politics. I remember Republicans in River Plaza, New Jersey, threatening the morning afterward to leave the country, but none of them did. They all stayed around to become millionaires.

There's a phenomenon called the "polling place syndrome" which defies analysis. The most well-read and well-informed citizen will suddenly become paralyzed by the levers. The inarticulate will suddenly realize a vote counts for someone, for some quality of life. Witness Millard Fillmore losing to Buchanan or Thomas Dewey losing to Truman.

The polling place reforms the folks like the oath in court reforms the pathological liar.

The long-haired bosses

Fifty years ago, it was a different story. The extreme left was short-haired. The members of the Wobblies, the famous IWW, cut their hair short and refused to wear moustaches or beards. The far right people wore their hair long. From the mine operators to the mill owners, everyone sported a luxuriant growth from chin, upper lip, and forehead. In fact, one of the reasons the Pinkerton private detectives commanded a pretty good salary was that in order to infiltrate the working men's groups, these fellows had to submit to the close crop with its attendant loss of respect and prestige. In 1899 the Wobblies used to sing, to the tune of "In the Sweet Bye and Bye":

You will eat, by and by,
In that glorious land above the sky.
Work and pray, live on hay,
You'll get pie in the sky when you die.

Long-haired bosses come out every night
To tell you what's wrong with what's right,
But when asked about something to eat,
They will answer in voices so sweet.

Chorus: You will eat ...

The far right today affects the short haircut and the clean chin and upper lip. The nonconformist, the mutinous, and the rebellious rather resemble lions, manes framing what is left of their faces.

The folk singers all have trouble freeing their thumbs from their locks so they can strum their tunes on a guitar.

This is not doing the liberals any good. First of all, I like my hair short and am worried lest I be mistaken for a reactionary or at least a man who puts some of his money into Pineville sewage bonds.

The depletion allowance

ONE OF the salient truths about Republicans is that they are the most loyal of bridegrooms. They married the nineteenth century, and they have spent over a half-century in absolute fidelity. But maybe the honeymoon is over. Even Walter Hickel, the Secretary of the Interior, was grumbling about the California oil slick. He went so far as to intimate maybe the oil companies ought to pay for the desecration they wreak on fowl, fish, animal, and public. In fact, he suggested they might use some of the money they save on their depletion allowance to repair the damage.

A token reduction of the depletion allowance has been made, and my guess is that before the century ends, the government will no longer allow oil companies the huge tax advantage they enjoy because they are "depleting" their resources.

After all, a cop doesn't get a break on his tax because he's depleting his resources by growing older, nor a writer, nor an airline pilot.

Nixon's hardest job

WHETHER INTIMATES, reporters, or politicians like him or not, one thing I've always heard them say about Richard Nixon is that he has a political intuition that amounts to genius. Only such a man could have survived the defeat in 1960, the subsequent defeat in 1962, and the Goldwater candidacy in 1964 to become President in 1968.

I don't think Richard Nixon is afraid of the American generals' mutinying if he pulls out of Vietnam, but I think he worries about polarizing the military and civilian structures. I think he may be worried about generals' resigning their commissions to run around exhorting the lunatic right as Curtis LeMay tried to do with George Wallace.

Reminding generals they were wrong about the Cuban people's rising up at the invasion of the Bay of Pigs, that the admirals pulled a bonehead play with the *Pueblo*, and that the military swore to God we were around the corner from victory a month before the Tet offensive of two years ago may be Nixon's hardest job as President.

Launched in blood

MY CITY of Charlotte, the largest city between Norfolk and Atlanta, has a new educational television station.

In response to its first scheduled program, Pete Seeger and

Joan Baez, the educational administration received eighteen postcards objecting to the program on the ground that "Seeger and Baez are leftists." The school authorities thereupon knuckled under and canceled the scheduled program.

There is a one-thousand-year-old tradition among the men who go to sea not to sail with a ship that had a serious accident at its launching. "Launched in blood," they call it.

The Charlotte school authorities have no idea what they have done. Who will take them seriously now? Long after we are all gone, the cancellation of its very first program will be long remembered and occasionally referred to when an essayist or historian wants to make a point in his writing of the John Birch Society and the 1965 Ku Klux Klan.

Marx was no prophet

RUSSIA AND China are vast, so vast and huge that it is with a shock we realize how wrong were the original estimations of the Socialists forty and fifty years ago. Never for a moment did any of them suspect a Communist revolution could take place in Russia, let alone in China. Marx, in fact, specifically said Russia would be the last of the great world nations to embrace Communism.

Everyone including Marx guessed the Communist revolution would transpire first of all in Germany, then in France. Germany was ripe for Communism, they said, because Socialists like August Bebel and many others had forced the admission of many Socialist techniques and institutions and legislation. Before World War I, 20 percent of the Reichstag was Socialist.

Even after the Communist revolution in Russia, the Leninists and the Stalinists constantly argued that a similar revolution could never take place in China. Communist revolutions, they said smugly, could not occur in rural, agricultural countries, nor could they gain impetus in any place but large cities. Well, we

know Mao Tse-tung never won the cities, but he did win the
countryside and the farmers.

We need a long story sometime about the Communists and
Bolsheviks and an explanation of how men could start such a
movement and be so ignorant of whom it would attract, just
as we need to know what in the world ever made us think Cuba,
subjected to a dictatorship we in America tacitly supported, exploited by foreigners, wouldn't turn to Communism when the
Cubans themselves turned out Batista.

Pincus Meyer Poole

ABOUT 1899, the district consisting of the Lower East
Side was in the control of Tammany Irishmen.

Mr. Scully, I believe, was one of the district leaders, and he
was quite anxious to have his protégé, another Irishman by the
name of Peter M. Poole, elected alderman.

But by now the district was almost 90 percent naturalized
Jews from eastern Europe. Scully wondered if they would take
to his protégé.

He solved this problem by having Peter M. Poole change his
name (on the campaign posters) to Pincus Meyer Poole.

All over the East Side Scully plastered election stickers in
Hebrew, exhorting all the Orthodox to send Pincus Meyer to
the board of aldermen.

Pincus Meyer went, too. I believe he even learned some
Yiddish expressions.

Between the lines

HUBERT HUMPHREY called for the "politics of joy" in
a year of riots, assassinations, and a Chicago civil war.

Politicians cannot avoid certain issues, but they are getting more and more adept at disguising what they mean to do about them. What makes American politics so fascinating a study is trying to read between the lines. Politicians who discuss "sharing" are really talking about the bussing of school children. When the electorate hears the word "bussing," it reacts like circus roustabouts who hear "Hey, Rube." The politician who discusses "community relations" is talking about the ghetto, just as some of the politicians are discussing the Negro when they talk about "law and order."

We liberals have "peaked"

THE SORRY pass we liberals have come to is in the realization we have "peaked," as politicians like to put it. We reached our peak with the great March on Washington in 1963, a movement which swelled with grace and justice. That demonstration capped the movement for civil rights because the movement was populated by people seeking justice, not by people looking for a fight.

It was a triumph of the liberal spirit that March; it made most of us feel that liberalism is a dynamic and viable political philosophy.

If liberalism has any thrust today—several hundred riots and contumacious demonstrations later—it is only because the conservatives and the Republicans are more inept.

PART 7

The Agony of Lyndon B. Johnson

The agony of Lyndon B. Johnson

AMERICANS USUALLY have a soft spot in their hearts for the President. They are ready to confer on him some degree of grace simply by virtue of his office. Americans insisted that Warren Harding's friends betrayed him rather than make the painful admission that Warren Harding was as stupid a man as had ever grown to adulthood. Though they refused reelection to Herbert Hoover, they said he was right about the Depression all along even if he was stubborn. Maybe they weren't going to vote for Harry Truman, but they said he was gritty and courageous. But Americans didn't love Lyndon Johnson. They conferred on him nothing, not even praise for the gifts he did possess.

They called him a "wheeler dealer." Well, a man with the reputation of a wheeler dealer is a man who keeps his word and owns up to his bargains. No one can wheel and deal otherwise. The wheeler dealer is the man who understands the *quid pro quo* of politics.

Franklin D. Roosevelt and Dwight D. Eisenhower were masters of the devious move. Some of the tricks they played would have left Lyndon B. Johnson in a state of stupefied moral outrage. But no one ever particularly wanted to hang the charge of deceit on F.D.R. or Ike. They hung it on Lyndon Johnson, even though he was more manipulative than devious.

213

One of the reasons the folks didn't love Lyndon Johnson is probably that the folks don't particularly love Texas wheeler dealers. Despite the protestation of the Lone Star State that its constituency is the biggest, the purtiest, the richest, and the best, I think Americans shy from braggadocio.

There is more to why Lyndon was unpopular. We as a nation are like a man approaching his fortieth birthday. A terrible realization overtakes a man at forty. He realizes then, with finality, that he is not going to own the whole works. We Americans have just had the same unsettling experience. We are not so powerful as we imagined. Bearded revolutionaries in Cuba defy us, and little men in black pajamas in a jungle halfway around the world stymy our military machine. Nor are we so rich. Our cities erupt volcanically. The poor loot and riot. We are sure we gave the Negro and the poor man everything he needed, and the answer is a resounding no, they want more. These two problems are never going to go away. Which means we are going to live in an unpleasant world, just as the man who turns forty lives with unpleasant realizations. And Lyndon Johnson, the President of all of us, did not make the world clear and delightful to our vision. In fact, it was he who insisted on a Civil Rights Bill and he who escalated the war in Vietnam.

It was all his fault we turned forty.

Any sensitive American could sense Lyndon B. Johnson's agony over Vietnam. Johnson was not cut out to be a war President.

He could never be a war President in the way that Lincoln, Wilson, and Franklin D. Roosevelt were.

He was a Southerner who wanted to be remembered as the President who finally smashed the last vestiges of racial segregation. He was the poor boy turned millionaire who wanted to help the poverty-stricken unemployed and those who lived in slums and ghettos. He was a schoolteacher with Mexicans for his students who accomplished more in legislation for education than any President in history.

But Johnson could not say of his Great Society, "General

Win-the-War will now replace Dr. New Deal," as Franklin D. Roosevelt did.

Johnson, an old Populist, was in his heart an insular man. It was amazing indeed that he had the firm understanding he did of America's place in the world and the need to perpetuate the United Nations.

Alone, I suspect, his thoughts always returned to the slums and to Appalachia and to the unlettered kids in the rural South. His dreams were of big shiny apartment dwellings for the inhabitants of the slums, of a vast medical complex for the elderly, and of eyeglasses and dental care for millions of kids. And even while talking about Vietnam and the Communists, Johnson thought wistfully of a million new classrooms, with a new teacher standing at the blackboard in every last one of them.

In the provincial days of America, at the turn of the century, Woodrow Wilson had already written a dozen essays about American foreign affairs. Franklin D. Roosevelt, from the Eastern Establishment, was always attuned to Europe and its affairs.

But Lyndon B. Johnson remembered when cotton sold for five cents a pound, and he kept thinking of the poverty and the illiteracy of a rural and mountain America lost in the industrial age of the twentieth century.

Lyndon Johnson was a proud man and a man with a lot of corn pone within him. There was an apocryphal story in Washington that Johnson asked a former Cabinet member, "Why don't people love me?" and the Cabinet member replied, "You're not a particularly lovable man, Lyndon."

As for myself, I subscribe to the notion that love is just another word all too frequently bandied about in serious conversation. It is a dandy word for movies and poems, but one should no more look for love in politics than one should look for happiness in marriage.

Ralph McGill's Atlanta

ATLANTA, GEORGIA, had Ralph McGill of the *Constitution* and Birmingham, Alabama, had Bull Connor of the police dogs. That is the difference between the two cities. Atlanta is the most progressive city of the Deep South, and Birmingham is the city of George Orwell's future, symbolized by a boot stamping on the human face.

The difference between Ralph McGill and Bull Connor is the difference one man can make. Atlanta is a city of reason, and Birmingham is a city that literally should arrest itself.

It wasn't easy. The night Ralph McGill's wife lay dying, someone fired a shot through his living room window. When Ralph McGill wrote an editorial, Southerners called him "Rastus."

Ralph McGill is dead, and Atlanta is poorer for it. Bull Connor still strides the streets of his hometown, and I wonder how many industries and government agencies have said, we cannot locate there, we could not possibly lure college personnel.

Ralph McGill championed integration in the very city Sherman considered the heart of the Confederacy. Sherman burned the city. Atlanta was the very city which gave birth to the Ku Klux Klan. On Thanksgiving Day, 1915, the Knights of Mary Phagan climbed to the tip of Stone Mountain and burned a cross there for all to see. Three times Atlanta has had race riots that beggar all description.

Yet there was one man. As Clarence Darrow said, "There is always that one man who says no."

Ralph McGill had said *no* since 1929. And Ralph won. He made his *no* stick. Ralph said *no* in the city which once considered an ordinance requiring builders to install segregated elevators.

He said first the separation of races by law is wrong and un-

Christian; he said, next, the South denies itself a vast wealth by insisting on such.

When he joined the Atlanta *Constitution* over thirty years ago, Atlanta prided itself on the Five Corners and on the old folks who could show a visitor the streets through which Sherman's bummers had marched. When he died in 1968, Atlanta had a skyline, the third largest on the Eastern Seaboard. It has a Negro legislator who has been placed in nomination for the Vice Presidency. It is the richest city in the South, and it is the city which led the fight for reapportionment in the Supreme Court.

A casual visitor to Atlanta these days is amazed at the city's growth and vitality. It is a little New York, full of industry, art, and culture. It represents the most amazing transformation of a Southern city in this century. The city which could lynch a Leo Frank in 1915 because he was a Jewish capitalist has elected Sam Massell, a Jew, as mayor. Truly this is Atlanta's proudest moment. And all of this in no small measure was the work of Ralph McGill.

Carl Sandburg on the wide veranda of his home in Flat Rock told me one afternoon that when he left Chicago he thought he would probably die of loneliness. "But," he said, "down here in North Carolina, I got Frank Graham to the east and Ralph McGill to the south."

David Selznick

THE DEATH of David Selznick, who produced the classic *Gone With the Wind*, saddened me because it recalled a story my friend the late Jimmy Street once told me.

Jimmy Street was a very successful writer, but before that he was—well, let's put it gently, fond of bending the elbow. Editors broke their codes, and some of them rehired him four and five and six times. Jimmy needed rehiring often because

he was—well, let's put it gently, fond of bending the elbow morning, noon, and night (in later years, of course, Jimmy was a
guiding beacon in the Chapel Hill Alcoholics Anonymous.
Whenever an alcoholic needed help, he always called Jimmy
because Jimmy was a lot more interesting than any of the other
reformers.)

In the midst of this sobriety, Jimmy told me one night, "David
Selznick is the greatest Jew in America."

The statement amazed me. I had never met Mr. Selznick. I
could safely presume he was an upstanding man, a credit to the
movie business, generous to his temple, perhaps, but in Jewish
affairs? Never heard of it.

By what virtue did Jimmy, a Catholic turned Baptist turned
Unitarian turned Episcopalian, instruct me on "great Jews"?

It all went back to the time a tough editor fired Jimmy for
the fifth time. Jimmy decided not to ask for his old job back.
He bought a copy of the *Saturday Evening Post*, secreted himself in a hotel room, and counted the words of the short story,
and when he had the requisite number of words, he quit and
mailed the story off. The *Post* bought it. Jimmy called it "Nothing Sacred."

Two weeks later he had a check, with which he proceeded
to bend his elbow. During the celebration, David Selznick con-
tacted Jimmy and said he was interested in buying the story for
a movie. Jimmy, on the telephone, said sure, anything. And
soon enough Selznick arrived at Jimmy's apartment with a
check for the movie rights.

Said Selznick, "I forgot to discuss with you the future rights,
I hesitate to ask you now." And, said Selznick, with discretion,
"Have your lawyer or agent get in touch with me and we will
complete that part of the deal."

Jimmy grabbed the movie check and forgot all about future
rights. *Nothing Sacred* as a movie starred Fredric March,
John Barrymore, and Carole Lombard. It was made later into
another movie with Jerry Lewis and into a play and then into

a musical called *Hazel Flagg*. It is still playing somewhere in one form or another.

"That's why David Selznick is the greatest Jew in the world," said Jimmy. "Had he offered me five hundred dollars extra for those future rights that night, I would have signed anything. But he was a gentleman. He wouldn't take advantage of a man— not himself."

Through his whole life, Jimmy Street was always receiving a royalty check of one sort or another from "Nothing Sacred." And according to his lights, David Selznick remained "the greatest Jew in America."

Joe Louis

WHEN WAS the first time any of us ever heard of black power? We heard it on a Wednesday night, June 22, 1938, when Joe Louis stopped Max Schmeling in two minutes and four seconds of the first round.

I saw the fight, and I can still hear the screams Max Schmeling gave that went above the roar of Yankee Stadium when Louis hit him in the ribs. Schmeling's mouthpiece shot from his mouth, and I think they're still looking for it.

Max was the heavyweight who won the championship on his back (when Jack Sharkey fouled him) and lost it on his feet (when Sharkey outpointed him in a rematch). Two years before, in 1936, Schmeling became the first man to beat Joe Louis when he knocked him out in the twelfth round. The upset made the Germans very happy, since it seemed to prove their racial theories. Adolf Hitler even forgave Max for fighting a black man and invited him to lunch. The Nazis called off their boycott of the North German Lloyd Lines, which had advertised excursion fares for the fight in New York. Max vented a few views on the superiority of the Nordics.

The second fight brought thousands of visitors to New York.

I was in the hotel business at the time, and that June night is one of the few nights during the Depression that every room was taken. Visitors spent three million dollars in the city that week, an unprecedented amount for hard times.

Eighty thousand people filled the stadium to watch Louis bounce Schmeling's head back and forth as though it were on hinges. Hitler and Goebbels stayed awake to hear the fight on wireless, as we called it in those days, and they surely didn't miss much sleep.

It was also the first time in my memory that I heard a great mass of white Americans articulating the hope that a Negro would win. Not everybody realized the political implications, but many did. As soon as Arthur Donovan, the referee, raised Louis' hand, Negro people poured into the streets of Harlem celebrating. In Negro ghettos all over the nation, people danced in the streets. In truth, they had something to celebrate. The first black champion, Jack Johnson, was careless, irresponsible, corrupt.

Joe Louis was everything a heavyweight champion should be —reserved, decent, and, in the ring, indestructible.

Now that's what I call black power.

Norman Thomas

THE LAST time I saw Mr. Norman Thomas was in 1963 when we met in Washington on the occasion of the civil rights march. He was concerned about getting a room in one of the hotels, and I said I had reservations adequate to take care of him; we might better spend our time in talk than in scurrying from hotel to hotel.

We talked about the lecture circuit. I had been traveling around making speeches for the last twelve years, and it was amazing to hear this elderly man remember all those same universities and banquet halls where he, too, had spoken many years before. I never had generosity pay off with such dividends. Mr. Thomas began recounting the early days of the Socialist movement and his part in it, telling me stories about men of whom I had written in *Carl Sandburg* but had never met. What a bonus I would have had had I spent a month interviewing him while I wrote that book!

This was one of the few times I met Norman Thomas. But I told him he had been such an active political figure for so long that I had long ago come to feel I knew him well and counted him as a friend. I reminded him of the first time he and I exchanged correspondence. In February of 1958, while I was on my way to Newark, New Jersey, a faulty flue in my home in Charlotte caused a fire. The office was completely destroyed, along with all my papers, books, clothes, and furniture. I was, I thought on the afternoon I returned, wiped out, because my subscription list for the *Carolina Israelite* was gone. But the police chief of Charlotte restored the list with infrared photography, the ministers lent me aid, a close friend got me an office, and another friend lent me a station wagon. Some people in Charlotte gave me a new typewriter, and within the week I was back in business.

It was about this time that he sent me a letter asking what he could do to help. I wrote him back and described to him the outpouring of goodwill which came from rich and poor alike —Presbyterians, Baptists, Catholics, Jews, and Episcopalians.

He answered me as follows: "I am grateful to the people of Charlotte; my grandparents are buried there. The city has good blood in its veins."

Norman Thomas's grandparents were Dr. and Mrs. Stephen A. Mattoon. They are buried on the grounds of Johnson C. Smith University, the Negro college here. Dr. Mattoon served as the first president of this institution, which now boasts a student body whose members come from all over the world.

All his life, which spanned eighty-four years, Norman Thomas preached the need for the reform of American economic life— for social security, old-age pensions, Medicare, low-cost housing, slum clearance, the five-day work week, unemployment insurance, minimum wage laws, and the abolition of child labor. He lived to see all these reforms become the law of the land.

But what the American people were willing to accept from a senior warden of the Hyde Park Episcopal Church who wore a Navy cape they could not accept from a Socialist. That's the whole story of Norman Thomas and the Roosevelt reforms.

W. C. Fields

ANYONE WHO ever saw W. C. Fields in the *Ziegfeld Follies* or in his movies misses him. Remembering W. C. Fields is like remembering a dearly departed friend; not that Fields would have been a dear friend, but his stage presence had the immediacy of a friend's. As some one remarked of another reprobate, "Just seeing him once in a while made you feel good for a week at least."

Why I most miss comedians like W. C. Fields is that the comedians who have replaced him see life through a suburban window or over a nightclub microphone. They all wear shined shoes, and when they are not in black tie, they are in gray flannel. I have never been to a nightclub and the one suburb I have seen is where my son lives, and that suburb to me is out in the woods, to say the least.

Fields is now among us in a new book published by the New American Library and the World Publishing Company titled *Drat!* It contains a series of stills collected from Fields' movies with suitable captions uttered by Fields.

In one of his movies, Fields tells a sheriff bound upon evicting him, "You're crazy." The amazed sheriff replies, "Why, you're drunk."

"Well," says Fields, "I'll be sober tomorrow, but you'll be crazy the rest of your life."

In another still, which reveals Peggy Hopkins Joyce in lingerie and Fields in pajamas, he is instructing a friend, "Tell my wife not to wait up for me because I won't be home for a month."

The truth that is never shown on the TV situation comedy is that men do on occasion stay out all night and not to play miniature golf either. Fields' rather practical approach is that she's going to be mad if you're an hour late and not much madder if you're a month late.

"Any man who hates dogs and children can't be all bad," remarked Fields. This revelation plumbs profound depths.

One of the sad failures of Hollywood is that the movie people never trusted W. C. Fields. They always costarred him with Gloria Jean or with Bing Crosby or with Edgar Bergen and Charlie McCarthy. In short, they dissipated. The movie makers tried to mitigate a clear ethic that Fields always enunciated. That ethic, in Fields' own words, was "I'm like Robin Hood— I take from the rich and give to the poor—us poor."

Namath's hall of fame

THE SPORTSWRITERS cannot say enough of what quarterback Joe Namath means to the Jets and to professional football. Far be it from me to add further praise over the Jet offense. Football got beyond me about the time Knute Rockne introduced the shift.

But I think Joe Namath has done something for us above and beyond his contributing to the sport. He is apparently a loudmouth and a swinger; he wears funny clothes and affects funny haircuts. He frequents bars and does not always obey the curfew. In short, he has set the cause of good living back two hundred years, and for that let us say amen. He has proved a man can be a winner without meeting an inspirational minister in his youth. He has proved you can lay it on to sportswriters and it doesn't change the score. It is a relief to learn we don't have to be nice guys to be number one.

Leo Durocher reminded us of this years ago when he declared, "Nice guys finish last," but the lesson always needs reinforcing.

Therefore I am soliciting for my own hall of fame. I haven't consulted an architect as yet, but I know the physical plant will contain spittoons and a brass rail, and the walls will sport several centerfolds from *Playboy* magazine. I am aiming, of course, for the atmosphere of a discothèque, rather than a shrine. Joe Namath is my first nominee.

Right after him comes Don Larsen, the New York Yankee pitcher who hurled a perfect game in the 1956 World Series against the Dodgers. When the sportswriters asked Don how he prepared for the game, he said, "I had a couple of beers last night and went to sleep when the Late Show was over."

No one can fail to appreciate Babe Ruth's credentials. There wasn't a secret left in life when the Babe hung up his cleats. He and Smokey Joe Wood once got drunk in Boston and married two waitresses. That's really tying one on. And he used to eat enough hot dogs occasionally to incapacitate himself.

Think, too, of Grover Cleveland Alexander, who, though he had pitched and won the day before, came on in relief in the 1926 World Series to strike out Tony Lazzeri and preserve victory for the Cardinals. When a nosy coach later examined the Coca-Cola Grover was sipping, he found it was laced with brandy.

As many people have been strangled by virtue as have been drowned by sin.

Harlem's Adam Clayton Powell

On April 11, 1967, the Supreme Court by a margin of seven to one returned Adam Clayton Powell to the House of Representatives. He defeated in a special election a handsome Republican grandmother named Lucille Pickett Williams and a thirty-eight-year-old Conservative named Erwin F. Yearling, a Baptist minister. Once again the House of Representatives had to face the discouraging truth that nobody is happy with Adam Clayton Powell except his constituency. But then a congressman doesn't need anybody else, does he?

It is hard to believe that Adam Clayton Powell would threaten anyone. For months he did no more than display his expertise at playing dominoes and judging female flesh, and this in the far-off Bahamas. One feels Powell no more menaces anyone than a college boy on vacation—except Adam Clayton Powell's Fort Lauderdale is the Congress of the United States.

When Powell was chairman of the House Education and Labor Committee, a post to which he ascended by virtue of seniority, he ran it much as a vigorous businessman runs any successful enterprise. He allegedly dipped into its capital to support a wife and a girlfriend. And who wouldn't dip into a business like the Education and Labor Committee? It is a business which cannot possibly go bankrupt. But it was for such practices his colleagues in the House expelled him.

In many ways, the display of high spirits ingratiates Congressman Powell to his constituents. The fact of the matter is that Adam Clayton Powell is having a good time, at least as good as any member of the white establishment. Powell has more imagination than most members of the white establishment, whose idea of a good time is reading stock market quotations. This good time is one of the reasons Harlem is for Powell.

Adam Clayton Powell, Jr., is the Colgate-educated son of Adam Senior, who made the Abyssinian Baptist Church in Harlem the largest Protestant congregation in the world. Adam Junior therefore descends from what we in the South like to call "family." And "family" probably means more in Harlem than it does in the South for the simple reason "family" in Harlem is more authentic. Harlem is a transient area. It is a poverty-stricken area. It is an area bereft of traditional manners, an area still waiting. Family there has a tougher time sticking together. In the South, the generations succeed each other into a sequence to power, just like the Rockefellers or the Kennedys or the

Lodges or the Roosevelts. Power is influence and money. Adam junior succeeded to both. He inherited a more than adequate competence from his father made from judicious investments in Harlem realty. Then, some thirty years ago, Adam Clayton Powell, Jr., took over his father's pulpit. The Abyssinian Baptist Church numbers 2,500 parishioners and, more important, over 15,000 dues-paying members. Adam Clayton Powell, Jr., who commands the adoration of these members even more than his father, has a head start in any election of 17,500 votes.

As the titular head of so large an organization, Adam Clayton Powell was certain to exercise influence in the Harlem community. His oratorical gifts and his compelling personality were enough to secure a forum as long as he chose to shepherd the Abyssinian Baptists. But in addition he was a reformer—and a successful reformer. In 1938 he organized the Greater New York Coordinating Committee for Unemployment and with other hard-nosed Negroes began picketing the stores on 125th Street demanding they integrate. The Woolworths, the Nedickses, the Davegas, the banks, and the liquor stores which lined the street employed only white personnel in those days. Negroes responded to Powell's campaign. They didn't cross his picket lines. Powell not only wrung concessions from these stores, he organized other boycotts which brought the telephone company and the bus companies and Consolidated Edison to a bargaining table.

No wonder Powell was a shoo-in when he ran for election to the New York City Council in 1942. With 64,000 votes, he became the first Negro to sit on that august if occasionally inefficient body. If the measures he constantly introduced to emasculate segregation didn't pass, still they made news. They proved an irritant and a goad. They served their purpose for Negroes and for Powell, too.

When the New York legislature reapportioned the state's congressional districts in 1943, Adam Clayton Powell announced his candidacy for Congress. New York's Eighteenth Congressional District (then the Twenty-second) is not wholly Harlem.

Adam Powell represents Puerto Ricans and Italians, Negroes and Hungarians.

Powell won handily in 1944. He has won handily ever since. More than a flair for politics, Adam Clayton Powell has a genius. In 1944, when Adam Clayton Powell became the first Negro elected to Congress from the Northeast, he was endorsed by Tammany Hall, the CIO, the American Labor Party, the Transport Workers Union, and even the Communist Party. In fact, his Republican opponent in April's special election, Mrs. Williams, once voted for him—in 1958, when the Republican Party also nominated him.

After the Reconstruction, the first Negro to take a seat in Congress was De Priest from Chicago's South Side. Mr. De Priest's election even shook the aplomb of Herbert Hoover, whose very own Republican Party sent De Priest to Washington. Hoover decided to avoid De Priest, and Mrs. Hoover, after arduous if short consideration, decided to invite Mrs. De Priest to her traditional tea for the wives of Republican congressmen. But she warned the other women of the ordeal.

When Adam Clayton Powell went to Washington, he told *his* party leader, Franklin D. Roosevelt, that he and his aides had every intention of integrating the congressional dining room. FDR, no mean genius himself, said, "Go right ahead." Adam did. He also succeeded in integrating the Capitol Hill police, whose appointment is determined by political patronage.

In the internal war for civil rights, Adam Clayton Powell was no slacker. He may not have been the Julius Caesar that A. Philip Randolph has been, nor a fiery St. Paul like Martin Luther King, but Powell has proved a pretty good Cicero. Like Cicero, too, he is a living paradox. A spell-binding orator, Powell only gets into trouble when he forgets to keep his mouth shut. Like Cicero, too, Adam Clayton Powell knows what Rome is up to.

To wit: Adam Clayton Powell makes no statements contra the administration's policy in Vietnam. Powell understands his constituency. Negroes are patriots. The proportion of Negroes who are combat soldiers is far out of proportion to their numbers in the population. Negroes are combat soldiers not solely because the basic sense of American injustice has decreed that the middle- and upper-class boys in college as well as the professional football heroes shouldn't fight the war; Negroes are combat soldiers because they love their country.

Fannie Hurst

THE FIRST person who congratulated me on my first issue of the *Carolina Israelite* was Fannie Hurst, the novelist. She sent me a postcard in red ink saying she looked forward to more issues and hoped my subscription list would grow. She sent her friends a year's subscription every Christmas, and I would guess all told she probably carried twenty or thirty subscriptions over the twenty-six years I published.

And the postcards kept coming. Every three months or so I got one, the words crowded onto the space as New Yorkers are crowded onto the subway cars. Come to think of it, the first fan letter I ever printed in the *Israelite* was signed by Fannie Hurst. I used to print fan letters from time to time not so much for the edification of my readers as to bolster my own morale.

I met her three or four times in New York. She lived in a huge rambling apartment in the East Seventies, I believe. One time she invited me to tea. When I said I preferred bourbon, that's what I got. She was a strikingly handsome woman with jet black hair combed straight back.

I remember this meeting because she told me solemnly that she was convinced the essay was the best form for the writer. This from the novelist who wrote *Back Street* and *Imitation of Life*, which alone made her one of the highest-paid writers in America. She wrote countless other novels during her seventy-eight years, and I believe her agent has two unpublished works. She knew the works of every essayist and recounted to me why the essay was provocative. "The passion is your own," she said.

In 1954 or thereabouts she asked me to join her on a television show she conducted for one of the New York channels. We talked about the immigrants who came to America in steerage, and she was so knowledgeable about the trip to the New World that it surprised me later to learn she had been born in Hamilton, Ohio, and spent her youth in St. Louis, the very town where T. S. Eliot was born. After the show she asked me again how she could help, and I said, "Keep them subscriptions coming."

Later I met Miss Hurst again at the Overseas Press Club in New York. It was a sad occasion—a memorial evening for Carl Sandburg, who had died that summer. Both Miss Hurst and I addressed the audience, telling them what Carl had meant to us.

I expected a red postcard from Fannie Hurst when I announced I was closing up my paper. She died the morning that the *Times* ran the story. I shall miss her. Fannie Hurst wasn't what was wrong with the novel, or this world.

Martin Luther King

THAT THURSDAY evening I was in Blacksburg, Virginia, scheduled to debate Senator J. Strom Thurmond of South Carolina in the auditorium of Virginia Polytechnic Institute. I was in an anteroom waiting for the debate to get under way when one of the student sponsors came in and told me that Martin Luther King had been shot in Memphis.

Our debate was under way before the dean of the school interrupted us and told the assembled students that Martin Luther King had been murdered.

The student body at VPI is all white. But no Negro audience could have been more shocked. I heard groans of despair. The dean then asked me if I would say a few words about Dr. King, since I had known him.

I said, "It is a sad day for the world and a sadder day for Americans. Like Pope John, Dr. Martin Luther King proved to all of us that Christianity has its uses. He borrowed an idea from Gandhi and transformed that idea of nonviolence into an American and Christian tradition. When Pope John died, however, he did not leave a vacuum, an ominous vacuum that may be filled not with love and brotherhood but with hate and terror."

I finished. The students were still too shocked to know whether to applaud the sentiments or not. As they fidgeted, Senator Strom Thurmond, who once ran for President on the Dixiecrat ticket, rose and said, "I disagree with Mr. Golden's estimate of Dr. King. He was an agitator, an outside agitator, bent on stirring people up, making everyone dissatisfied."

Then we went on with our debate. Senator Thurmond urged the answer to our problems was law and order, and I said the answer was law and justice. He said the federal government was too big, that it encroached on the sovereign rights of the states, and I argued there hasn't been a sovereign state since the original thirteen ratified the Constitution. The students applauded our arguments in equal measure.

Before I left the next morning, I learned a group of the students asked the president of the institution if they could lower the flag to half-mast. The president said the flag was lowered only by federal proclamation. The students thanked him and went out and lowered the flag anyway. As I was leaving the campus, I saw they had also lowered the state flag of Virginia.

If they can lower the flag for Martin Luther King in a state which once closed its schools rather than integrate them, maybe his life wasn't in vain. Martin Luther King's life was too short, but it made ours fuller.

The Wall Street shark

HE WAS the great Wall Street bear until the Securities Exchange Commission ruled that Wall Street was not a public preserve. Livermore's life and misdeeds are the subject of a brief but telling biography by Paul Sarnoff—*Jesse Livermore: King of Speculators*, published by the American Research Council.

One of Livermore's pet tricks was to operate a pool. Together with three or four other sharks, he would select a stock and run it up by "wash" buying. Wash buying is the process whereby the pool operators keep buying from each other. But the ticker tape records heavy orders, and when the stock hits a certain high, the operators turn and sell it to the public.

I wasn't particularly close to Livermore, but I saw him frequently downtown. As often as I saw him, he was with a beautiful woman. He had three wives, and he once boasted the one hobby he indulged was hopping into bed with a handsome lady. That and making money were the only two things that never bored him.

The Crash wiped him out. He came back, was wiped out again. He even wrote a book, *How to Trade in Stocks*.

I once watched Jesse Livermore selling United Drug Company short. United Drug I believe was then at three dollars a share, and Jesse Livermore was selling thousands of shares at two dollars and fifty cents.

"Mr. Livermore," I asked, "you are selling so many shares short, where do you think United Drug will go?"

Livermore looked at me and said, almost snarling, "When they are sick, they die." A few weeks later, United Drug went broke, was taken off the Big Board, and sold for pennies over the counter. It was another killing for Jesse Livermore.

He was a tall, spare man with rimless eyeglasses and a ready wit, sardonic perhaps and cynical. And he always sold short. His first killing came when he sold the Union Pacific Railroad short and the San Francisco earthquake made his hunch pay off.

In 1940 he shot himself in the hat-check room of the Sherry Netherland Hotel. He owed over a half-million dollars in lawsuits. He had written his own epitaph: "When they are sick, they die."

Marshall McLuhan

ONE OF the ways to deal with problems is not to deal with them at all. Which is the way I have dealt with the problem of Marshall McLuhan. Marshall McLuhan is one of my problems through no fault of his own. As a peripatetic lecturer, I must indulge at least half an hour of questions, and one of those questions from the audience always inquires what I think of Marshall McLuhan.

When it comes to the ABM, I am quick on the trigger; give me five minutes and I will recite the history of the Supreme Court; the prospect of civil rights is child's play for me. But I had a great deal of trouble trying to think up anything to say about Marshall McLuhan. I used to answer the question with "I have inordinate difficulty trying to make clear what I write without the burden of making clear what he has written." Lately, I have borrowed from Henry Gibson of Laugh-In, and when I get the question, I repeat Mr. Gibson's poem: "Marshall McLuhan—What're you doin'?" (I hereby give Henry Gibson free and uninhibited access to any of my written opinions, jokes, or causeries.)

What brings Dr. McLuhan to mind is the privilege I had of hearing him speak at the convention of the American Booksellers' Association. I myself once had the honor of addressing these dear men who try to fill a writer's pocket with silver. On this last occasion the luncheon was sufficient and McLuhan compelling. Except when he had finished, I was back with my problem again. The editors and publishers who are my friends asked me what I thought of the speech.

Since Dr. McLuhan had assured us that the book will persevere, I said I thought he was right, that he had better be right for all our sakes. Among other insights, Dr. McLuhan offered that the United States is the only country founded on literacy—on the Gutenberg press. Therefore it is having the hardest time adapting to the electronic age. What did I think about that?

I had been trying not to think about that until my editor pressed me. I wanted to say it was a solipsism, except I knew it wasn't, a solipsism being the theory that nothing is real or exists but the self. Instead I said that Dr. McLuhan would do well to restudy his logic and remember the caution about the law of the excluded middle. But that is what I mean about Dr. McLuhan —he brings out the worst in a man. Who uses words like "solipsism" and spouts the law of the excluded middle when he's trying to light a postprandial cigar? And anyway, I have grandsons so adapted to the electronic age as to be the despair of their parents.

This last insight was the least provocative of the many insights Dr. McLuhan offered. I remembered that Socrates once argued with Protagoras the Sophist that if they were to debate, they had to debate Socrates' way. Socrates reasoned that if a fast man races a slow man, there is no excitement unless the fast man promises to run slow. Since Protagoras knew everything and Socrates knew nothing, the contest was already over unless Protagoras went along with the dimwits. I have spent a lifetime trying to catch up to the twentieth century, and here the good doctor is already examining the twenty-first. The time is out of joint. No wonder I cannot satisfy my audiences.

Adlai Stevenson

ADLAI STEVENSON died in London in 1965. I was in London not long afterward, and I went to the spot where his heart stopped beating—a few doors from the American Embassy.

Adlai Stevenson's influence will be far greater than that of any other defeated Presidential candidate. Henry Clay, William Jennings Bryan, Wendell Willkie, Thomas E. Dewey never exercised such lasting influence. It is true that Bryan succeeded to Woodrow Wilson's Cabinet as Secretary of State, only to resign when Wilson drafted a strong protest to the German Kaiser. It is true that Wendell Willkie worked for Franklin D. Roosevelt and wrote a significant book, but his untimely death cut short his influence.

Stevenson succeeded to John F. Kennedy's Cabinet as Ambassador to the United Nations. Just how powerful and all-pervading an influence Stevenson has wielded was demonstrated after the Cuban missile crisis, when reporters Charles Bartlett and Stewart Alsop published an article in the *Saturday Evening Post* which purported to be the inside story of administration planning and strategy sessions. These journalists were critical of Adlai, charging that he had advised President Kennedy to go soft and negotiate with the Russians for the removal of the missiles.

But the story exploded in their faces. No one has to overhear administration councils under such conditions to realize men change their thinking from day to day and minute to minute. No doubt some of the men sitting in on these conferences called for war. But what was interesting is that these two journalists were charging that the man who counseled peace was suspect.

Even so perceptive a man as the late John F. Kennedy was amazed by the mail which inundated the White House following the story's publication. It ran ten to one for Stevenson, and it was evident that the scare word "appeasement" did not terrify

Americans. God help the world on the day when a Presidential council does not have a man willing to face up to the risks of peace.

There was a sadness about Stevenson in his later years. It was not that power eluded him—Stevenson knew why it had—it was rather that with the Kennedy administration of young men and new words, America did not give Stevenson the sense of personal security he so richly deserved. Ed Murrow summed it up best for me in a letter dated August 3, 1960: "In England Stevenson would be in Parliament, lighting the hearts of the people of the free world, but here he sits around waiting for a few tired old friends to come in and have a drink with him."

April 12, 1945

WHEN THE Charlotte newspaper carried the news in April, 1945, that the Roosevelt funeral train would pass through town a little after midnight on its way to Washington, I went down to the Southern Railroad Station. At eleven o'clock I found it impossible to get within a block of the terminal. I have never seen so many mothers with infants in their arms. It was a long wait. Then as the train passed I could hear whispered prayers. I edged through the crowd and saw dozens of Negroes on their knees, hands clasped.

It was a slow departure afterward. What fascinated me were the lights on both sides of the track stretching northward as far as the eye could see. These were the lanterns and flashlights of the rural folk who had walked down to the tracks.

I shall always remember those Negroes praying at the Charlotte railroad station and the rural folk coming out to wait for the funeral train. They came and they prayed because the President who died had attempted for the first time in the history of man to abolish hunger.

Whatever happens again in this country—depression or disaster, flood or dust storm—people need not starve. This is the important and central fact of the Roosevelt career.

But, of course, they are starving here in America, while the rest of us hold up protesting hands against the spoonful of sugar in our coffee.

The Charlotte doctor Raymond Wheeler, who saved my life, was one of several doctors who visited the Delta just over a year ago. He was able to testify under oath before Senator James Eastland that indeed Mississippi and Alabama were starving people to death, withholding surplus food so that more and more Negroes would emigrate from the state.

One of the reasons we can tolerate starvation is that so few of us have ever gone hungry. We have a vague idea of what hunger can do to a baby's stomach. We have no idea of what it can do to the mind and soul. We have no idea of how weak and subservient it makes men. We have no idea of what a morning is like which is immediately invested with the mystery of how to eat that night.

The greatness of Franklin D. Roosevelt was the New Deal. It restored the promise of the American Dream. It was the progressive era's new nationalism. He inaugurated the philosophy of government as the agency of social reform. That this philosophy has become the touchstone of America's future can be seen from the fact that Eisenhower, the Republican President, confirmed the New Deal and enabled Presidents Kennedy, Johnson, and Nixon to proceed with social reform. Another great facet of Roosevelt's presidency was that he turned the American Negro away from his traditional Republicanism. Eleanor Roosevelt had a lot to do with that. Befriended by Mrs. Roosevelt, and constantly assuming a more potent political influence in the larger Northern cities, the Negro was ready in the thirties to abandon his traditional allegiance to the Republican Party. Harold Ickes, Secretary of the Interior and a former president of the Chicago Branch of the NAACP, began hiring Negro intellectuals as advisers and set an example which other Cabinet officers and bureau chiefs gradually followed.

Franklin D. Roosevelt's New Deal was the most significant political and intellectual movement in twentieth-century America.

The trial

HE WAS an old man on trial. He was near ninety, and his hands and head were palsied and shook when he rose and when he talked. He was facing a terrible test.

His children had accused him of senility and had argued persuasively that he was no longer fit to handle the family fortune. It was true that during his lifetime he had added to that fortune. But the fortune had descended to him from his father, and in this city and in this time it was expected he would hand over that fortune to his sons. Now his sons were impatient.

He himself had lived so long that his sons were no longer young; indeed, they had grown sons of their own. They no longer heeded his advice on the disposition of the family's energies. They had challenged him: It was their turn.

But he was averse now as he had always been averse to letting others direct him. He had managed for himself. The years left to him were his and, family or not, he was entitled to their direction. So he rose, facing men in a jury box appreciably younger than he.

Younger though they were, they were tired men, for the city had fallen upon evil times. When he was young, this city had bested the invaders from the east. But now civil war was about to bring it to ruin, although he was sure he himself would not see that ruin. Yet it saddened him.

His children charged he had spent his life in worthless pursuits among wicked people. Granted he had gained success among these people, they charged he demeaned his aristocratic name. Now they said he was too old even for old pursuits.

He held one parchment before him which he unrolled, and

then modestly he told his jurors it was true he had also been a poet and a playwright, he had indeed won several prizes in Athens for his works. He was Sophocles, the Sophocles who dealt with myths, but it was not true he was senile, that he was incompetent. The only proof he would offer was the reading of recent verses. Sophocles read some of the choruses of *Oedipus at Colonus*. Finished, he told the jury he believed the profession of poetry made men virtuous and that he was still able to apply himself.

The jury returned no judgment against him.

Threats from Mr. Buckley

I HAVE received a communication filled with passion and anger from Mr. William Buckley, editor in chief of the *National Review*. Mr. Buckley says I called him bad names on a television show and that if I call him names, I am insulting principal intellectuals throughout the country, all the Founding Fathers, dozens of senators, and hundreds of congressmen. My goodness! I wouldn't want to say mean things about anybody, especially about them herd-riding intellectuals, congressmen, and senators.

Mr. Buckley takes a back seat to no one when it comes to name-calling, himself. He has called me on occasion a Liberal Yahoo and says that though I terrified the Communists on the Lower East Side, I did not terrify the Communists who dominate the Emergency Civil Liberties Committee. I wasn't aware there were Communists on the Emergency Civil Liberties Committee, but if he wishes to furnish me with their names, both of us will see about legal soap and water.

I find Mr. Buckley a brilliant young man, and for that reason it seems strange to me that he puts so much energy into making the 1890's a better time for everybody.

Even if he did really want to retreat unto the days of Grover Cleveland, the pressure from progressive liberalism would not let Mr. Buckley do it. Little housewives around the world are learning English so they can order an electric can opener from Sears Roebuck, and Eskimos are actually buying electric refrigerators in which they store their TV dinners, which they consume when they come home from working as mechanics on a government project.

Don't be mad, Mr. Buckley. Come along.

It's a tie, Nancy

NANCY DICKERSON of NBC, the Washington reporter, interviewed Dr. Harold Graning, then Assistant Surgeon General of the United States. Dr. Graning and a staff of American medical experts had covered six thousand square miles of Russia studying Soviet hospitals and progress in medical science.

Nancy was interested in one thing: Who's better, we or they? Dr. Graning said, "The Russians have made tremendous advances."

Well, Nancy wanted to know, where would you be happier to have a brain operation, here or there?

Said Dr. Graning, "I would not be happy having brain surgery anywhere."

Nancy tried again. Which people are healthier, we or they? Dr. Graning said the Russians work harder, walk a lot, and do not have our luxuries.

Nancy tried three or four more times without success. I think, Nancy, it's a Mexican standoff, tie score.

P. D. East

The Petal Paper, which is published in Alabama by P. D. East, my friend, is still going strong. It is no easy task to publish an integrationist newspaper in the South, let alone in

Alabama, but P. D. manages. His advertisers are from such diverse places as Livermore, California, and Mountain View, Alaska, and as long as they are not paying him with due bills, I suspect P. D. will get along.

The Petal Paper does not endear P. D. East to his neighbors. Once, when he stopped for a red light, a fellow-Alabaman recognized him, walked over to the car, and said, "If you get out of that car, I'll kill you."

P. D. thought the invitation over and replied, "That ain't incentive enough."

Errol Flynn

ON THE night of Errol Flynn's death, 17,000,000 middle-aged American men suddenly took stock of themselves and stopped drinking. On the same night in Los Angeles and in other metropolitan centers, the whores did absolutely no business. The town was as quiet as if a police crackdown had swept everyone into jail.

Twenty-four hours later, however, things began to perk up. Those 17,000,000 men learned that Flynn had had two previous heart attacks. The liquor stores got back in the thick of things again, and the whores were back taking taxicabs to and fro.

PART 8

Yiddish Humor

The fifty-first civilization

MARK TWAIN made our language when we were an agrarian society. At least we thought we were an agrarian society, which makes a lot of difference in how we laugh. It is true that while Twain wrote, railroad magnates spanned the continent, brokers manipulated the market, manufacturers perfected the machine and exploited the men who manned it. But by and large, we thought of ourselves as a nation whose roots were in the soil and not in the city.

Certainly much of this was true. The great movement from farm to city had not gained real impetus, and Mark Twain's great virtue was describing the essential innocence of Huck Finn uncorrupted by the social context of the farm and city, Huck Finn cleansed and kept innocent by the Father of Waters, the Mississippi.

Long before Mark Twain's death, however, we recognized ourselves as an industrial-urban society. Twain's genius was never in doubt, but let us say Booth Tarkington's is. *Penrod* remains a juvenile book because it is essentially a fantasy. It is about boys in a never-never land.

It was written, I believe, while hundreds of thousands of immigrants were landing in America, transforming our society from an agrarian one into an industrial one. It was written while other thousands of boys and girls labored in the sweatshops. There was nothing funny about boyhood in those times. Our humor thus became an ethnic humor.

We found hilarity in the differences between the rude immigrant and the native born. Where we had always enjoyed a stage Irishman, now we laughed at a stage Jew and a stage Italian and a stage Negro. We laughed at their fumbling attempts to be Americans—they misinterpreted every custom so readily.

Vaudeville was our focus in those years, and in their way Weber and Fields, Gallagher and Shean, and Bert Williams the Negro comedian were great comics, utilizing and tickling society's attitudes. There is even an apocryphal story about Williams. A stagehand remarked to him one night that he was a good nigger because he knew his place, and Williams replied indeed he did, and his place was in dressing room number one with the star on it.

Immigration was halted by the ethnic and racial provisions of the 1920 restrictive law and by the evil McCarran-Walter Act of the 1950's. The funny stage immigrants were now in their third generation. The fellows waiting for vaudeville to come back are not aware of the fact that the basis for it was this ethnic and racial humor. The true artists among the old vaudevillians transferred easily enough to the movies, radio, and television, precisely because they were artists.

The ethnic and racial joke vaudevillians will wait forever and in vain. You cannot tell a Jewish dialect story today when the fellow's daughter goes to Radcliffe and his son wears an Ivy League yarmulka at Harvard.

The Negroes fight the same battle today. They threatened to blockade the parade in Philadelphia of the white men painted black, and more power to the Negroes. The time has come for the stage Negro to go the way of the stage Irishman, the stage Jew, and the stage Italian. It is silly to portray Uncle Remus with Dr. Ralph Bunche around.

Yes, vaudeville had its day. We all became Americans, native-born, and world catastrophes overtook us as Americans. The ethnic jokes diminished in number and quality from year to year. Stepin Fetchit is gone, and even Rochester is now an old man.

There is without doubt a correlation between humor and the economic and psychological health of a society.

Steve Allen has written that one of the requirements of the humorist is to be Jewish. Mr. Allen was exaggerating, of course, but he was eager to make a valid point. The historian Ernest Renan, who was not particularly friendly, wrote, "when you write of Jews, write of their humor."

There have been three waves of Jewish immigration to the United States: Spanish Jews from Spain, Portugal, England, and Holland in Colonial times; a much larger immigration of German Jews from 1848 to 1870; and finally a great wave of immigrants between 1880 and 1920 from eastern Europe, Russia, Poland, Hungary, Rumania, and Austria. And since the 1880's much of the American humor has been spoken by Jewish performers and written by Jews for non-Jewish performers.

Why?

The church fathers put the Jews into ghettos in the twelfth century, as punishment. The church fathers had no idea they were giving the Jews a one-thousand-year seminar in living in the industrial age of the twentieth century. The Jew was an urban man before there was a word for it. But the Jew developed a high sense of humor as part of ghetto life.

In the ghettos of Europe the Jews developed this protection against the hostile society outside. But in America there was political and economic freedom, and so the one great challenge in this ghetto was to get out. And the Jews prepared for the challenge, as always, with humor. Looking back upon it, it is still to me the wonder of wonders that laughter always rocked the Lower East Side of New York. Times were hard. Fate was cruel. Life was often dreary. But people laughed. So it does not seem strange at all that for the next two generations all America was entertained by Jewish comedians, or *komikers*, as we called them. Jews learned to laugh at dire fate because they have an intimate relationship with dire fate.

Indeed the hostile society lends itself to humorous review and criticism. Dr. Freud suggests that one of the reasons for the hostility is that the Jew has been the eternal critic of mankind. And no one really likes a critic.

I personally figured out, for instance, the reason for Dr. Arnold Toynbee's hostility. He found the pattern of the rise and fall of fifty civilizations—beginning, rise, fall, and silence; beginning, rise, fall, and silence. When he came to the Jews, he found beginning, rise, fall, rise, fall, rise, fall, and rise, and he didn't know what to do with that. It just didn't fit. This fifty-first civilization made him mad.

After all, it is something to survive Titus, Vespasian, Hadrian, the Moslems, the Crusaders, the Middle Ages, the feudal system, the czars of Russia, Hitler, and the Communists.

The Jews have a keen insight about this. They know the hostility is not because we claim to be the Chosen People but because of the fear that we really are.

Blessed be the tie that binds

PRESIDENT RICHARD NIXON, ever diligent in his attempt to bring us together, asked Rabbi Louis Finkelstein, chancellor of the Jewish Theological Seminary in America, to conduct the weekly pray-in at the White House. The President invited a great many of his Jewish constituents, a more than unifying gesture. But Mr. Nixon dumbfounded this makeshift congregation when the service led off with the Doxology, a Christian hymn, one of my particular favorites:

> Praise God from whom all blessings flow!
> Praise Him all creatures here below!
> Praise Him above, Ye heavenly host!
> Praise Father, Son, and Holy Ghost!

A close friend who was in attendance but who has sworn me to secrecy confessed he was at first embarrassed. He hadn't seen the inside of a *shule* since 1946, and he at first thought liturgical reforms had caught him unawares. It wasn't until the New York *Times* informed him that he realized the Doxology was not a new part of the Jewish ritual. Since he didn't know the words, he hummed.

Certainly President Nixon intended no slur, desecration, or slight to Jews. But the history of Jews in America is the history of such confusions.

I was in attendance that day in South Carolina when Senator Olin Johnston addressed a congregation of Jews on the celebration of Israel's statehood.

Olin Johnston liked Jews. He told me once his best friend in Charlotte was one Tony Castellano, who was an Italian, but Olin said it would make no difference if Tony were Jewish. On this occasion, Olin mounted the rostrum and told the congregation how in Ezekiel in the Old Testament God promised Palestine to the Jews. Now the prophecy had come to pass. God works in many ways His wonders to perform, Olin concluded, and all that made him sad about Israel was that he would miss seeing the people before him, all of whom, of course, would be proceeding to Israel right away to fulfill God's holy promise. Some of the Jews who were in that assemblage are still shaking.

Not to be outdone, Ross Barnett, when he was governor of Mississippi, addressed a Jewish congregation in Jackson. Barnett was then in a lot of trouble with the federal government, and he wanted to ingratiate himself with all the citizenry. He said the nicest thing he could think of to these Jews. Throughout his sermon he kept calling them "fellow Christians."

Years ago I worked for Mr. I. D. Blumenthal, a Charlotte Jew deeply committed to the interfaith movement. I. D. owned Wildacres, a beautiful estate in the Carolina mountains, where often he invited Protestant, Catholic, and Jewish clergymen for seminars.

I remember one particular minister who was taking his leave of I. D. after a week of horseback riding, swimming, picnicking, and good talk. I. D. pressed a basket of apples into his hands, and in genuine appreciation, the minister said, "Mr. Blumenthal, you would make a wonderful Christian."

But I also remember one of the Wildacres seminars over which Bishop Spaugh presided. The bishop said, "Let us first sing a hymn." And we all sang, "Blessed Be the Tie that Binds."

Thus I feel about the Doxology, if it bound up ties, it's all right with me.

A school prayer plan

ONCE AGAIN my spies tell me the kids are praying in the public school classrooms. A lot of folks have told their school boards the Supreme Court is mistaken. Prayers belong in the public schools. Many of my delightful contemporaries feel that, because they helped make the law, they can disobey it whenever it restrains or inhibits their natural buoyancy. Moreover, the educators argue that since they were required to remove prayers from the curriculum the kids have been going to the dogs. These school officials feel that if part of the day were reserved for beneficial exercise, perhaps less LSD and marijuana would be peddled from the schoolyard telephone booths. There is no doubt that we have reached an impasse over the matters of school prayer. Parents do have some say in what their children should or should not be taught. The question is, how can we accommodate the desires of the pious and still preserve our Constitution?

It behooves me to offer my answer: A Golden Plan for Resolving the Prayer in the Public School Issue. We should in every community petition the school board to schedule the start of school one-half hour later each day. This new schedule would give all the kids a chance to go to church before classes start. This plan would not only give the school day a reverential start, but it would cut down on the time the kids can spend loitering around that phone booth.

This plan has long been operational in the South among the

Baptists. The Baptists by and large are intransigent on the separation of church and state. They have long opposed the recitation of classroom prayers. The Baptists were the only denomination among Southern Protestants to cheer and applaud the Supreme Court decision in 1963 which held that public school prayers "coerced" children. Hundreds of thousands of Baptist children go daily to church before school. I must point out the reason for the Baptists' intransigence is not a zeal for civil liberties but rather the fear that any devotional exercise not theirs is inspired by the Pope in Rome. Since, however, so many people are wrong for the right reasons, I suggest we cheer on those who are right for the wrong reasons.

Jews and Communism

When he left the United States on the way to join the Revolutionists, Leon Trotsky said, "There will be no more Jewish problem, because all the Jews will become good Communists." This was another way of saying, "There will be no more Jews." Unfortunately, this is not the way the world understood Trotsky. The world remembered the pogroms of the czar.

It was during the 1920's and 1930's that quite a number of Jews joined the Communist Party. There were two main reasons for this. First, the Communists had passed a law making anti-Semitism a crime. It was understandable that young Jews, heartsick at the impending fate of Jews in Germany and distressed by the Nazi pamphlets circulating around the United States, were taken in by the Soviets. They did not know, of course, what the Communists had in mind with this law against anti-Semitism. The Communists had decided to eliminate anti-Semitism by eliminating "Semitism." Nevertheless, there were many fooled. Second, the Communists exploited an issue uppermost in the minds of Jews. They made noises against Hitler. They made noises when no one else made noises. This, too, was a fake. The Communists made a pact with Hitler later and betrayed their fraud. For many it was too late. It was too late for those who had become so deeply enmeshed they could no longer see that the entire ideology involved a renunciation of logic.

Nor were these individuals wholly to blame. We liberals as a group, all of us, in America made this serious mistake in the thirties. We hated Hoover more than we hated Stalin. The fact that the reactionaries in America hated Roosevelt more than they hated Hitler is beside the point. We paraded every martyr in the Mussolini-Hitler world but intended to neglect, if not forget, the martyrs the Communists created every day. Here again the Communists were a little too smart for everybody, it seems. My father, who recognized the nature of Communism, made this very point in a Yiddish article in 1934. Harry Lang of the Jewish *Daily Forward* had gone to Russia with the credentials of the late Senator William E. Borah of Idaho. Mr. Lang hit a bull's-eye with the most accurate analysis of what the Communists stood for that had ever appeared anywhere, and Mr. Lang did this in the early 1930's. His articles, which were translated in the New York *Evening Journal*, were the first important insights into the Communist fraud. Mr. Lang stated: "Hitler creates many flames in smoke which the world at least can see; the Communists are just as bad except that there is no flame and no smoke, because whatever they do is in a dungeon." This is the devastating thing about Communism. You wrote a letter to the Soviet Embassy and asked them about some intellectual or poet whose work no longer appeared, and they wrote you a formal note saying that they had never heard of him.

In thinking back to the Jews who joined the American Communist Party, we must bear in mind several pertinent facts. Communism made its inroads primarily in the urban communities, and the Jews are an urban people.

The idea of a United Front, which the Communists inaugurated in the 1930's, had great attraction to people who were honestly interested in a few of its stated goals like slum clearance or fighting anti-Semitism. Moreover, if we say that in the thirties Jews were in the Communist movement beyond the proportion of their numbers, so too were they in the fight against Communism far beyond their numerical ratio. There were many Jewish liberals who fought Communism when it wasn't at all fashionable to do so. The late Lord Bertrand Russell said he lost more friends by criticizing Russia in 1920 than he did by refusing to serve in the armed forces of his country while she was fighting for her very life.

Elihu Root, the "Mr. Republican" of his day, likened the Bolshevik revolution to our own War of Independence. A J. P. Morgan partner publicly urged recognition of the Bolshevik government. While America was listening to them there were Jews like my father and Harry Lang and, the most effective of all, David Dubinsky, who were out-and-out opponents of Communism. Dubinsky had very little outside help in those days. There were no congressional committees to which he could appeal. With one or two exceptions, the press was indifferent. This was in the thirties, and Dubinsky and his group of liberals put the entire International Ladies' Garment Workers Union on the line. They would either beat the Communists who had won control over some of the locals or lose their entire organization, if not their lives, too. Dubinsky won, and won almost single-handed.

Long time between lunches

ONE OF my readers was kind enough to send me a clipping from a Spanish paper. It was a news item describing the luncheon of the Judeo-Christian Society. What made it especially noteworthy was that this was the first time that Spanish Jews and Christians in Spain had broken bread together at an advertised and publicized event.

Appropriately, the meeting took place at the Restaurante

Sinai, the only kosher restaurant in Spain and perhaps the first Jewish restaurant, since no one is sure whether the Jews had eating places before the Inquisition. Three priests sat at the head of the table. There was no rabbi, for the simple reason that there is only one rabbi in all of Spain, and he lives in Barcelona.

There are 32,000,000 citizens of Spain, 8,000 of whom are Jewish. Twenty-five hundred Jews—Spanish, Hungarian, and Moroccan—live in Madrid.

In 1965 the Franco government permitted Jews and Protestants to worship openly. Jews had had less difficulty in worshiping than Protestants, since Judaism does not advocate proselytizing. In the Madrid synagogue, services took place every evening, and, as elsewhere, the temple was filled to overflowing during the High Holy Days.

The luncheon was a first since the Inquisition. The guests, after praying for universal peace and brotherhood, ate Sinai chicken, served with stewed prunes.

Albert Elmalmen Cochren is the proprietor of the Restaurante Sinai. He spent most of his life in Morocco, and when he came to Madrid, friends said a kosher restaurant would certainly make him a buck if the government didn't interfere. For the government in Spain often does take things in its own hands. The Jewish community, for instance, is allowed to import only one thousand gallons of kosher wine every year. This time the government said nothing. Biblical and Medieval Jewish paintings decorate the walls along with "Visit Israel" posters, and there are pictures of Moshe Dayan, everybody's idea of a defense minister.

One kosher restaurant does not a fellowship make. Franco has yet to recognize the state of Israel.

Southern Protestantism, 1970

IF A man held a gun at my head and said, "Become a Christian or I shoot," I would not take the martyr's route as so many of my ancestors did. I would join one of the Protestant churches. There would be very little there that would offend me. The minister conducts the service just as the rabbi does. He reviews the latest book, talks about the current movies, and delivers his once-a-month sermon on juvenile delinquency.

It starts out honorably enough. When they build the edifice they turn it over to the big givers because "they know how to spend the money." Then when it comes to building the Sunday school, the big givers are still in there because they know how to spend the money. In short, the laymen have taken over. And the clergymen reflect the culture of the layman and often his prejudices. "Stick to religion," the word goes down from the layman to the minister and the rabbi, "Stick to religion and stay away from controversial matters, politics, and sociology."

We'll never know how many Protestant clergymen were fired in the last fifteen years because they said a word above the battle on the race issue, from which the Protestant churches and the Jewish temples of the South backed away. They backed away from the great moral issue of the twentieth century.

In April, 1955, Mr. Joseph Sidney Rigell in the pulpit of St. Paul's Presbyterian Church in Chester, South Carolina, urged his congregation to relax its rigid condemnation of the Supreme Court. Mr. Rigell asked his membership to stand to show him support. Only one rose, Mrs. Rigell. The minister sighed, told his congregation he could not let his wife stand alone. He left the pulpit, stood beside his wife for a moment, and walked out.

The refusal of the main Presbyterian church of the South to support the March on Washington elicited a critical letter from Dr. John Randolph Taylor, who wrote: "We as a church will have to pay a high price for withdrawal. If we do not identify ourselves with men's needs how shall we ever be able to establish communication with men effectively enough to present the Gospel?"

I quote this letter from Dr. Taylor not to reinforce his plea, for he doesn't need me, but to show that astute members of the Southern ministry are aware of the price the Protestant Church will pay for its withdrawal. Had the Catholic clergy dissociated itself from the struggle of the Irish immigrant and workingman to unionize, then the Catholic Church in America would have been irreparably damaged in the 1890's, for the Irish workingman was the backbone of American Catholicism.

The number of clergymen who lost their pulpits because they supported the Supreme Court decision of May 17, 1954, is hard to determine. The number fired outright because of their moderate or liberal views are but a handful of those who found themselves out of work because they were "too controversial" or because they "devoted too much time to community affairs." One minister in the South, a personal friend of mine, condemned racial segregation one Sunday. The next Sunday his congregation let him out because he wasn't visiting the sick as often as he should. But there was one occasion when the board failed to renew a minister's contract because "he is a stooge for the Supreme Court." The rise of a Southern middle class in the last forty years not only secularized many of the urban churches and dampened their influence but also robbed the minister of his classical function. It may be said that the South is no longer the "Bible Belt." Southerners spend a lot of time at church, they are punctual in their attendance, but for the last twenty years a casual observer cannot sit through most of the Protestant services without thinking of George Bernard Shaw's comment that Christianity would be a marvelous philosophy if only the folks would try it. This secularization is even reflected in the work of the itinerant tent evangelist. Forty years ago the hymn-singing tent evangelist who staged a tent-meetin' revival asked the converts for a sacrifice to prove good faith. A man was redeemed because he gave up smoking or drinking or consorting with

painted women. The sawdust trail was a trail of personal abnega-
tion. Today the revivalist simply asks the sinners to believe and
the Berlin Wall will come down; television will abjure violence;
the Chinese Communists will become missionaries; and anxiety
will only be another name for a headache. Today the secretaries
do not have to forswear sin with commercial men, nor does the
advertising salesman have to abjure beating his wife. Redemp-
tion is a tranquilizing experience. There is no longer a conflict between body and spirit.

Baptists, Methodists, even Presbyterians who rose in the world
might have joined the Episcopal Church, which throughout the
South has always been the aristocrat's church. But material wealth
is so much more eagerly come by since 1940 that many of the
Methodists, Baptists, and Presbyterians have turned their own
churches into an Episcopal church, insisting on a much more
formal religious service, on more elaborate vestments for their
clergymen, on a more imposing edifice for their place of worship.
They leave the Elm Street Baptist Church and organize a new
congregation with the world "Park" or "Heaven" in it.

The middle-class parishioners remade their church in their
own image. One consequence of their efforts has been to rob
the minister of his authority. He no longer makes more money
than members of his congregation. He makes less. He no longer
accounts to the officers for a charity financed by men of great
wealth. He accounts to fuel oil distributors who were once
mechanics and to contractors who were once carpenters.

As the middle class proliferated, its need for self-expression
also grew. Lacking the talent or inclination for politics, traditionally the province of the rich man's ambition, the well-off
layman found that he could fulfill his hunger for expression by
managing his church. He gave the church money, then formed
a church committee to decide how to spend it. Eventually, too,
this committee began to oversee the content of the Sunday
sermon. As a result, the Protestant Church throughout the South
was rarely the champion of the unpopular cause, not even the
unpopular cause remote from the racial crucible. The Church

conforms in almost all respects to prevailing beliefs of the over-powering majority.

All the candidates in the South proclaim their belief in reli-gion—Christian religion, they call it. In all political advertise-ments the candidate's most important boast is that "he is an elder of the Second Presbyterian Church" or "he had been a member of the First Baptist Church for forty-three years." "He teaches a Sunday school class" is the most effective of all.

But in the South religion does not instruct the middle class; the middle class instructs religion. The new uses to which people put religion are manifold. Mr. W. W. Taylor, a former member of the North Carolina House of Representatives, appeared before a legislative committee in March, 1959. He came as a representative of small businessmen who opposed passage of a seventy-five-cent minimum wage law for the state. Said Mr. Taylor, "Jesus Christ would be out of place if He returned to earth where employers were told what they could pay their em-ployees." Clearly he implied that Jesus would have opposed the minimum wage of seventy-five cents an hour.

And up in Kannapolis a clergyman was fired because during a Sunday sermon he used the sentence, "The wages of sin is death." The big giver called him in and said, "Why are you talking about wages? I have a union election coming up in my plant."

If anything, the dilemma of the Jewish clergy in the South is more excruciating than that of the Protestant. Where some Protestant clergymen definitely believe in what they say, pro or contra, and say it, the rabbi is frustrated. It is, without quali-fication, impossible to find a rabbi who does not hold segrega-tion in contempt and does not hold in contempt those of his congregation who insist on his silence.

The Jew missed an opportunity, an opportunity to give the sort of help he himself has had to ask all through these long centuries. The Jew missed this opportunity not because he lacked sympathy for the Negro and his cause, but because the Jew feared his own security depended upon conforming to the habits and the prejudices of the surrounding society. Like their Protestant counterparts, the Jewish middle-class congregants told their clergymen, "Stick to religion." While Protestants imposed the silence on their clergy because they feared the Negro, Jews imposed a silence on their rabbis because they feared the white Protestants. Only the Negro was without fear, and the Negro was more threatened and deprived than whites, Jew or Protestant.

I remember visiting with my rabbi and two officers of my temple one night when I mentioned that a new Jewish family had come to town. The officers whipped out their notebooks and asked his name, the size of his family, his wife's age, and finally, "What does he do?" I said the newcomer was the CIO organizer in the area, and the two officers immediately closed their notebooks and said no more. For all they cared he might just as well have been a grand inquisitor. This anti-union attitude reflects the culture of the local Protestant churches.

In my city they would make Muhammad Ali the mayor tomorrow if somehow we could guarantee them no minimum wage for laundry workers and no collective bargaining contracts.

The Passover

THE FEAST of Passover is probably the only religious holiday which is as old as recorded history itself. Some scholars believe it began as a festival in which the people performed rituals to keep their houses free of disease, sickness, and hunger. When the Hebrews left Egypt, Passover became an agricultural festival.

"And they baked unleavened cakes of the dough which they brought forth out of Egypt, for it was not leavened; because they were thrust out of Egypt, and could not tarry, neither had they prepared for themselves any victual." (Exodus 12:39.)

Every ritual at the Passover Seder is symbolic of the history of the Jews. Next to the plate with the shank of bone is the dish of salt water, beside it a few sprigs of parsley. Each of us dips the parsley into the salt water and tastes it. The parsley is green, the new and happier life out of the tears, freedom out of slavery.

But the whole idea of Passover can be summed up by a toast Jews drink: "Next year in Jerusalem." Jews have drunk this toast for centuries. But the proposal is not a literal one. The toast is another way of expressing the hope that the family will persevere another year, another decade, another century, until all the Jews collect in Jerusalem, as the Bible prophecy goes. "Next year in Jerusalem" is important to Jews because it reminds them that their ancestors were the first people to seek freedom, and in seeking it, the first Jews founded a long history.

There were centuries past when no Jew ever expected to see Jerusalem. What he hoped for when he proposed the toast was that his Bible, his religion, and his freedom would justify him before God.

For the Jews of course Passover means the escape from bondage and slavery and the beginning of a history as a people. What is even more important is that Passover is a family holiday celebrated in the home. On Passover night, 1970, Jews everywhere in every nook and corner of this world, in battle, in camps, in the desert, on land and on sea, will observe the Passover, and at the Seder (Passover meal) they will read the Exodus story in a book called the Haggadah which asks that "in every generation let each man look on himself as if he came forth out of Egypt."

This undiminished vitality the Jews have lent to Christianity and to Western civilization. The Plymouth Bay Colony expressly drew up its constitution on the same principle of Nehemiah after the Jews' return from the Babylonian exile. The Massachusetts Bay Colony also obeyed Moses in framing its laws.

And on the Liberty Bell in Philadelphia is the Passover prayer from Leviticus 25:10: "Proclaim liberty throughout all the land unto all the inhabitants thereof."

Hitler's other war

HITLER FOUGHT two wars. One against Russia, France, England, and the United States, and one against the Jews. The war he fought against the Jews is the war he won. Germany is almost *Judenrein* (Jew-free) today. From a pre-Hitler population of 650,000 Jews, there are hardly any left.

In its way, the war against the Jews was a hard war. It took almost as long to win as the other war took to lose. It has burdened Germany and Germans with a guilt which will last for centuries. It annihilated 6,000,000 innocents.

In Germany today the neo-Nazi Party, called the NPD, is still trying to generate anti-Semitism. Often this party frightens German Jews and German liberals. But the party works against insuperable odds. In the first place, the Bonn government has passed laws against anti-Semitism. In the second place, the Germans do not like constant reminders about their guilt. And in the third place, and most important, there are almost no Jews in Germany. The way to rid the Germans of anti-Semitism, it has been proved, is to rid them of Jews.

The East Germans have succeeded in this. My information comes from Leo Katcher, who wrote *Post Mortem: The Jews in Germany Today*. Like the Nazis, the East Germans are determined to kill Judaism. But they are not going to kill Jews. The Jews can exist if they deny their existence as the Chosen People, if they deny God, if they deny the First Commandment. The Communists want no cantors, no rabbis, no Hebrew teachers. The old and infirm can remain Jews, for the East Germans intend to bury Judaism with them.

In West Germany, the neo-Nazis have become impatient with the ever-continuing trials of war criminals. They are impatient with the pro-Israel attitude of their government. They are anxious to become once again a great nation. The neo-Nazis are constantly serving notice if Germany does not become great, Germany will become Communist.

The automatic identity

IT SHOULD be taken into consideration that the search for identity, the greatest of all human projects, presents a singular advantage to the Jew. The Methodist is a Methodist by reason of his membership in the Methodist Church. If he asks for his letter and takes it to the Baptist Church and asks to be admitted, he is henceforth a Baptist. But the Jew needs no card, letter, or admission. Neither the Gentile world nor his fellow Jews give him a religious test before recognition or identification. His identity is permanent. If he doesn't go to *shule* often or at all, the Gallup fellow would make a mistake to record this as either disloyalty or indifference. Nonsense. Incidentally, this clear-cut, permanent "identity" has obtained for over four thousand years, and yet I never cease to wonder at it with day-to-day fascination. You get out of bed in the morning, and you are already a Jew. You don't have to do another blessed thing.

Yiddish humor

IN YIDDISH humor there are no jokes about honeymoons —Jews did not have honeymoons. There are no jokes about paternity suits or homosexuals, but plenty of jokes about women. The predominant figures in Yiddish humor remain the same: the *schnorrer* (panhandler), the *gvir* (rich man), the *poyer* (peasant), the *poretz* (feudal baron), and of course the *bala-goola* (ignoramus).

A word to the Protestants

IT IS hardly a coincidence that the Protestants initiated the "God is Dead" movement.

Since we Jews found Him originally, we'll keep Him healthy until the Protestants regain their common sense.

Hail to the Swedes

MY FRIENDSHIP with Carl Sandburg made me 100 percent pro-Swede. The Swedes are seafaring men who did not suffer the frustrations of their cousins, the landlocked Germans. The Swedes got around; they met people and had a fine time. Even to this day unusually tall blond boys bob up in the best of families around the world, even in Charlotte, North Carolina, and one must be philosophical and try to understand how the Germans felt left out of things. And the Swedes are workers. A railroad magnate once said, "Give me Swedes, snuff, and whiskey, and I will build a railroad to hell."

Bad news for the Christians

ACCORDING TO a Gallup poll, the Protestants gained 7,500,000 adherents to their fellowships in ten years, and the Jews lost 300,000.

If this trend continues, it will be bad news for the Christian world.

I do not believe Christianity could survive the disappearance of the Jew by more than a decade.

I suspect that is one of the hidden reasons for anti-Semitism across the last two thousand years—the resentment of being so completely dependent upon us. You resent someone you can't do without.

Roll call

A TEACHER in a progressive school announced she would call the roll. She asked that each child rise and express any thought that came to mind. She began:
"John Allen."
"I like to play with my electric train."
"Michael Baker."
"I like summers 'cause then I can go to East Hampton."
"Donald Cohen."
"I pledge a thousand dollars."

Two Jewish mothers

FIRST MOTHER: My son's a homosexual.
Second mother: Dat's nice, where's his office?

PART 9

Duet on Fifth Avenue

The Sabbath is here forever

IF ISRAEL launches a space cap-sool, as we Americans love
to call it, it will go by the name *levonoleh,* which means "little
moon."

While space orbits are complex processes, the Israeli orbits
will be more complex than most. *Der Tag,* one of the morning
papers published in Yiddish in Israel, recently reported the
rabbinical decision regarding the Orthodox astronaut. The American rabbinate sent a series of questions to Rabbi David Chelouche of Jerusalem asking for complete instructions, just in case
the National Aeronautics and Space Administration suits up a
Jew in the near future.

From the horse's mouth came the word: The Orthodox astronaut must observe the Sabbath twice daily. The reasoning behind
this is that the spaceship or "little moon" revolves around the
earth once every one and one-half hours. Crew and passengers
experience a sunrise and a sunset every revolution. Each sunrise
and sunset must be considered a separate day. What else?

Therefore: every sixth and seventh revolution is the Sabbath,
and any mathematician can count there will be two Sabbaths
every twenty-four hours.

Sunrises and sunsets will keep the astronauts busy. But they
will get a break with the moon because its motion will appear
the same to the folks in the capsule as it does to the folks on

earth. While observant astronauts will have to exercise the same piety with the moon's phases, it will take no more time from their maneuvering than it would on earth. They must, of course, bless the new moon. Rabbi Chelouche concluded also that the astronauts must wear the four-cornered *Tzitzeth* whenever the space ship is in natural light.

Nor can the astronaut put aside his daily prayers to fool with the retro-rockets. He must recite them once every twenty-four-hour period. Whenever he reposes for sleep, he must also recite the *Shema* whether it is light or dark outside. And the astronaut should wear his phylacteries only if it is light when he recites his morning prayers.

The British Rabbi Jakubovitz upon reading these requirements remarked: "These questions require further discussion before definitive rulings are made. Meanwhile I would advise every Jew venturing into space to repeat the *Shema* until his safe return to earth."

Some of the rabbis may not take this information with high seriousness. They may complain they have enough trouble finding the observant in one of the temples on earth, let alone worrying about the observant zipping through space. However, it is always wise to provide for all contingencies.

Christian fervor

I SANG the union song "The Mill Was Made of Marble" on Johnny Carson's *Tonight Show* (keeping wonderful pitch as I often do). Joe Glazer wrote this classic, and now I have had a welcome letter from him. He tells me he received letters and good wishes from all over the country. Right now Joe is working for the United States Information Agency in Mexico.

He told me the interesting history of the song "We Shall Overcome," which is pretty well accepted as the theme song of the civil rights movement. Joe thinks he probably made the first recording of this song in 1947, having heard it from Agnes Douty, who in turn had heard it sung by Negro tobacco workers when she was working at the Highlander Folk School in Monteagle, Tennessee. The song is derived directly from the Gospel hymn "I Will Overcome," and Joe says he recorded it under the title "We Will Overcome," but now everyone has made it "Shall." Joe says he heard it sung by the Southern textile workers all over the South, and it was even included in a movie by the unions in the late 1940's.

Most of the labor songs came out of the churches. The hymn "I Shall Not Be Moved" became the militant strikers' song "We Shall Not Be Moved" in the 1930's. "We are Climbing Jacob's Ladder" became "We Are Building a Strong Union" during the Marion, North Carolina, strike in 1929.

A large proportion of American folk music has come from North Carolina, so it is not strange to learn that these same Tarheels turned "Let the Light of the Lighthouse Shine on Me" into "Let the Light of the Union Shine on Me" and "Since I Been Introduced to the House of the Lord" into "I Been Introduced to the CIO."

These union songs, freely borrowed from gospel hymns, always keep the same spirit or fervor, if you will. They inspired the workers, who sang them as ardently as the worshipers.

During the long strike in Henderson, North Carolina, the workers sang two songs every day. One was the famous "Solidarity Forever" and the other "Onward, Christian Soldiers." Interestingly enough, the workers never changed any of the lyrics to "Onward, Christian Soldiers." They sang it just as the choir sings it. The strikers could not see any difference between their cause and the Christian ethic.

Are the jets dinosaurs?

SOME FORTY years ago, to get from New York to Montreal I took a limousine from the hotel out to the airport. The limousine was not a bus, but a touring car so big it accommodated five of us plus the driver. We drove over some bumpy roads to Hasbrouck Heights, which was just outside Newark, New Jersey. It took us roughly half an hour to negotiate this distance, so in the past four decades the superhighways, the tunnels, and the bridges have not appreciably speeded traffic up.

Hasbrouck Heights, of course, has long since given way to Newark Airport, with its mammoth terminals and vast parking lots. In those days, however, the airport was a jerry-built shack with a wind sock flying above it. The runways were grass on which a shiny two-motored airplane stood awaiting the twelve passengers. When the motors started, the whole plane shivered as though in the wake of an Arctic blast.

A single pilot flew the plane. He boarded, said hello to all of us, and disappeared into the forward cabin. He wore a leather jacket, goggles, and a white scarf, and his dungarees were tucked into riding boots.

Over Tarrytown, New York, I noticed one of the wires which strutted the ceiling of the plane had snapped and was in my lap. I knocked on the door, and the pilot beckoned me into the cabin, where I told him about it. He replied he would check it out as soon as we landed.

Two and a half hours later we landed at Albany, New York, and the pilot looped the wire once around the others and then took on some new passengers. Two and a half hours later we were in Montreal. On the way back the wire was still where the ragged pilot had looped it.

Now I fly all the time. Newark, at which I land frequently, no more resembles the old airport at Hasbrouck Heights than the Boeing 707 resembles the old two-motor airplane. There are no more wires to unsnap, and the pilots dress like rear admirals.

The airlines are now flying the new jumbo jets, which carry three hundred to nine hundred passengers per flight. I have asked airline personnel what they anticipate with these mammoth planes, and they all reply they anticipate headaches. What will happen when two jets with five hundred passengers apiece come in at the same time? It will take these one thousand passengers as long to retrieve their luggage tomorrow as it did for me to fly to Hasbrouck Heights yesterday. The runways will be as long as California highways, and the residents in the neighborhood will be permanently deafened litigants.

This situation reminds me of the dinosaur, the poor reptile of gigantic proportions who ruled the earth millions of years ago. The dinosaur went out of business because he grew so big he couldn't manage survival anymore. He sank quickly if grudgingly into the primordial ooze until Sinclair Oil rediscovered his decomposed carcass made aviation fuel. They will use this fuel to grow even bigger reptiles which may also choke themselves with inutility.

The philosophy of protest

JESUS BELONGED to the tradition of Hebrew prophets who established the philosophy of the protest.

When people asked the meaning of the local disturbance—Why the parade? The clutter? Why can't the merchants from Antioch pass with their camels?—the answer was, "Jesus, the Prophet of Nazareth: He's protesting."

Protesters have existed in all countries and at all times.

According to Gibbon, there were protesters in Rome: small groups parading, protesting the war with Carthage.

This idea came into full flower with the Hebrews. The Jewish prophets gave protest a meaning, and this meaning inspired the Christian saints and the Moslem agitators.

The Jewish prophet was an amazing individual. He was crude and thoughtless and showed disregard for everything except his own idea, which was always obsessive. With all of that, when the prophet opened his mouth, he held the people spellbound. It was the Jewish prophet whose thoughts moved in terms of the parable, a literary and religious convention he gave the world. He created the effective idea of accepting his own punishment, which was later adopted by the Christian martyrs, by Gandhi, and by Martin Luther King. Gandhi in his loincloth and King in his business suit went to prison every month, and no one could gauge the attendant outrage. The Jewish prophets invented this gambit. The prophet knew he had little chance in the highly stratified society of the kingdom. An ordinary man making a complaint would have little chance—indeed, he would risk his property and even his life expressing a protest against the existing political structure.

The tyrant was heavily protected in his palace, sitting there levying taxes, thoroughly protected by the outward forms of the religion. So the prophet went into the hills and let his beard grow and let the clothes rot and ate berries and never washed, and after a while he felt he was ready for his protest. He walked through the street with a wild stare in his eye. The people looked at this strange figure and paved the way, and the fellow walked right into the palace, and the guards stood aside because what's there to do with a fellow like that? He stood before the king pointing a bony finger. "You are doing wrong."

The Jewish prophets succeeded in showing up those who used ceremonial law to maintain power. The prophet declared that God did not care for all of these trappings and festivals and sacrifices. "Cease to do evil," said the prophet. "Learn to do good, relieve the oppressed, do not judge the fatherless, plead for the widow."

Letter of introduction

AT SIX-MONTH intervals over several years a pretty young girl would come to my office from one of the distant towns of North Carolina. The girl always carried a letter of introduction, normal enough in itself. The letter was always from the same leading citizen, and he introduced the young lady as one interested in a job as stenographer or as commercial artist or as reporter.

Of course, in all these cases I had no such opening, but I tried to help. I gave the girl a few letters to other people in Charlotte who might be able to consider her. I also questioned her, and once in a while I recommended that she go back to school or take a course in journalism. I wanted to be kind.

Sometimes there would be a visit by a young girl who carried a letter from the leading merchant of the town. It never struck me as unusual that these letters of introduction should come from this one town and why these two men engaged in the project of placing different stenographers, commercial artists, and reporters.

Along about 1962 the last of these girls came to see me with the inevitable letter. Only this girl was a little older than the others, say twenty-eight, and she told me she had been married and divorced and hoped to settle in Charlotte. She wanted to know what the prospects were for a job on a newspaper. This is what she liked, what she thought she could do—reading proofs or correcting copy or editing or going out and getting a story. She had a letter of introduction from the leading citizen.

As I spoke with her for the first time, I gleaned the secret of the letters. This twenty-eight-year-old redhead opened up in such a way that only Balzac or Maupassant could do justice to her story and therefore to the stories of the five or six girls who had preceded her.

This is what she said, very quietly but with passion:

"I did a lot of shopping at Mr. So-and-So's store [the merchant]. And one day I told him about my hopes of coming to Charlotte to get into newspaper work or commercial art. And he said he thought he could help. He would give me a letter to the town's leading citizen, a man who had tremendous influence. I was all for it. But he kept stalling me for three months. Meanwhile, I was getting laid all the time. Finally I said to him, 'I've come across often enough, how about you coming across with the letter?' So he did.

"I took the letter to Mr. So-and-So [the leading citizen], and I thought I was on my way. After all, he'd been a member of Congress, and he had a big law practice with lots of important clients. He said to me, 'I think I can help. I know Harry Golden in Charlotte. He is a world-famous author. I'll mention you the next time I see him, and then I'll give you a letter of introduction.'

"I started to thank him just the way I thanked the merchant. He kept me waiting for the chance to talk to you, which took about three months. Meanwhile, twice a week on his couch I was getting the business again.

"Now I got the letter to you, and I suppose you're going to give me a letter to somebody else important?"

At Cape Kennedy

WATCHING THE blast-off at Cape Kennedy, I met Governor Lester Maddox of Georgia. He told me I didn't understand the Southern way of life. I said those three men in the space ship were getting off for the twenty-first century and he was still living in the eighteenth.

The Southern way of life, whatever it was, can't really have much meaning when we are about to colonize the moon, to my way of thinking, and Lester Maddox presumes me a radical out to destroy happiness and motherhood for motives of simple jealousy. And our differences are a microcosm of the perilous twentieth century. We live in the same time and the same place and from the press section at the cape watch the same awe-inspiring venture, and still we have nothing to say to each other that makes sense.

Alfred Nobel invented dynamite, which he thought would help twentieth-century man make this planet more inhabitable, more accessible. When instead dynamite made men only more warlike, he bequeathed his fortune to establish the Nobel Prizes. We have spent billions to put astronauts on the moon in the hope that this is the first step to taming the universe. Yet one of the refrains I heard at Kennedy was that the next war will be won by the side which best exploits and controls outer space. What prize will compensate for that?

I saw the blast-off, as did 25,000,000 others. It was Jules Verne come to life. As a boy I read every word Jules Verne ever wrote. Jules Verne was my idea of imagination at its height, its full powers exercised. Here was a spaceship bound for outer space, people in every remote corner of this globe able to watch its ascent.

Yet there might be something about the scene Jules Verne would not comprehend. Jules Verne's world was a stable world, or at least the world of his imagination was stable. It wasn't rent by hunger in Africa, inequities in the United States, tyranny in Russia. Touring the world in eighty days meant a man needed access to the Middle East and to the Orient. There are many of us who have a better chance of walking to the moon than of ever seeing Cairo or Peking.

Senator Richard Russell has voiced the hope that if we are doomed virtually to destroy the planet, he hopes what few survivors are left will be American citizens. Why someone would wish this upon Americans I have no idea.

These are the sobering thoughts I think we should entertain as men open up the door of the twenty-first century. If we are sending men upstairs to help obliterate ourselves, save a precious few who will be able to remember the Pledge of Allegiance, then I say the sooner the better. If we are sending them upstairs and declaring a holiday to take the populace's mind off hunger, inequity, and oppression, then we had better study history. Bread and circuses didn't work for the Romans, and they had a smaller world to manipulate.

If saying, "Jules Verne, we are here," is at least a promise that the conquest of space may help Earth, possibly we have spent the money wisely. The thrill of the matter will be meaningful.

Duet on Fifth Avenue

MANY YEARS ago in a stray paragraph I wrote that the taxi drivers are all hanging jurists. I didn't mean only taxi drivers hang defendants, I simply meant that the workingman is not the paradigmatic example of mercy in the twentieth century. I should have said the buttonhole sewers, and I would have saved myself a lot of trouble. Because once the phrase escaped my pen, the taxi drivers' newsletter picked it up, and I have been lectured ever since by taxi drivers in New York City.

I have traveled from the Algonquin to the East Side terminal and departed my cab washed by a profound shame at my inadvertency. Sometimes I even prefer to walk rather than hear again an account of how I have abused and maligned one of God's noblest professions.

But the dark days may be over. The last time I was in New York and hailed a cab, the driver looked me over and, watching my reaction in his rearview mirror, began to sing:

"*Ich bin* a boarder by *mein veib.*"

He asked me if I remembered the words, and I said sure, and we joined in a duet down Fifth Avenue. "*Ich bin* a boarder by *mein veib*" is an old Yiddish song that was a vaudeville favorite on the Lower East Side. It recounts the loneliness of a man who, upon getting a divorce from his wife, finds there is absolutely nothing to do. He lives in a rooming house with strangers who never speak to him. He is always broke because his alimony is high. So one day he proposes to his wife that she take him back into their old apartment as a boarder. She will get his rent and he will have the surroundings that are familiar. She does.

The verses get a little lustier after this, for the boarder confesses he never had it so good.

I asked the taxi driver if he had been on the *Ed Sullivan Show*, and he replied, "No yet." As we pulled up to my destination on Sixth Avenue in Greenwich Village, he started to sing an old Jewish favorite: "Off'n *Pripachuck brent* a fire'l."

This song enjoins the young Jewish boy to study his Talmud. In English it would conclude:

> When you are grown older,
> Oh, my little ones,
> You will one day know
> All the tender love and all the burning hope
> That in these letters glow.

I am sorry I said the taxi drivers were hanging jurists. No, they are not. They are a resounding chorus of joy cruising the Empire City.

The German nudists

THE TROUBLE with this world is that there is room in it for two senior partners but not three. The trouble with the Germans is they have always wanted to be the third senior partner. They are at it again, this time setting the French and the Swiss at odds. The Swiss Lovers of Light and Sun, a respectable nudist colony whose members neither smoke, drink, nor have outdoor barbecues, are in competition with the French outfit which, though nudist, is like most things Gallic—dedicated to the carefree life.

The German nudists form a significant segment of the Swiss

nudist colony, but they have deserted the Lovers of Light and Sun and are moving by the hundreds into the French camps.

The result is now that Europe has German-Swiss nudist colonies and German-French nudist colonies.

The European nudist colonies are an armed camp, needing only an Agadir or a Sarajevo to touch the fuse off.

Ireland and Iran

IRELAND AND Iran are separated by a significant geographical distance. Their climates are diverse. Their languages bear no similarities. Their industries are unrelated. Their political systems are as different as can be. Their gods are different gods. They probably never think about each other. But they should. They have a common problem. The marriage rate is low.

Irishmen and Iranians do not get married because they put such a high value on their women.

The dowry is as much a part of Irish tradition as the Church or revolution. A penniless woman is a spinster. That's the long and the short of it. And there are a lot of penniless women and consequently a lot of young buckos wasting the best years of night and life in pubs. True love conquers time, space, and the neuroses, but there are some obstacles too formidable for it to surmount.

Precisely the opposite tradition prevails in Iran. If the Irish husband is the most expensive on earth, the Iranian girl is the dearest bride. The young Iranian is expected to buy his precious object several rings, bracelets, and necklaces of precious stones. Then he has to outfit the bride. He has to pay for the wedding banquet and, alas, provide her mother with gifts equally as beautiful as those he gave the daughter. It is easy to see what happens when money enters into the marital equation. Not only does the monetary equation result in low birth rates, but the marriage clerks are living in disaster areas.

In Ireland the priests keep repeating Paul's exhortation: "It is better to marry than to burn!" In Iran the government is considering a law to make marriage compulsory. The law would prohibit an employer's hiring any man unable to produce a marriage certificate.

Both Iranian and Irish girls are noted for beauty and fidelity. There aren't better girls in the world to put up storm windows for. But I doubt you can change Benedicts by law. If the Irish Parliament passed a law prohibiting bachelors from entering pubs and the Iranians pass their law prohibiting employment to single fellows, why, Ireland will become a nation of teetotalers, and widespread indolence will afflict Iran.

America solved the marriage problem by making divorce easy. While our divorce rate is scandalous, it is still surprising the number of folks willing to try marriage over and over again. That's a step in the right direction. Convince a young man or woman the money doesn't commit them for life. Or the Irish could devalue their pound and the Iranians could up it. Or the other way around, I'm not sure.

Getting controversial

THERE'S AN old theater expression that tragedy is what closes Saturday night, while comedy is a serious business. Probably nothing is harder to write than humor. But you know when you succeed with it in the same way a poet knows when he succeeds with a rhyme. It is much harder to determine when you are and when you are not being controversial.

Almost all the major magazines have an Outspoken Corner or Get-Me-Mad Page. Editors ask writers to take some very positive attitudes about the issues of the day. From time to time I get my turn at bat. As often as that happens, I go mad trying to dream up some issue about which I think people ought to have opinions.

"Listen," I suggest, "how about an article on the disgraceful way we Americans treat the elderly?"

"Naw," says the editor. "People don't really get worked up about old folks. Everyone knows they're always grumpy. Whatever happens serves them right."

"I happen to be old myself," I retort.

"That's what I mean," says the editor.

Eventually I address myself to the failure of the public school system. It has signally failed to instill a sense either of equity or of discipline in the children. Nor are the children literate. I research the problem thoroughly. I find the folks couldn't care less about the New Math. What the hell, by the time the kid grows up, adding machines and computers will be a dime a dozen. What the parents really demand of the school system is that the dietician publish the cafeteria menu for the whole week. That way Junior can take the money if he likes what they're serving or his sandwiches and orange if he doesn't.

"I could have told you that," says my editor. "What we need, Golden, is a real think piece on what to do about year-round game poachers."

"What do I know about hunting?" I ask. "How about politics?"

"Too soon before election."

"Why Lyndon B. Johnson is the greatest President of the twentieth century?"

"Wait a minute, pal," he says. "We got advertisers."

Modestly I offer that my fame rests on my ability to analyze the race issue. I find the magazine did that controversial subject *last* month. I rack my brains. Maybe I could offer that we encourage nudity in the movies. *Playboy* magazine has beaten us to it. Discourage nudity in the movies? My heart isn't in it.

I ask, "Is *Is Shoveling Snow Better Than Mowing Grass?* a suitable subject?"

"My friend," says the editor, "you are cooking with gas."

"And you too went to school a long time ago," I say.

1917

I AM convinced that one of the great events, probably the greatest event, of the twentieth century was the Bolshevik Revolution. I say this because fifty-three years ago Russia was a country populated largely by illiterates. I am not arguing that the Russians could not have made the same advances if the revolutionaries of 1917 had opted for democracy. They could. I am arguing that Russia would still be largely a nation of illiterates if there had been no revolution. Indeed, Russia has paid dearly for its scientific progress. It took the mechanical Soviets fifty years to produce a poet like Yevtushenko where once Czarist Russia could boast such writers as Tolstoy, Dostoievsky, Chekhov, Gogol. No composer growing up in the Soviet has ever begun to compare with Moussorgsky, Rimsky-Korsakov, Borodin, or Tchaikovsky.

Ironically, our election day in 1967 fell on the fiftieth anniversary of the November Revolution, the day the Bolsheviks took over Russia.

Both countries have come a long way. In November, 1917, the British and French generals were annoyed at Woodrow Wilson for his insisting that he was sending an American army to the front, not replacements for decimated British and French divisions. Pershing made it stick, too. In November, 1917, the Russian Army was literally unable to continue the war against Germany. The Germans could have taken any Russian city they chose; to concentrate their troops against the Allies they let Lenin make peace with them.

In the 1930's America and the West suffered through the ravages of the Great Depression, to which Russia contributed, as Professor Sidney Hook argues, because the Communists withdrew from the world market and left a dead spot. Russia suffered through the same depression compounded by a famine, and in addition Stalin initiated the purges, which took thousands upon thousands of lives. Indiscriminately the Russian dictator struck down peasant and general, patriot and skeptic, for reasons which elude not only historians but Stalin's own daughter.

Think of the slogans the world has believed since then. Lenin, wrestling for power, kept promising "all power to the Soviets," knowing in his heart he intended a rigid dictatorship. Americans went to war to make the world safe for democracy and to guarantee a war to end wars. The curious thing is that so many people believed. The Russians had a five-year plan, and we had a New Deal. Without the five-year plans Russia probably wouldn't have defeated Germany, and without the New Deal neither would we. But Russian life remains gloomy, Russian cities are cold and forbidding, and the folks wait in line for two days to buy the simplest of consumer goods. We, the most affluent people in the world, have spent summers watching in utter fascination as one by one our cities have exploded with the riots of the poor and marginal.

Fifty-three years ago there was room in this world for two senior partners but not for three—so Britain and France told Germany. Today there is still room for only two senior partners —so we keep telling China.

Which leads me to expect that the next greatest event of the twentieth century was the independence of India. If India had not achieved her own independence, neither would Africa, and neither would a score of new nations have emerged peacefully. It is true that India today is racked by famine and overpopulation. But it is also possible that India will solve these severe afflictions. Should she, then that independence, India's presence on the world scene, will perhaps prove more significant than Russia's.

Certainly the emergence of Israel as a nation will figure prominently among the great events. This is no chauvinism on my part, although I have always subscribed to the notion there is no ism like chauvinism. Israel is a great event because she is the first nation to emerge from what the United States State Department categorizes as Underdevelopia and produce what within this generation will prove a viable economy. The point is if she can do it, everybody can—the Congo, Southeast Asia, literally everybody. The trend throughout the world for the last century has been urban growth. People abandon the land for the city factories. Israel reversed this. In Israel an essentially urban people is wresting a livelihood from the land. Israel managed this by the invention of the kibbutz, the communal farm. There are areas of this world where the kibbutz will prove more valuable than electricity.

Last, I shall say that Franklin D. Roosevelt's New Deal is of monumental importance. The implementation of the New Deal literally saved the world's largest and most powerful democracy. It is hard to imagine that America would have remained either a capitalistic society or a democratic one without the New Deal reforms. Realize now that Medicare and civil rights are really the last tying together of these reforms. Throughout our history we have been a "bridge" nation. We became the first republic in 1789, and there is every chance that by 1989 we will be the bridge nation between the have-not nations and the haves, between the white race and the colored races (we are now the nation with the second largest Negro population in the world). If we do achieve this, it will be by the legislative and social programs we are able to improvise from the original New Deal reforms.

The English

THE ENGLISH are a race which has lived three thousand years in the rain. This sort of habitat makes them cold and reserved and formal but often intemperate, their wisdom at bottom nothing more than sheer, outrageous courage.

Hope for the future

My HOPE as a liberal is that someday there will be no such thing as a pool of unemployed, that someday the future will look back on us with the same awe and bewilderment for allowing such cruelty as unemployment with which we look back on the Middle Ages for its cruelty in burning witches.

PART 10

More Complaints and Free Advice

One lifetime's progress

AMERICA IS better than ever. This country is going to the dogs, people will grumble, but things are not bad at all. They are much better than when I was a boy.

The greatest development in the sixty-seven years of my life has been sanitation. When I was a boy, the alleys were filled with refuse and filth, and the dead horses were left on the ground for days with insects swarming over them. The development of sanitation during these sixty-seven years has been phenomenal to the point where we are all living enclosed in cellophane. When I was a boy the life expectancy of the American male was forty-seven years. Today it is seventy years.

Then we come to education, where we have realized the dream of Horace Mann that America must educate the entire mass of the population. The community colleges multiplying all over the country are the most singular development in this process. They take everybody at no cost, and you learn at your own pace.

Next in development is medicine and pharmacology. When I was a boy, during the influenza epidemic all you could do was hang a piece of camphor around your neck to ward off the Evil Eye. The wonder drugs have enhanced life and productivity. Infant mortality is down to almost nothing. Tuberculosis, which was endemic when I was a boy, has been cured. Social security and pension benefits are making life much better for all the people.

All we need now is to find some balance between the wonders of technology and humanity. But it will come as sure as anything. We are a nation of laws and not of men, and it shall come.

This is a good country, the greatest experiment in freedom ever known on this earth.

The plague

IT IS beyond belief that more people will die in traffic and swimming accidents over a three-day holiday than will be killed in Vietnam in a month.

Whether it happens because of speed, mechanical failure, dangerous highways, or fate, it will continue because no one can digest the statistics and realize the carnage.

I urge responsible legislators in each of the fifty states to introduce resolutions which would revise the present calendar so that there would be no three-day holidays in spring, summer, or fall. Independence Day can fall on July 3, 4, or 5, as long as one of those days is a Wednesday. Labor Day doesn't have to be a Monday. It, too, can be a Wednesday, the first Wednesday in September.

State policemen, driving experts, governors, and safety authorities have spent a generation warning motorists, with absolutely no effect. On a three-day weekend we are out to decimate ourselves.

Just as we try to stop the potential suicide from his grave wrong, so we should stop the heedless from endangering themselves and others.

Over a holiday, the tolls on the highway should be trebled, quadrupled if necessary. Every red light should operate for four uninterrupted minutes. If we can close liquor stores on a legal holiday, why can we not close highways?

The most complex set of rules has been devised to guide welfare workers in the administration of payments to the indigent and needy. I urge that we devise the same sort of complexity to keep motorists off the roads. Let us insist on holidays a motorist needs a passport to traverse the distance between cities. We will have to dig into the federal kitty to pay off the motel owners and concessionaires who depend on legal holidays, but the savings we will gain in lives, in sparing doctors and police, will more than offset this expense.

Apparently all those songs, homilies, and bromides about the American home are a collection of myths. Home is where the folks don't want to be. We shall have to jazz up the neighborhood with more parades, clambakes, charity balls, and, if need be, topless waitresses in the local restaurants. We must implement a variety of programs to keep the folks to home, as we say down heah.

One case of bubonic plague would marshal an entire city, a state, the federal government. Our accident rate on the highways is no less a plague. We cannot sit by and let the disease spread. The trouble with this plague is that there is no antitoxin. The only effective warning is the sound of metal crumbling.

Secrets of the ice box

THEY SAY that CIA operatives look through wastepaper baskets to discover important security secrets, even infrared photography. Out in the suburbs they say you can tell everything about your neighbors by rummaging through the garbage, and intellectuals have always insisted everything you want to know about a man is revealed by his library.

I claim you can tell everything by examining the ice box. If you see a lot of Clapp's baby food, you know there is either a new baby in the house or an elderly parent with no teeth.

Several toupees in the ice box mean you are in the home of an aging male dress designer or interior decorator. Orange juice in one of those waxed cardboard containers indicates a health fanatic who believes this orange juice is more healthful than frozen or canned juice. If you find nail polish and lipsticks, you are probably looking at an ice box which belongs to a lady of easy virtue. I get this information from a friend who strayed from family hearth and fidelity only once and then only during the war. He says all ladies of joy keep cosmetics in the ice box, which explains the rather curious food they often serve their clientele. He himself, he confesses, had to sup on some canned meatballs in gravy that resembled molten plastic. The experience has since kept him on the straight and narrow path, and I say amen to that.

If you have a terrible hangover when you wake up and you don't know where you are and find halvah in the refrigerator, then you are in California, which is how they store the precious candy out there. If it seems the ice box is filled with tiny bananas and oranges and apples, you are not in the home of midgets. You are still in California, because the Christmas gift boxes of marzipan are mailed out from New York in the shape of little fruits, and Californians also store marzipan in the ice box.

And the FBI reports that there is no better security risk than the bachelor whose ice box is completely filled with local beer.

Our corporate profits

EVERYBODY talked about President Kennedy's action in settling the steel crisis. When the President, using the powers conferred upon him by the Constitution, forced steel to back down on its price rise, the *Wall Street Journal* said this was Government by Fear. James Reston in the *Times* worried about the President's initiative, too. Roger Blough, who was a momentary villain, became, if not a popular, at least a technical underdog.

What nobody said, because they didn't want to believe it, is that this is the way it is going to be. The years since the

Kennedy incident have convinced me more than ever that this country will have to move into some sort of profit and wage rationing to prevent inflation. I believe it will be properly legislated, and I believe it will make more people unhappy than income taxes ever thought of doing.

I neither urge nor condemn this innovation. I am simply projecting it. The idea of drafting men into military service was a heretical idea until the Civil War.

During World War II the country voluntarily undertook rationing and price and wage stabilization on a *pro tem* basis. The day will come when the country will accept it as the stabilizing factor in the economy.

Of course, I admit this is a dangerous prophecy. Nothing affects tempers like talking about money. Liz Taylor and Richard Burton, I believe, made the front pages as part of a gigantic conspiracy to keep the country's mind off the falling stock prices in the rear of the newspapers. But there are two things we ought to consider: One, profits will be still profits whether the government legislates the percentage of profits a corporation or an individual can realize or not. As long as there are profits, I don't think there's any appreciable change in a capitalistic economy. Two, we are often guilty of allowing a historical configuration to color everything we plan to do in America. That there once was an Old South in 1860 was advanced as a sufficient reason for segregating American citizens in the 1960's. Because small corporations thrived during 1860 was advanced as the reason monopolistic and gigantic corporations had to continue to thrive unrestrained in the 1960's.

We must remember that most law is based on man's responsibility to his society, but just as much has been legislated because man and corporations by nature are irresponsible.

Whither the diner?

THE FIRST time I ever saw a paper napkin I was in one of the old-fashioned diners which resembled a railroad car with entrances at both ends. There was a long counter which stretched the length of the place, and the clientele sat on stools whose seats twirled. The old-fashioned diner was an ever-ready place for the man who wanted a quick lunch or cheap dinner. All the cooks were short-order cooks and all the gravies very thick.

I wonder what happened to these diners. They were on every street corner in the 1930's and 1940's. Now there is hardly one to be found. I wouldn't complain about their disappearance if the drive-in restaurants were an improvement, but most of the drive-in restaurants represent dining at its entropy.

What made the diner attractive was that the customer on his stool could see all the food prepared before his eyes. Lined along the wall were an electric range and a griddle, a gigantic refrigerator, the pit for the deep fry, the cutting boards, and the other paraphernalia which lent a minimal comfort to the hungry. I can still see the exceptionally sturdy water glasses the waiter would set before you as soon as you entered.

These old diners used to encourage a certain camaraderie lacking in the drugstore restaurants and the pizza palaces today. There is little joviality exchanged over a constantly wiped plastic table. First of all, the food these days is all prepackaged and precooked, and one never sees a piece of raw meat or a basket of raw vegetables. Most of the sandwiches dished out are some sort of salad—chicken salad, turkey salad, egg salad—all of them, I suppose, coming from the same case lot of tuna fish.

Admittedly, the diner was hardly a culinary treat. The short-order cooks could make an appetite vanish if they chose, but you always saw what you were getting, and you made your complaints directly and personally, not through channels.

At the beginning of the war I used to talk to a counterman

daily about life, love, and food. He had a real flair, this fellow. He was quite proud of his advertising on the back of his matchbooks: "It's smart to eat in a diner." He spent a frenzied week after Pearl Harbor composing a song, the title of which was, "You Have Liberty in Your Hand—Now Hold It." He was sure it was going to return him a fortune. He sang it often for the benefit of his clientele, but I never remembered hearing it on the Hit Parade.

Eventually he sold his diner and small back lot to a developer who squeezed thirty-eight houses into the space. Neither the counterman nor the developer needed hit songs after that. Maybe thus the way of all diners.

The electric toothbrush

I HAVE ventured that the three greatest inventions of the twentieth century are movies, Scotch Tape, and the eight-hour day. We cannot really understand how movies, Scotch Tape, and the eight-hour day have improved the quality of life until we see how the three most useless inventions of the twentieth century did absolutely nothing.

It is hard to see how anything can beat the electric toothbrush for sheer inutility. Not everyone subscribes to the notion that we all need a toothbrush. Carl Sandburg used to gargle with a mouthwash every morning, and at eighty-eight he still had every tooth in his head. I will not, however, condemn the innocent toothbrush. Children dote on them, and anyway I believe it was invented several centuries ago. If nothing else, the toothbrush serves a cosmetic desire. But the electric toothbrush? Was it for this Benjamin Franklin risked electrocution?

Certainly the gossip column is something the twentieth century could have done without. While it has made some gossips rich and helped some newspapers increase circulation, its intrinsic value is a big zero. Most of us have minds cluttered by minutiae, and the gossip column only compounds the clutter.

The devoted newspaper reader is your average sports fan. Spare him no detail no matter how insignificant, but no sports editor has ever included a gossip column on his pages. Ball fans are interested not in a first baseman's marital problems but in his batting average.

Last but not least in the useless sweepstakes is eggplant Parmigiana. It is a hard word to spell and a harder dish to enjoy. I have maintained before and maintain now that eggplant is the signal mark of the bad cook. Eggplant is a felon of the cuisine. It has probably ruined more pleasant get-togethers than photograph albums. The eggplant was originally cultivated for opera lovers who armed themselves with the fruit to throw at tenors who sang flat.

Rivaling eggplant Parmigiana in mediocrity, of course, is the eggplant cookbook. That does not legitimately count as an invention but rather as an aberration.

We preserve error

THE LIBRARY has been variously and sentimentally called the storehouse of all knowledge and the treasure-house of the mind. Its real virtue, however, is that as a repository it preserves error as well as truth and nonsense as well as sense.

We know a great deal about the Egyptians, not only because the pyramids are preserved with their hieroglyphics but because they preserved their speculations about the astronomical system. We call it the Ptolemaic system. It is the system which insists the sun goes around the earth. We know the Egyptians took the immediate evidence of their senses, which by and large stands most people in good stead.

But guiding life by the senses is a matter of habit. The habit of one generation is often the folly of the next. This is so in science, theology, philosophy, and politics.

There is, to be sure, a large amount of innate knowledge in all of us, including animals. Who taught the ant to bite every grain of corn carried to the ant hill so that it will not take root and grow? The biting of each grain of corn represents the ant's instinct for self-preservation. Only man, however, has developed his instincts beyond the bare intelligence he needs for survival.

It is the library which celebrates this advance.

The Communists find it necessary to obliterate the record of the past. They change their ideology from day to day and in the process change the names of streets and whole cities to rectify the mistakes encountered along their historical pathways.

It is only by recording error that we take some pains to insure it will not occur again. The greatness of the United States is that we preserve error and do not fear the past.

On inanimate objects

I DON'T know who coined the phrase about the perversity of inanimate objects, but it is certainly one of the most descriptive in the English language. It is a shame that there are so many machines and conveniences and comforts, all so complex. Nothing should be more complex than opening a bottle of bourbon, but alas, everything else is more and more intricate.

When the ice cube tray no longer makes cubes, when the phone is on the blink, when the dictaphone suddenly starts spouting algebra instead of sentences, I find it is enough to reduce a man to a nervous state of hypnotic imbecility. What compounds this whole process is that when the repairman or engineering expert arrives, all he really does is take the thing apart and put it back together. Apparently inanimate objects need love and affection and will receive it only from certain types. In that respect they are much like women, although I am sorry now I brought in the image of the repairmen.

This you call a postal system?

MY FATHER came from the little town of Mikulinca in Galicia, a province in the old Austro-Hungarian Empire, now Poland. For as long as he was in America—until the advent of Hitler—he never lost touch with the relatives he left behind. He wrote them with a punctuality Emily Post would have admired.

When he forgot the addresses, he used to describe the location of the house. "Four streets in from the river, two houses up from the police station." One of the ways I realized there was a relationship between different languages was guessing *Polizei* meant "police." Not one of these letters ever went astray. Nor did either my father or his correspondents suspect they ever would. Mail has a sanctity everyone adores.

Veteran postal workers remember when Italian immigrants used to send home gold. These workmen used to purchase gold dust or ingots. The weight and destination revealed the contents. The Italians sent gold to Genoa or Palermo, where it was banked for retirement. I suspect Mussolini put a fast end to these dreams, though these packages unfailingly reached their destination.

But now I read in this age of jets and superservice we are not to get properly addressed, innocent letters and bills. Congress is balking at appropriations, and during recent years some small stations have closed and some deliveries have been curtailed.

This government will subsidize everything except the letter. Frenchmen enjoy four deliveries a day. Not to get the daily mail is inconceivable to a Rumanian. Disturbed cynics the world over write to the editor or the deputy or the commissar. Getting a letter is a kind of minor Christmas for the folks. It is true that bills come in the mail, but the really bad news invariably reaches us through the telephone and telegraph.

The tragic aspect to the whole situation can be summed up

by reminding the constituency that some of the towns scheduled to surrender their post offices were Adamant, Vermont; New Russia, New York; Seven Mills Ford, Virginia; and Ninepoints, Pennsylvania. Just think of the postmarks that have surprised and delighted people over the years from those romantic places.

I miss the scissors man

THERE WAS a fellow who used to come around twice a year to sharpen scissors. He drove an old bus which he had converted into a workshop. There were grinding stones and pliers and screw drivers and all the apparatus a scissors sharpener could use. On the outside of his bus, hand-painted, was the legend "Scissors, knives, clippers sharpened."

One of us from the office always collected all the scissors and letter openers and went out and waited our turn.

I don't see him anymore. I guess we haven't seen him in several years. In fact, I wonder who does sharpen scissors anymore. Getting the scissors sharpened is hardly the *raison d'être* of a day. At best, it's an afterthought. But our scissors sharpener is gone, and while it would be fatuous to say I miss him—for I doubt I ever talked to him save to ask how much I owed—I wonder what happened to the man who used to come around.

One fellow who came around wore a handlebar moustache. He sold horseradish, homemade horseradish. I always bought a couple of bottles. Until I met him, I had no idea where horseradish came from. But he told me he made it from a root which grows in swamps. Horseradish, like sharpened scissors, is hardly a necessity of modern living, but on the occasions when I had some guests in for short ribs, that homemade horseradish was at least a conversation piece.

Thirty or forty years ago, I remember, we bought eggs from a candler who came around twice a week. Everyone in the neighborhood usually had a standing order for one dozen eggs a week or whatever number he needed. Once every three months he toted up the bill.

Twenty years ago there were still bakeries which dispatched whole fleets of trucks with fresh bread and doughnuts and pastries. Now all the bread comes off supermarket shelves wrapped in layers of waxed paper and plastic. Jewish rye bread is the only bread that comes unwrapped, but in Charlotte you can only buy it at Leo's Delicatessen.

I started business in Charlotte at the tail end of the Depression. There was always a hobo who stopped and asked if there was an odd job or two he could do in exchange for a meal and some money to get on to the next town. To have the rain gutters cleaned now I have to call a contractor who will not deign to consider cleaning the rain gutters unless I also commission him to put a new gable on the roof.

When scissors are dull, an office manager chucks them out and buys new ones. Our society has no time for small chores.

Eggs from a butter and egg man are not much different from those shipped in every day from Eggville, USA, out on Route 7. The disappearance of these men I suppose makes little difference. What worries me, however, is how many other kinds of men have disappeared with them?

Absolute democracy

THERE ARE four of us at luncheon, all of us drinking friends, and our conversation is animated by a discussion of the local school system. All of us are parents, which of course gives us some authority, and two of us have been career teachers. Apropos of nothing, I suppose, I offered the observation, "We all know kindergarten teachers are stealing the money."

At which point the waiter interrupts: "Wait a minute! My wife is a kindergarten teacher." We are effectively cowed and are apologetic enough to suffer the waiter's evaluation that kindergarten is the most important step for a child in the educative process.

Such sheep!

We are sheep because we subscribe all too superficially to the principle that all men are created equal. We are such absolute democrats we let the waiter lecture us. We may or may not be right about kindergarten teachers, but what right does a waiter have to interrupt us just because he's married? Not one of us had the guts to say, "Please, please. Enough talk. I'm waiting for my Bloody Mary."

At the other extreme are the militant college students who presume to dictate to the faculty and the administration who shall and who shall not set foot upon the campus. It is hard to believe that every demonstration on a college campus is motivated by antiwar sentiment. At Berkeley apparently one of the privileges college students wanted was the right to shout obscenities.

No, some of the demonstrations seem to me democracy at its entropy. Which is to say if you have the numbers, you throw your weight around as a majority and get your own way. But no majority should have its own way by virtue of its majority. It is for that reason we have checks and balances written into the Constitution. Left to their own devices, the collegians would elect Bob Dylan President and Joan Baez Secretary of State.

Not long ago I watched Eric Hoffer spell out his views to Eric Sevareid on a nationally broadcast television program. Hoffer is a unique thinker. What momentarily dismayed me about the presentation was the narrator's insistence over and over again that Hoffer was a longshoreman. Mr. Hoffer has some penetrating insights about the mechanics of mass movements, but he doesn't have them because he is a longshoreman. If the equation worked, the audience would be better off listening to one of the Mafia Anastasias who control the New York docks or to Harry Bridges, both of whom are more interesting longshoremen than Hoffer. That either of these two men will appear seems a remote possibility. But Hoffer's audience was beguiled by the notion that he was a workingman. For some reason Americans firmly believe the workingman is not only the paradigmatic democrat but that the workingman has all the answers to the unsettling problems of the world.

Expertise and experience are values too sophisticated for us to honor.

Key to a good restaurant

I HAD luncheon the other day at a restaurant which had the folks waiting in crowded lines to get at the food. Any restaurant for whose convenience diners will tolerate inconvenience and delay is sure to serve good food.

The restaurant was the New York Exchange, which I believe is part of the nationwide complex of Woman's Exchange clubs. There wasn't a man in the jammed dining room save in my party. The place was absolutely chock full of dowagers. And rich dowagers at that. In fact, if a bomb dropped on the Woman's Exchange building at noontime, probably millions upon millions of dollars would straightaway escheat to the state.

It is probably the only restaurant over whose tables no dirty joke has ever been bandied.

I was in New York working on a book and was accompanied by a photographer, Jay Maisel, and his assistant, Pete Lerner. We were wining and dining Mr. Harvey Orkin, theatrical agent extraordinaire. Harvey had offered his help so we could write and take pictures of the New York theater. It was he who steered us to the Woman's Exchange because it was near his office. I don't know whether the hostess whisked us by the dowagers because Harvey is so celebrated a patron or whether she figured four men mean a lot more action on the tipping, but we all exulted in the preference.

They had lentil soup, roast pork, and salad, and I had corned beef hash and coleslaw. It came to roughly ten dollars. It would be cheaper to feed a growing family at the Woman's Exchange than cart back and forth to the supermarket sales.

What made the lunch memorable was that experience provided me with a formula for detecting a good restaurant.

Carl Sandburg taught me never to eat in a restaurant not light enough to read the newspaper.

A. J. Liebling advised to trust the prices and the food of any restaurant in which two priests dine together.

And I say if you see a line of rich dowagers waiting to get at the food, get at the end of it.

Getting organized

IN HIS novel *The Cat's Pajamas and Witch's Milk*, Peter De Vries has a hero named Tattersall who writes letters to himself. I always read a De Vries novel from start to finish the same night because he writes about men who have passed the point of quiet desperation and have exploded into noisy disorganization. This time I put the book down.

Writing yourself a letter, I thought. What a marvelous way to get organized next week. My best plans for getting organized usually come to me about noon Monday when it is too late to put them into practice for *this* week. It is as self-defeating to come upon the strategy for organization at mid-Monday as it is to find the resolve for a diet late Friday afternoon.

Disorganization plagues modern man as the Furies plagued Orestes. As soon as a reasonable schedule is laid out, the pipes will freeze, which necessitates putting everything aside in order to importune plumbers.

A Cook's Tour through Europe is perfect organization except that it doesn't lead to accomplishment. I find little trouble in organizing a vacation but a great deal in getting the work out. Writing myself a letter not to take a vacation may be a great help.

I envy politicians who are always the product of organization. Richard Nixon is our President by virtue of his organizational and administrative skills. I got out a newspaper for twenty years only by virtue of a printer who always reminded me my deadline was two days away. Then I would work all day and night to get sufficient copy to him so I could publish on the dates I promised the United States Post Office I would. It might seem the man who writes books is superbly organized, but do not forget behind every writer is a gang of editors and publishers politely but constantly inquiring, "What's with the book?"

One of my sons wrote himself reminders every night before he went to sleep. He was as punctual about this as other children were about prayers. His notes would say: "Do not forget to get up. Wash. Comb hair. Put on suit. Eat breakfast. Buy newspaper. Go to work." These nocturnal injunctions helped him work his way through a PhD. His internal life I believe is all of a piece. His external life is a turmoil. He is always forgetting his keys. He never remembers where he parked the car. He loses things. His children slide down the banister in my living room, than which nothing is less conducive to organization.

The real push I get toward organization is from my brother, who never fails to put all the long-playing records back into the proper folders whenever he visits.

Prepackaging

I CAN remember the close examination my mother gave each item she bought. If she wanted apples, she picked up one and studied it, held it against her ear, thumped it with her middle finger, put it in her basket, and repeated the whole process until she had a dozen.

My mother would have a hard time today. Everything comes to us in cellophane or plastic packages. Our health is supposed to be better for this prepackaging, but I do not know that it has improved our tempers or our dispositions. I know I can't get the Swiss cheese out of the package. In the dairies in which my mother shopped, there was always a big cheese barrel with a lead scoop sticking in it. The proprietor scooped out cheese to my mother's specification, always giving me a healthy piece to chew on. If my mother wanted Swiss cheese, there was a big round hoop of cheese covered with a cloth, and the wedge she'd want would be deftly sliced off with a knife. The French say every cheese has a soul, but you'd never know it from the packaged cheese. The cheese, too, is a victim of conformity. I remember watching other boys carry beer in a pail. But the beer cans are jampacked tight in the six-can carton, and most of those old-timers would go thirsty rather than struggle with the cardboard.

No butcher ever sold my mother a piece of meat without holding it on high and twisting it so she could see how fat it was. You take the meat as it comes today wrapped in plastic and half hidden by cardboard trays out of those refrigerated boxes in the supermarket. If babies came in plastic the way our food does, the world would be filled with waifs.

Naked in solitary

THERE'S A terrible story out of the Norfolk, Virginia, prison farm. A sixteen-year-old boy who was sentenced to the farm for "traffic violations," no less, was confined to solitary confinement for refusing to work. The guards took away all his clothes and confined him to a cell with only a blanket to wear and sleep upon. His diet consisted of bread and water for two full days, and on every third day he was given a full meal. After nine days this boy went mad and tore a strip from his blanket and hanged himself.

Throughout history men in solitary have saved their sanity by ripping off their buttons and scattering them about the dark room to find them one by one. Many of these men have been hardened killers, many of them imaginative. But this was a six-teen-year-old convicted of traffic violations, with nothing but a blanket.

This sad event should remind us we Americans do not "coddle" criminals, as we often hear from the easily outraged. The United States, in fact, is more severe with convicted people than any other society in the world save Saudi Arabia, where the law provides for chopping off a thief's hand. The average sentence for convicted felons in this country is nearly three times as severe as that meted out in the United Kingdom.

Just what kind of punishment is it to strip a sixteen-year-old of his clothes and place him alone in a solitary confinement cell? To strip a man naked is the oldest trick known to dehumanize him.

The school buses

THE LAST of the endless marches seems to be that of the school buses, which never stop prowling Charlotte. School buses seem to stop at corners so obscure that police cars cannot find them. I can see why you have to have school buses in the coun-try, where a child might have a fifteen-mile round trip to school, but why are there so many in the city? Why don't they subtract school buses and physical education at the same time? Make the kid walk to school, which will do the little darling good, and make all the physical education people into guidance counselors.

The spiritual recession

MANY YEARS ago I remember going to West Virginia to do a job for a "puff"—the advertising special newspapers put out two or three times a year. I could not happily describe what

I saw. The people worked five days a week, and they worked hard. But on Saturday morning the line wound serpentine around the corner to the liquor store. I am no Prohibitionist, but I thought then and think now this is a serious problem of our times—that our leisure is so unregulated and formless that we fill it with a conscious desire for the unconscious—the essential purpose behind drinking.

Is it because our work is not work at all but what Hannah Arendt calls labor? I think so. The end product of what we do is not worthy of us. And because we are not proud of it, we are not proud of our weekdays. It is hard to celebrate on Sunday.

We worry about an economic recession every two years, and yet we have a spiritual recession every weekend.

Memo to the airlines

I THINK the airline companies should make a joint New Year's resolution to take the money out of advertising and invest it in the food. I fly frequently and far, and in the last decade, while the advertising has become glossier and more appealing, the food has become more and more like a gigantic leftover.

Serving food, snacks, champagne, and peanuts to the passengers is part of the airline business. It takes the passengers' minds off the sense of impending disaster. I am all for it. But that rubbery omelet I've eaten countless times on the morning flight to New York is a disaster of sorts, too. An airplane has one virtue: It gets you there fast. The advertising agencies ought to come down heavily on that with significant safety statistics to comfort me, not those cafeteria steaks.

The trivial question

ONE OF the rages sweeping the country now is the trivial question. The trivial question tests one's ability to remember facts absolutely unimportant to ordinary everyday existence. The trivial question can be distinguished by its salient characteristic: It is even more pointless than the questions they used to ask on quiz shows.

Sometimes the trivial question simply poses a direct challenge to memory, like name four of Alice Faye's leading men. And you have to remember the movies you saw in which Alice Faye costarred with John Payne, Don Ameche, Cesar Romero, Tyrone Power, or Tom Ewell.

Why anyone would want to remember movies the like of *In Old Chicago, State Fair, By the Light of the Silvery Moon, Down Argentine Way,* or *Rose of Washington Square* is beyond me and mine, who are trying to forget them.

Sometimes the questions are more elaborate, like name three pairs of men with the same name who distinguished themselves in different fields at different times. Then you have to remember that William Shakespeare was a playwright as well as a Notre Dame All-American in the mid-1930's, that Henry Morgan was a pirate as well as an actor, and that Paul Douglas was both a senator and a movie star.

The majority of folks can not only think these questions up but answer them as well. Yet I distinctly remember that two weeks before John Kennedy's assassination, a poll revealed that something like 40 percent of the populace did not know who Lyndon B. Johnson was. More recently, the Gallup poll sadly announced that 50 percent of the citizens who vote do not know the names of their congressmen. And you can probably stump anyone by asking for the names of the Supreme Court justices.

I think the trivial question betrays a certain failing in the American educational system. If the folks wanted to concentrate on the order in which the states were admitted to the Union, I would cede this was historical fact. It would not in my estimation be knowledge *per se,* but facts do constitute part of that which we call knowledge. Knowing the names of "Baby" Pignatari's wives is pseudo-fact.

Despite the skills and moneys we pour into the school system, the best we've learned is how to retain what we read in the gossip columns.

Pizza and hamburger

AN ALERT tourist could probably eat three hundred different varieties of hamburgers between here and Asheville.

There is no doubt the hot dog also is here to stay. It is standard fare at the ball park and the Boy Scout jamboree. There is no easier way to feed a growing family of six than with a dozen hot dogs.

No, what presses the hamburger, what has made the hamburger dress up, is the pizza. The pizza has always been as varied as the hamburger. Down here in Dixie we have always been able to avail ourselves of the eggplant pizza, the meatball pizza, and the sourdine pizza, as Southerners put it. Along that highway between Asheville and Charlotte a tourist can buy as many varieties of pizza as he can hamburgers. And in the supermarkets he can buy frozen pizzas and pizza mixes.

In Shea Stadium a ball fan can buy a pizza as readily as he can buy a hot dog, but it is my impression hot dog devotees stick to hot dogs but hamburger devotees are switching.

While the pizza is Italian in origin, I am willing to bet more pizza is consumed in South Carolina in one day than in Tuscany in a month. In fact, there's a pizzaburger stand outside of one South Carolina town that has yet to construct a library for its citizenry.

Why cookies?

CHRISTMAS IS over and done with, and I have no wish to relive its carnage and joys. What I need to know is: What am I going to do with all the Christmas cookies? Why grown-up

Jews always collect Christmas cookies beats me. I put a tree up every year; I give the newsboy a puzzle or a chess set; I exchange gifts with pals; but all the ladies think that cookies are a goodwill compromise between the Christian and Judaic ethics.

It has long been my opinion that cookies are no food for a growing man. A man needs a layer cake or a mincemeat pie or even a four-and-twenty-blackbird pie. It has been given to me that baking cookies is as much a chore and an extravagance as baked Alaska. I have found a piece of Gruyère cheese on a chocolate drop cookie kills the taste.

For some other reason, I am a guava jelly man. Neighbors and friends and the Welcome Wagon hostesses are always depositing guava jelly in my office. They always inform me they chopped up the hoof themselves (guava jelly comes from horses' hooves, doesn't it?). I put some cream cheese and guava jelly on a piece of matzohs and put that beside my soup, and then I crumble up a piece of matzohs in my soup and throw out the other. That way I can always tell them it was delicious.

The mobile society

WE ARE a mobile society, one literally on wheels, but I think there are other reasons why we travel. Many Americans cannot be that interested in a Miami adventure in the sun or the edification of a tour of Williamsburg.

We are a tense competitive people, afflicted with ulcers and anxiety. And we travel all over the world to forget ourselves and the petty problems we think are so important. That would-be writer goes to Paris to forget American publishers who don't think his books will sell. The accountant spends three thousand in a Puerto Rican hotel to relax. His relaxation consists of as many sets of tennis as he can squeeze in before noon and as many rounds of golf as he can squeeze in before dark and as much money as he can lose at roulette before they close the casino.

Losing things

IN COLUMBUS, OHIO, some years ago I lost my wallet and all my credit cards, which provided the lucky but corrupt finder with a six-month-long vacation.

I lost the typescript of a book once, and it stayed lost for three whole days. I wanted to beat my employees with a cane during that time. I lost my eyeglasses not too long ago and found them, despite the agonizing headache, in the refrigerator behind the buttermilk.

Now I've lost my keys. There's nothing to do except kick the door in.

I think of Mahatma Gandhi, who reformed India and won its independence from Britain simply because he never wasted any time looking for things he had lost. Gandhi didn't lose anything because all he wore was a towel, and he couldn't carry anything to lose.

Child-oriented culture

SHOULD THE city council decide the time has come to build a town garage in which to store the snow sweeper and sanding trucks and all the lawn mowers, they will commission the mayor to find an appropriate spot. The mayor will come to the next meeting with the news that there are six acres out on Route 42 which should suit. What's the next step?

The next step, of course, is taking to the barricades. All the folks out on Route 42 who don't want a town garage near them descend upon the open meeting.

If you build the town garage out there, say the folks, actively backed up by the PTA, the truck drivers will be running down all the school children.

That is what the sociologists mean when they say we are a child-oriented culture: You can always tell the folks are desperate if they couch consequences in terms of their children.

When the police chief starts banning all the paperbacks which deal with sex, his reason is always that such and such a book or books will corrupt and contaminate children. The largest volume of outrage I've ever heard mustered occurred one Christmas season when the local movie booked a Brigitte Bardot instead of the usual animal film over the holidays.

In the schools they teach language arts because courses directed to English or French are liable to confuse children, just as civics might prove too intractable and becomes Effective Living.

You can see we worry about children. We are afraid the truck drivers will run them down and that a paperback book or Brigitte Bardot or even civics is not to be trusted behind the wheel.

Pornography

HARD-CORE PORNOGRAPHY, so called, has only two models. One is the *Song of Songs*, which is Solomon's, and the other is *Justine* and *Juliette* by the Marquis de Sade.

The second first. *Justine* and *Juliette* are verbal exercises in sadism and masochism and are hardly the thing to recommend to a young swain. Not that they will inflame him, but he will find virtually no practical advice in them. Going around with a whip is not the way to make an impression.

The *Song of Songs* derives its chief amorous effects from its luxurious verbiage, which, while uninhibited, is still disciplined.

It is my impression a young fellow is better off with a box of good chocolates, a bunch of flowers, and/or a bottle of heady wine.

Listen to the men

THE MEN have taken up where the women left off. They have evolved huge programs for losing weight and are constantly opening their jackets to display knotted belts cinching baggy trousers. If it's not their weight, it's how soon they are going to stop smoking. They opt for either the apple-instead-of-the-cigarette, cold turkey, or the I-will-smoke-one-cigarette-less-each-day method. As observed before, we are a people afraid of silence and a people victimized by our own biology.

Three dollars for the market

EVERY TIME I pay three dollars for two tickets to the local movie I remember what my mother bought for one dollar. For one dollar she bought vegetables, bread, milk, and flanken, which she boiled. In addition, the butcher gave her a pound of liver for the cat. As a matter of fact, watching my mother bargain while she shopped was a better show than most of the movies I've paid the three dollars for.

The penny

CARL SANDBURG wrote that the penny was the most humanitarian coin we have. It is the coin the newsies used to use for their gambling, and it has Lincoln's face upon it. Today, no one bothers to stoop to retrieve a penny from the street. Yet

I remember very well tradesmen on the Lower East Side shouting, "*Veiber zvei fer* penny." Housewives, come and get them, two for a penny. The penny was humanitarian because the East Siders used to send their kids to college with those pennies.

On economics

WHEN MRS. JACOBS didn't hang out her usual shining line of clothes, we knew something was amiss. My mother went to see what she could do for her. When Mr. Jacobs got a raise, we saw a proud array of new clothes and household linens. But when things were mended, we knew there was trouble, bills to be paid or sickness. We looked out the kitchen window and got all the information that today Sylvia Porter works so hard to get.

Today I am a fountain pen

AIRPLANE TICKETS are issued now by a UNIVAC machine which makes no mistakes, and garbage disposal will soon no longer be a problem with the new radar incinerators. We have gone forward in the big items certainly, but with regard to fountain pens, we have gone backward.

Fifty years ago a boy got a fountain pen at his bar mitzvah, and thirty years later he still wrote his prescriptions with it as a doctor.

I defy any pen to do the same today. I admit, today's pens do some jobs more easily than the old fountain pen. They are much better when it comes to writing on butter and much, much better when it comes to writing under water. But, after all, how much butter (or as the advertisers say, expensive table spread) do you want to waste just to write a letter, and how long can you last under water?

Terri and Randi

JILL, TERRI, CANDY, RANDI, AND ROBIN were the names of girls who recently graduated from Hebrew school, according to a temple bulletin I hold in my hands.

The same temple listed the names of six new baby boys. Four names began with Barry. I hardly think naming a kid Barry can be called the fault of Barry Goldwater. That kind of popularity he just doesn't have.

Years ago Gentile mothers used to name their daughters Shirley. Then the Jews thought it was a pretty name, and the Gentiles dropped it like a hot potato and began naming their daughters Rebecca. When the rest of the country finds out how many Barrys are going to start school soon, I predict there will be a tremendous wave of naming the baby boy Jacob.

How is the market?

"How IS the market doing today?" is a phrase guaranteed to stop fellowship. Anyone who makes his living in stocks or bonds or depends upon his dividends for income indeed knows how the market is doing. Anyone who continually interrupts some delightful gossip with "How is the market doing today?" invariably owns ten shares of an over-the-counter issue which he bought at two dollars three years ago. I have two answers. If it is a good friend I reply, "I wonder if Bob Gibson won last night?" I don't care whether Gibson pitched or not, but if he did pitch, everyone hopes he won. If I am going to end the conversation and the fellow asks, "How is the market doing today?" I answer with "The market is still going down, but as it descends it teaches a moral lesson. It teaches us there is no substitute for working for a living."

I recommend writing a book

IF NOTHING else, writing a book helps jazz up or tone down your obituary. Take Polly Adler, the most beloved of all the whorehouse madams. I would hate to count the number of cops Polly corrupted with bribes, not to mention the number of girls Polly just generally corrupted. I would even hate to count the number of gangsters who were "fingered" up at Polly's.

When Polly cashed her chips not too long ago, what did the obituary headline read? Of course. "Author Dies." Polly wrote a book. Publishers in trim morning coats and editors with pipes went to her funeral.

What it means to be a humanist

I BELIEVE that the first requirement for being humane is the recognition of humanity, and humanity is essentially the human story no matter how high we go into space or how many planets we eventually explore. The human story remains the same as it was a thousand years ago and as it will be a thousand years from now, the story of a man, a woman, and a home and the relationship of one to the other.

I've always liked what St. John says in the Gospels: "If a man boasts of loving God and hates his neighbor, he is a liar." Or the words in the Talmud, when the young man asks the high priest what time of day is it proper to say the first morning prayer, and the answer: "When it's light enough to see a fellow human being at ten paces."

The wonderful progress of science has brought no improvement to the hearts of men; the direct responsibility for the universal disaster from which all nations are seeking to emerge belongs to the nation where the cult of science was most intense and diffuse. All the forms of wealth directed by technical knowledge, and that knowledge directed in its turn to disinterested research, lead to the most unexpected results. The intense aspiration toward material welfare has become universal.

The increase in wages and salaries, fruit of just social vindications and active economic laws, is still below the growing needs of men. We become impatient; we find the evolution that is taking place too slow. And we wonder whether the empire of man over nature keeps pace with the empire of man over himself. Is moral progress in accord with material and political progress? Are social laws the effects of goodness or of fear? It is interesting to note that in the South not a single Southern councilman or mayor got up one morning and said, "Today we will do such and such" in the integration of the schools, parks, public facilities, or restaurants. Not a single voluntary act was offered. It all came about through the pressure of law, fear of boycott, fear of sit-ins or pray-ins, fear of the law.

How can humanity escape such fatal contradictions? Why do we not see the saints of morals rise next to the saints of knowledge? Somehow we must reestablish the balance between the miracles of science and the miracle of kindness. We need a little of St. Francis of Assisi's, or Albert Einstein's simple wisdom; the scientists of the present day have great need of such celestial spirits that prevent their destruction in spite of their scientific and political glories. We need men who can tell the bellicose spirits of all countries these great truths that spring from the heart. They and they alone can succeed in giving us, among the cruel struggles of classes and nationalities, that internal peace which may herald universal peace.

Solomon wrote, "There are three things which are too wonderful for me; yea, four which I know not. The way of an eagle in the air, the way of the serpent on a rock, the way of a ship in the sea, and the way of a man with a maid." We have solved the puzzle of aerodynamics that the eagle uses, and we know about the principle of friction such as the serpent uses; and we imitate them. As far as the way of a man with a maid, we have grown accustomed to it. We can add a fifth mystery: how to recognize humanity, to accept humanity; and we have yet to achieve the greatest miracle of all, the miracle of human kindness.